Friendships Between Women

THE GUILFORD SERIES ON PERSONAL RELATIONSHIPS

Steve Duck, *Editor*
Department of Communication Studies
The University of Iowa

Friendships Between Women
Pat O'Connor

Conflicts in Intimate Relationships
Dudley D. Cahn

Friendships Between Women

A Critical Review

Pat O'Connor

The Guilford Press
New York   London

© 1992 Pat O'Connor

Published by The Guilford Press
A Division of Guilford Publications, Inc.
72 Spring Street, New York, NY 10012

Printed in Great Britain

This book is printed on acid-free paper

Last digit is print number: 9 8 7 6 5 4 3 2 1

Library of Congress Cataloging-in-Publication Data

O'Connor, Pat, 1950–
    Friendships between women: a critical review/Pat O'Connor.
      p.   cm. — (Guilford series on personal relationships)
    Includes bibliographical references and index.
    ISBN 0-89862-976-4.   — ISBN 0-89862-981-0 (pbk.)
    1. Women—Psychology. 2. Friendship—Sociological aspects.
3. Interpersonal relations. I. Title. II. Series.
HQ1206.025 1992
158'.25—dc20   92–13770
                                         CIP

For Stella

Are there no men present? Do you promise me that behind that red curtain over there the figure of Sir Charles Biron is not concealed? We are all women you assure me? Then I may tell you that the very next words I read were these – 'Chloe liked Olivia . . .' Do not start. Do not blush. Let us admit in privacy of our own society that these things sometimes happen. Sometimes women do like women.

(Woolf, 1977: 78)

Women have been friends for millennia. Women have been each other's best friends, relatives, stable companions, emotional and economic supporters, and faithful lovers. But this tradition of female friendship, like much else in women's lives, has been distorted, dismantled, destroyed – in summary, to use Mary Daly's term, 'dismembered'.

(Raymond, 1986: 4)

The question of female friendships is particularly elusive; we know so little or perhaps have forgotten so much.

(Smith-Rosenberg, 1975: 3)

Contents

Foreword   ix

Acknowledgements   xi

1 Women's friendships: an underexplored topic?   1
2 Towards a theory of friendship: identifying the elements   27
3 Married women and their friendships   56
4 Friendships: a refuge for single women?   90
5 Elderly women and their friends   118
6 Is there something special about the friendship tie?   145
7 The future of women's friendships   173

Bibliography   194
Index   225

Foreword

Treat your friends as you do your pictures,
and place them in their best light.

In *Friendships Between Women*, friendships are more than placed in their best light, as Jennie Jerome Churchill advised. Pat O'Connor brings them fully into the light, examines them from every angle, evaluates their strengths and limitations, brings into focus the social and cultural context which shapes them, and sets them squarely before us in all their sublime dimensionality. Her integration of psychological, sociological and feminist perspectives presents the reader with a bold new synthesis of the nature of friendship. Western notions of friendship as a strictly privatized relationship are challenged, as she deftly illustrates how structural variables such as class, power and resources affect and are affected by what is presumed to be one of the most intimate relationships. Thus, her work is an important contribution to the fields of Women's Studies, Psychology of Women and personal relationships.

By exploring the factors that shape women's friendships, previously unasked but significant questions are raised, such as: To what extent has the much exalted greater intimacy of women's friendships been shaped by women's subordinate social status and lack of concrete resources, such as time, money and physical space? What are the limitations of intimacy as a defining feature of friendship? What role does friendship play in maintaining social norms? What are the costs of friendship to the individual?

The comprehensive analysis O'Connor provides expands our conceptions not only about the nature of women's relationships, but about how friendships operate in general. For instance, the value placed on equality in

ix

friendship has been widely accepted and idealized. A closer examination, however, reveals the unacknowledged structural limitations placed on friendship by this criterion. As people with vastly different resources or life stations are unlikely to ever be equal – race and gender are two such differences – friendships are circumscribed by and maintain an established social order. Repeatedly, the hidden-from-view or politely concealed supporting social structures of friendship are brought into focus beside traditional, more personalized concepts to allow for a more wholistic understanding.

The power of friendship to validate, heal or transform the individual or pair is not neglected in this thoughtful review. Friendships as a source of joy are celebrated, their mental health benefits fully noted, and the potentially radicalizing effect of bonds between women are addressed. Moreover, this is done in the context of how friendships function at different life junctures – the effects of marriage, being single, and ageing on friendship are examined thoroughly. For instance, in addition to illustrating the emotional and psychological benefits of married women's friendships, the relationship of friendship to the marital relationship also is depicted.

Friendships are not solely a force for good in people's lives. As O'Connor points out, this 'rose-coloured' view actually denies the rich, complex reality of friendship. Friendships may be a source of conflict, anxiety and personal pain, as well as of rewards. They involve costs and disappointments as well as joys and satisfactions. They may be an oppressive, confining force, as is sometimes the case for battered women, or a liberating, affirming one. Clearly, as O'Connor argues, there is more to be gained by demythologizing friendships than by treating them as unambiguously positive. Only then will their true scope and impact be appreciated.

The critical analysis presented in this book opens the way for constructing a theory of friendship which 'highlights the wider structural and/or cultural context in which friendships are created and maintained' – one of the author's major goals. By bringing together emerging theories of personal relationships, empirical research on gender and friendship, and feminist perspectives on relationships between women, O'Connor has forged the beginning of a broad path toward her goal. This exciting new direction holds considerable promise for understanding not only key issues in women's lives, but the place of personal relationships in both private and public life.

SUZANNA ROSE, PHD
Associate Professor of Psychology
Director, Womens's Studies
University of Missouri-St. Louis

Acknowledgements

My debts of gratitude are many and varied. They are owed to George Brown at Bedford and Royal Holloway College, University of London, and David Morgan, University of Manchester, who were the examiners of my Ph.D. thesis on this topic. The encouragement to work on this book came directly and indirectly from many sources. I should especially like to thank Clare Grist, the commissioning editor who has been unfailingly courteous, reassuring and helpful. I am grateful to Graham Allan and Steve Duck for their thoughtful criticisms and generous help. Julia Brannen, Jonathan Gabe, Janet Finch and Ian Sinclair commented fully and helpfully on earlier drafts and/or related papers and I should like to take this opportunity of acknowledging this. I should like to thank Stella Reeves for her discreet interest and much appreciated help with proofreading. Ailbhe Smith and Carol Goodenow directed me to interesting and important literature, and for this I am very grateful.

This manuscript could not have been written without the trojan efforts of Terry Moloney and her library staff at Waterford Regional College. I am indebted in diverse ways to my former colleagues and students at that college. In a special way, however, I would like to thank Sandra Sheehan for her stoical patience in typing the first draft and Harryet Hoff of Transtype Services for her intelligent and meticulous attention to detail in producing the final draft: their calm efficiency in dealing with my maverick script is typical of the competent professional service they provide.

I have been part of a series of women's groups (women's studies;

running groups; reading groups) and these, together with my individual friendships, have contributed in no small way to my thinking.

I should like to remember my parents, Denis and Sheila O'Connor, in gratitude and sadness. Most of all, I should like to thank Stella and Tommy, Emma, Suzanne, Margaret, Claire and Elizabeth, who know, I hope, how much they all mean to me.

— 1 —

Women's friendships: an underexplored topic?

INTRODUCTION

The study of friendship can, even today, be viewed as a rather trivial exercise. It can be seen as reflecting a concern with the emotional, the tangential. Friendship, it is implied, is not concerned with the realities of sex or money, and hence is not worth serious attention. Indeed, until relatively recently, a similar attitude existed as regards the study of most aspects of personal relationships. Simmel (1971) rather wryly suggested that this reflected the predispositions and, indeed, arguably also the gender, of those engaged in academic work:

> For since they personally are men of a passionate drive for knowledge, but seldom of a passionate drive for love, their *subjective* nature is reflected in the fact that they continually make cognition the object of their thought, but most infrequently do the same for love.
>
> (Simmel, 1971: 235)

In Western society we have become accustomed to think in terms of the separation of the public and private areas of life. Personal relationships, whether those of heterosexual love or friendship, have been assigned to the private area – an area variously viewed as 'natural', 'irrational' and 'feminine', but in any case not suitable for serious study. Friendships between women have shared in this general neglect, although, as will be shown later, their treatment reveals additional processes.

1

The move towards recognizing the significance of friendships has been most directly facilitated by an increasing concern with the association between personal relationships and various indicators of emotional well-being such as psychiatric health (see Brown and Harris, 1978a, b; Thoits, 1984; Brown *et al.*, 1986; Fleming and Baum, 1986; Hobfoll and Stokes, 1988). However, a number of other developments have made extremely important, if less obvious, contributions. Firstly, the rise of the Women's Movement in the 1960s, with its slogan 'the personal is the political', implicitly legitimated a concern with personal relationships. Secondly, the emergence of a 'science of relationships' (Hinde, 1979, 1981; Duck and Perlman, 1985) in the late 1970s and 1980s facilitated the study both of relationships as psychological constructs and of the processes through which they were created and maintained. Thirdly, cross-cultural anthropological work (Rosaldo and Lamphere, 1974; Reiter, 1975; Brain, 1977; Caplan and Bujra, 1978; Bernard, 1981, 1987) highlighted the importance of locating discussions of friendship within a particular social and cultural context (looking, for example, at the way in which friendships reflected and reinforced class position). This concern with the wider social consequences of friendship derived further strength from the critique of the failure to see the public dimension of private areas (with Finch, 1983, arguing forcibly that the idea of mutually exclusive spheres was dubious on several grounds: empirical, theoretical, analytical and ideological and that it served to obscure certain important features of social life in both areas). Finally, the interest in 'talk' as a way of creating 'discourses' and/or 'shared understandings' and 'shared knowledge structures' further heightened an interest in friendship (Duck, 1986; Morgan, 1990).

It is obvious, then, that a wide variety of perspectives have contributed to the increase in interest in women's friendships. This book is concerned with drawing together the work done in these various traditions. It looks at the existence of such relationships and their content and quality at various stages of life and in different marital situations (ranging from adolescence to old age; and including married, single, widowed and divorced women). An attempt is made to explore the nature and effects of friendships; the processes operating within them; the factors facilitating and constraining their development and the ways in which they reflect and reinforce the institutional structures of society. It provides an overview of work done in the area and raises issues which might well be explored in future work. Because of the relative paucity of work on friendship within specific countries, the review ranges widely – drawing mostly, but not exclusively, on British and American material.

In this first chapter, it will be argued that friendship, although a human attachment, is also a culturally constructed form of relationship which varies both historically and cross-culturally. It will also be argued that, until relatively recently, there was a strong tendency to trivialize and derogate friendships between women – seeing them as culturally 'suspect' (i.e. as in some sense lesbian and hence 'sick'). It will be shown that such relationships are important in women's lives and that they not only have an effect on the individual's psychological well-being, but also play a part in reflecting and reinforcing class position and marital structures. In Chapter 2 theoretical perspectives on friendship will be outlined and evaluated. It will be argued that the nature of women's friendships can only really be understood within the context of an understanding of their lives in structural, ideological and situational terms. The main elements which might be included in a theory of friendship will be referred to in this chapter.

The following three chapters will look at trends and issues in studies dealing with various categories of women: married women (Chapter 3), single women (Chapter 4) and elderly women (Chapter 5). Chapter 6 will compare and contrast friendship with other kinds of relationships – including sister–sister relationships, work-based friendships and lesbian relationships. It will raise the question of whether there is or is not anything special about the friendship tie. Finally, Chapter 7 will involve a speculative discussion of the key issues which need to be addressed in future studies of friendship.

FRIENDSHIP AS A FORM OF ATTACHMENT: THE HUMAN CONDITION?

Friendship is one form of personal relationship, and hence much of the theorizing on the needs met by such relationships, their relational provisions and/or the styles of relating in them are at least potentially relevant to a discussion of friendship: 'While realizing that relationships of love and friendship function in many different ways, many theorists and researchers assume that these personal relationships serve, in part, to fulfil internal needs or motives that are central to healthy personality functioning' (McAdams, 1988: 8). One may identify four traditions of work in this area which are potentially relevant to a discussion of friendship. Firstly, there is the work of the personality and personal relationship theorists who see such relationships as meeting fundamental needs (e.g. for self realization or belonging: Maslow, 1968). Secondly, there are those who are concerned with describing the actual experience of personal relationships in terms of love styles (e.g. Lee's, 1973, six types of love: eros, ludus, storge, pragma, mania and agape). Thirdly, there are those who are concerned with love as an attachment process, and who, building on Bowlby's (1971; 1975; 1979; 1980) and Ainsworth *et al.*'s (1978) work on types of attachment, have attempted to identify adult versions of secure, avoidant and anxious ambivalent styles of attachment (e.g. Shaver and Hazan, 1988). Indeed, other work in this tradition attempts to look at the association between these styles of attachment and Lee's (1973) types of love relationships (e.g. Levy and Davis, 1988). Finally, there are those who have been concerned with identifying relational provisions (e.g. Weiss, 1969, 1974). This section will provide a brief overview of these four 'streams' in so far as they have dealt with friendship.

In fact, with the exception of McAdams (1988), theorists who have been concerned with needs, love and attachment styles have shown very little interest indeed in the friendship relationship *per se*. Thus for example, although it is noted that one of these styles (storge) is 'in some ways not a romantic style at all', being characterized by calm affection, companionship and shared interests (Shaver and Hazan, 1988: 496), it has not been used specifically in the study of friendship. This is particularly surprising since it is recognized that friends are important to those who have this type of orientation to love relationships.

McAdams (1988) does identify two styles of friendship which he sees as reflecting two types of personal needs (for power and for intimacy); two types of relationships (helping and self-disclosure respectively) and two types of fears (concerning conflict and public disgrace as opposed to separation and private betrayal respectively). He sees these as linked with sex-role orientations (masculinity and femininity respectively). He suggests that those high in power motivation are more likely to report friendship episodes involving groups, and that this pattern is linked with a need to consolidate individuality, assert, separate and expand the self; whereas those high in intimacy motivation are likely to report more dyadic interaction and this is associated with the need to merge; to surrender the self through openness, contact and co-operation. In these terms, they sound very similar to the gender-differentiated pattern which will be discussed later (in Chapter 2).

Those who have been concerned with what relationships provide (i.e. at a social and/or emotional level) have offered more insight into friendship. Weiss (1969, 1974) was amongst the first to discuss the supportive potential of relationships, and to suggest that they could be conceptualized in terms of six provisions. He argues that each of these is usually associated with a particular type of relationship, although this element in his work has tended to be overlooked. Similar, although less comprehensive, schemes have been put forward by others (e.g. Brim, 1974; Tolsdorf, 1976; Lopata, 1979; Solano, 1986). Weiss' ideas have, however, been particularly influential. The six provisions he identifies are as follows:

1. *Attachment*: this is provided by relationships from which respondents get a sense of security and place. He sees it as being typically provided by marriage, although he recognizes that it could also be provided by sisters, mothers, 'buddies' or close female friends.
2. *Social integration*: this is provided by companionable relationships where there are shared experiences and common interests which involve social activities or social and intellectual stimulation (e.g. friendship relationships).
3. *Opportunities for nurturance*: this is provided by relationships where the adult has a chance to take responsibility for a child and to feel needed by them.
4. *Reassurance of worth*: this is provided by relationships which recognize the individual's competence in a social role such as at work or in the family. He suggests that for women who stay at home 'relationships with husbands, children and acquaintances who recognise their homemaking skills, make this provision' (1974: 24).
5. *Sense of reliable alliance*: this involves the provision of assistance, regardless of the warmth or hostility of the relationship. He suggests that it is most likely to be provided by kin relationships.
6. *Obtaining of guidance*: this involves not only emotional support, but also advice about a line of action. He suggests that it is most likely to be provided by a trusted authoritative figure.

Weiss' work is a very interesting attempt to conceptualize the supportive properties of relationships and to link the absence of these to particular emotional effects. He was particularly concerned with the first two provisions: the absence of attachment being, he argued, associated with emotional loneliness; and the lack of social integration being associated with social loneliness and boredom. Many of those who claimed to have been influenced by his thought in fact attenuated his scheme still further by being concerned only with attachment (e.g. Henderson *et al.*, 1981). This exacerbated the tendency within Weiss' work to focus exclusively on the psychological rather than the social consequences of relationships.

This tendency can be illustrated by juxtaposing Weiss' categories with Solano's (1986). Solano's categories are in many ways very similar to Weiss' but are less amenable to reduction to an exclusive concern with attachment. Solano identifies three functions of friendship, namely those meeting material, cognitive and social–emotional needs:

1. *Material needs*: she differentiates between the actual provision of fairly concrete help by friends (e.g. giving money, goods, services and even information about job opportunities) and the feeling of inner security created by the presence of people who are willing and able to help out, or whose presence is simply felt to be an asset (e.g. having someone with you when walking home on a dark night).
2. *Cognitive needs*: here Solano includes the need for stimulation in the sense of providing conversation, ideas, interesting experiences etc. However, she also adverts to the role played by friends in constructing identities and versions of social reality, as well as providing a frame of reference to assess oneself and one's position relative to others.
3. *Emotional needs*: Solano sees these as clearly related to the giving and receiving of love. Thus she refers to acceptance, self-disclosure, trust, understanding, etc. However, drawing on Foa and Foa's ideas (1974), she also adverts to the way in which the existence of friends in general, as well having one particular friend, can satisfy a need for social status.

It is obvious that in many ways Solano's schema is similar to Weiss'. Indeed, in some ways Solano's can be seen as more primitive and less conceptually sophisticated. It does, however, highlight distinctions which are obscured in Weiss' one. Firstly, within the concept of a 'sense of reliable alliance' (Weiss, 1969) a distinction can be made between receiving help and feeling that it is available (and indeed, the latter is sometimes used in definitions of attachment). Secondly, Weiss' focus on 'reassurance of worth' obscures the extent to which having a friend in and of itself may be status enhancing. Thirdly, Weiss' work clearly makes no real reference to the 'discourses' created by friends and the way which these build and/or maintain a social reality. Fourthly, Solano's schema highlights the extent to which those who have attenuated Weiss' schema to a concern with attachment have omittec vital insights into the nature of the friendship relationship. Fifthly, whereas Weiss' work, and particularly his concept of a 'fund of sociability', directs one's attention to the whole question of the extent to which friends and husbands are functional alternatives, Solano's schema enables one to consider a much wider range of functional alternatives to friendships. Furthermore, it encourages one to explore the social and cultural conditions which facilitate and/or inhibit the emergence of particular types of friendship relationships. These types of issues are also, of course, entirely precluded by a preoccupation with needs or motives – a preoccupation which seems particularly inappropriate in view of the recognition that friendship as a cultural form varies at different points in time and across different societies.

FRIENDSHIP: ITS VARIABILITY AS A CULTURAL FORM

In Western society today we have become accustomed to see friendship simply as a human personal attachment. At the very least, this type of perspective ignores historical and cross-cultural evidence as regards variation in the form of friendship relationships in different societies. Thus, for example, Contarello and Volpato (1991) note that in France the concept of friendship was used during the high medieval period to refer to basic solidarity between kin; in feudal times it was used to refer to relationships characterized by patronage: 'Only later did the term take on a meaning closer to that of today i.e. of a mutual relationship of intimacy, freely entered into . . .' (Contarello and Volpato, 1991: 70). Although they argue that social conditions facilitated the development of friendship in France from the seventeenth century onwards, they go on to note that only in literature in the twentieth century was there a clear distinction between sexual love and friendship. A similar argument that the emergence of the Western form of friendship relationship dates from the early twentieth century is implicit in Faderman's work (1981). On the other hand, Hannan noted that, amongst his 1970s Irish respondents, the '. . . concept of friend as a freely chosen confidante and intimate to whom one is joined in mutual benevolence, is still used by the older people in rural areas to refer to kin' (1972: 176). Similarly, Allan (1979) noted that, in his British study, concepts of friendship were interwoven with kinship amongst his working class, but not his middle class, respondents. Such work clearly suggests that it is not sufficient to see friendship simply as a personal relationship which meets important needs. Indeed, Allan's later work (1989) implicitly endorsed this in its attempt to develop a sociological perspective on friendship. Anthropological evidence – albeit mostly on friendships between men – certainly supports the argument that in certain settings friendship is a specific cultural form. Thus for example Brain (1977) identifies various institutionalized forms of friendship relationships including the *compadrazgo* or co-godparent-hood, which he describes as a ritualized friendship between the parents and godparents of a child christened in church. This was common all over Europe and still exists in parts of Greece, Spain, Italy and Russia. This was regarded as a closer and less ambivalent tie than kinship itself, but with similar long-term obligations as regards social support and emotional satisfaction (Brain, 1977: 91–107), although it was still a friendship relationship.

Baker and Hertz (1981) note that comradeship is the form of the friendship relationship in the kibbutz – reflecting the communal ideology there and the homogeneity and common cultural origins of those involved. In Chile, friendship as a cultural form even more clearly transcends the private world, according to Adler Lomnitz (1990). There, this emotionally close relationship facilitates access to resources – albeit within sharply defined parameters. Thus, for example, it is acceptable to ask for certain favours from a friend but not for those which might threaten their job, a concept of friendship which is reminiscent of Boissevain's (1974).

It has become popular to see friendship in Western society as lacking a social form. McCall has challenged this, arguing that friendship 'is an objectified social form – an institutionalized mode of social organization' (1988: 469). Similarly, Argyle and Henderson (1985a, b) argue that friendship is 'rule-governed', and identify rules governing both the maintenance and termination of friendships. The issue of the form of friendship which is institutionalized in Western society and its similar-ities/differences with other forms of relationships (e.g. close kinship, workmates, etc.) is taken up more fully in Chapter 6.

Simmel (1971) vividly highlighted the tension between the continuity of life and the forms of social life – a tension which he saw as becoming increasingly acute in all 'forms of sociation' in Western society. In this context, friendship arguably represents the relational genre of the future. It is arguable that the attractiveness of friendship in Western society lies in its very fluidity as a cultural form and the extent to which individuals can shape it in particular situations, within the general cultural context of an understanding of friendship relationships. Friendship thus offers the possibility of individualizing the cultural form, and of terminating the relationship when the friendship is no longer desired. At this stage, it is worth noting that less attention has been paid to this issue than to the question of the actual content of friendship relationships or the nature of personal attachment.

However, before dealing with this, it is important to explore the issue of the level and the type of attention which has been paid to women's friendships – a topic which is explored further in the next section.

THE ATTENTION PAID TO FEMALE FRIENDSHIPS

Up to the mid-1970s, the topic of women's friendships attracted very little attention. In fact, it is hard to escape the idea that it was systematically ignored, derogated and trivialized within a very wide variety of traditions (including history, anthropology, sociology and psychology). Thus, in the mid-1970s, Smith-Rosenberg noted that:

> The female friendship of the nineteenth century, the long-lived, intimate, loving friendship between two women, is an excellent example of the type of historical phenomena which most historians know something about, which few have thought much about, and which virtually no one has written about.
>
> (Smith-Rosenberg, 1975: 1)

Anthropologists have typically been most interested in cultural variation in relational forms, yet Brain (1977), on the basis of his review of the literature on friends and lovers, asks: 'Do women have friends, allies, among the men and other women? Apart from my experience of the Bangwa, I am afraid I have to answer, through paucity of evidence, that I don't know' (Brain, 1977: 44). Yet he wryly notes that most people, including himself, would have little trouble bringing to mind examples of friendships between young girls, wives and older women 'which are just as binding and loyal as the most glamorous male friendship' (Brain, 1977: 48). This absence of descriptions of friendships between women was also noted by Contarello and Volpato (1991) in their examination of five French novels, all written by women and spanning eight centuries – from the twelfth to the twentieth century. They noted that, despite the fact that there was evidence of the existence of such friendships in France during this period, female friendships were 'underportrayed' in the texts they considered (chosen on the grounds of being available, relevant and popular). In contrast, there were frequent and detailed descriptions of male friendships (friendships being defined in both cases as including any relationship where those involved were referred to as 'friends'). Furthermore, in a genre as completely different as that of Grimm's German fairy tales, there is a similar paucity of depictions of friendships between women – especially amongst those fairy tales which have survived in popular series such as the Ladybird Well-Loved Tales series (see O'Connor, 1989). Thus across a variety of disciplines, there is evidence of a lack of attention to friendships between women.

There has, in fact, been a widespread tendency to trivialize them (portraying them as 'two-faced', 'gossipy' or as a juvenile phase in the progression towards 'normal' psychosexual development). Faderman (1981) has argued that, since Freud, close physically demonstrative friendships between women have effectively become impossible for many women: 'since love necessarily means sex and sex between women means lesbian and lesbian means sick' (Faderman, 1981: 311). There has been no systematic attempt to explain these phenomena, although Brain refers to male bias, lack of encouragement to women to 'rejoice in their own kind and in their femininity' (1977: 47), as well as the absence of mythic endorsement for this type of relationship: 'There are not even any myths of devoted women friends comparable with those of Achilles and Patroclus, Roland and Oliver. And Sappho and her friends have been relegated to the dark limbo of lesbianism – on the shaky grounds of a few lines of verse' (Brain, 1977: 47). Early feminist scholars saw this tendency as serving a very clear purpose for patriarchal society: 'The purpose it serves for the patriarchal society in which we live is to reinforce women's dependence on men. For if women cannot trust or work for or be friends with women, then they must of course turn to men' (Seiden and Bart, 1975: 194). Later work, however, has recognized that the relationship between the two patterns is more complex, since, in turning away from other women, women could turn to paid employment, children or indeed to non-social activities in addition to and/or instead of relationships with men. However, the viability of these alternatives in practice is questionable in view of women's typically high orientation to personal relationships, combined with their typical pattern of at least partial financial dependence on men.

An attempt has been made to portray women as incapable of friendship – an attempt which reached a pseudo-scientific peak in Tiger's (1969) argument that women were not genetically programmed to bond with one another. Others have argued that hostility between women is almost inevitable, rooted as it is in sexual jealousy and/or in that desire for male approval which is almost inevitable in patriarchy (Gilbert and Gubar, 1986). Indeed, O'Connor (1989) argues that one of the less frequently noted characteristics of patriarchy is its concern to suggest that relationships between women are invariably 'bitchy', jealous and hostile.

Within a sociological perspective the neglect of friendships between women can arguably be seen as indicative of a lack of interest in personal relationships and what Simmel (1971) called the 'forms of sociation'. Thus, sociologists, until relatively recently, remained preoccupied with institutional realities and structural forms: topics which obviously did not lead them to explore friendships. Simmel's insights into sociability (which he described as a 'play-form of association' (1971: 130)) could have stimulated a discussion of a type of friendship expressed in fun and pure sociability. However, as Simmel himself noted, the very recognition of such a phenomenon was inimical to rationalist thought, which saw it as 'empty idleness' (1971: 129), and so there was little interest in exploring it.

In the late 1970s and 1980s the emergence of an interest in friendships between women seemed more likely because of the growth of the 'science of personal relationships' (Hinde, 1979) and the gradual emergence of women's studies (see Oakley, 1989). Yet, ironically, friendships between women became central in neither of these traditions. Thus, although there has been considerable interest within the personal relations field in the topic of romantic love, love styles and attachment (e.g. Hendrick and Hendrick, 1986; Shaver and Hazan, 1988) such attention as was paid to women's friendships became to a very considerable extent simply obsessed with establishing whether or not gender-differentiated patterns of friendship existed (an issue discussed at greater length in the next chapter).

Within the women's studies tradition, although an interest in caring as a form of labour and/or of love was established early (Stacey, 1981; Finch and Groves, 1983), attention has continued to be disproportionately devoted to issues related more to labour (i.e. to domestic and paid work) than to love. Furthermore, attention has tended to be paid more to a critique of romantic love than to an exploration of friendships between women. (There are a small number of notable exceptions such as Faderman, 1981 and Raymond, 1986, both of whom have documented the varieties of women's friendships which have existed historically, as well as indicating the obstacles to the development and maintenance of such friendships.) Their work, however, can be located within a radical feminist tradition which has been more concerned with celebrating than with analysing '. . . the culture of female friendship – a culture that has vitality, élan and power of its own' (Raymond, 1986: 21).

Prior to looking at these topics, we turn in the next section to a general discussion of the importance of friendship and its effects in women's lives.

FRIENDSHIP BETWEEN WOMEN: ITS IMPORTANCE IN THEIR LIVES

As previously mentioned, the Women's Movement in the 1960s and 1970s was associated with an increasing awareness of, and interest in, all aspects of women's lives. Interest in their friendships, which emerged as part of this wider phenomenon, has been considerably slower to develop than interest in issues related to the nature of production and reproduction, public power and class – issues arguably centrally related to 'male' concerns (Oakley, 1989). Amongst liberal and marxist feminists, women's friendships, as an aspect of the personal dimension of life, were not seen as a potential avenue for understanding or changing patriarchal society. This position was challenged by the radical feminists, who stressed their importance in creating what Jaggar (1983) called a 'woman culture' as a way of bringing about change. One stream within their general tradition (namely cultural feminism) has equated women's liberation with the development and maintenance of such a culture (Ringelheim, 1985; Alcoff, 1988). This tradition celebrates woman's attributes and lifestyles, albeit in a way which implicitly endorses an essentialist view of women, and which idealizes women's friendships with each other, thereby discouraging any systematic analysis of them. A paradox implicit in the cultural feminists' stress on the importance of such friendships has been faced by Ringelheim (1985), herself formerly a cultural feminist. Thus, she asks: 'does cultural feminism in spite of itself glorify the oppression of women? Is women's culture [i.e. friendships between women] liberating? How can it be if it is nourished in oppression' (1985: 758). The initial work, largely by historians, (e.g. Smith-Rosenberg, 1975; Faderman, 1981), vividly documented the vitality and importance of friendships between women in other historical periods. Smith-Rosenberg's work dealt with the correspondence and diaries of women and men in thirty-five American families between the 1760s and 1880s. It highlighted the centrality these relationships had in their lives: women shared joys, sorrows and tasks; they encouraged each other; enjoyed each other's company; valued each other; regularly slept together and showed what to us appears to be an almost shocking level of physical demonstrativeness and florid verbal expressiveness. Indeed, as she notes: 'An undeniably romantic and even sensual note frequently marked female relationships' (Smith-Rosenberg, 1975: 24) These women typically lived very much within a sphere which was inhabited by children and other women. It was a world which was seen as having an integrity and independence. Yet its very structure was, to varying degrees, influenced by the men's world. Smith-Rosenberg (1975) argued that this pattern could be understood in terms of the rigid gender-role differentiation within the family and in society as a whole at that time.

> Such female relationships were frequently supported and paralleled by severe social restrictions on intimacy between young men and women. Within such a world [i.e. the female world] of emotional richness and complexity, devotion to and love of other women became a plausible and socially accepted form of human interaction.
>
> (Smith-Rosenberg, 1975: 9)

These relationships encompassed both kin and friendship ties. They typically were embedded within highly integrated networks, and lasted 'with undiminished, indeed often increased, intensity, throughout the women's lives' (Smith-Rosenberg, 1975: 26). Faderman (1981) went even further and noted that 'it was virtually impossible to study the correspondence of any nineteenth century woman, not only of America, but also of England, France and Germany and not uncover a passionate commitment to another woman at some time in her life' (Faderman, 1981: 15/16). Furthermore, she argued that these relationships appeared in the seventeenth and eighteenth centuries – with women friends confiding in each other and writing to each other in the intense romantic way that we associate with heterosexual love. Faderman argued that most of these relationships were not lesbian in the sense that they were genital.

Nevertheless, they were clearly a very real aspect of women's lives, and were, up to the end of the First World War, treated in a very casual accepting way by society. Indeed, she implies that it was the economic independence of women which allowed relationships between women to move from a romantic to a lesbian status (1981: 20).

This pattern was not atypical. Thus, Raymond (1986) drew attention to the rich history of such close female relationships – including the Beguines in Belgium, economic and social sororities among African women and Chinese 'marriage-resistance sororities', all of these women having various kinds of intense primary relationships with other women. This picture of strong, emotionally important relationships between women received cross-cultural validation in, for example, Abu-Lughod's (1985) work on Bedouin women. This patrilineal patriarchal society was characterized by very close, physically demonstrative ties amongst women who were very sharply segregated from their menfolk. It was a world characterized by denial of sexuality. These women were most at home with other women. Their preferred topic of conversation was other women. Together they talked about themselves, and shared their experiences and their knowledge; they orientated themselves towards other women rather than trying to please men; they valued competence and self sufficiency and saw themselves as constituting a separate society with its own internal structure. This community regulated its own internal affairs 'far from the interference and often the knowledge of men' (1985: 644). In it, women 'correct each other well into adulthood through gossip, teasing and other forms of indirect criticism, even poetry' (Abu-Lughod, 1985: 646). They did not tell the men their 'secrets'; the older women 'covered' for the younger ones if spouses or male kinsmen returned unexpectedly. The women saw this world as existing parallel to, rather than subordinate to, the men's world. It has been suggested that the very segregation of the women's world is conducive to the formation of strong ties between women. Other anthropological work (Leis, 1974) suggests that in itself this is not sufficient. Thus, she argues that amongst the Northern Ijaw the emergence of strong ties between women are associated not only with the existence of patrilocal residence patterns, patritineal kin structures, but also economic independence and polgyny. Such insights are not, however, readily transferable to a Western cultural system, one of whose dominant features is monogamy.

It is indeed difficult to get a picture of the importance of friendship in women's lives in Western society today. The form of relationship which we have come to define as friendship is located in the private area. It

presupposes a structural and cultural setting dominated by the institutions of the family and the economy. It has been argued that

> From the Edwardian wash-house where women gathered to do their
> laundry, through the door-steps of Bethnal Green, to the factory canteen
> and teenage bedrooms of the present day, come accounts of close woman-
> to-woman relationships that provide the emotional, and sometimes
> material, support which makes life worth living.
>
> (Green *et al*., 1990: 143)

A small number of studies have implicitly questioned the secondary status
which is popularly given to women's friendships within a culture in
which women's relationships with their husbands and children are in
some way seen as more conducive to their happiness and well-being than
any other relationship. Thus Holmes (1972: 357) noted that, in a study
he himself conducted, women friends were mentioned more often than
husbands amongst the three people his female respondents most liked
being with (a finding that he located in the context of the fact that
American married couples spent an average of only about twenty minutes
per week in direct conversation with each other). Indeed, Oliker (1989)
also noted that in her study, women were more able to identify easily the
unique provisions of their friendships than the unique provisions of their
marriage. Furthermore, 'these accounts often portrayed the beginning of a
new friendship in terms of excitement, heightened energies, frequent
thought about the other, invigorated self-regard – in short, in terms of the
ardent sensibilities of romantic love' (Oliker, 1989: 5). In Goodenow and
Gaier's study (1990: 17) friendships between women were no different in
emotional strength from their relationships with their husbands or lovers
(although their friendships were significantly more likely to be equal).
Deem, on the basis of a study of over 350 British women, suggested that
women, 'far from disliking the company of other women, actually seek it
out' (1986: 26), while Green *et al*. drew attention to the 'sheer pleasure
women experience from the company of other women' (1990: 143). The
Hite Report (1987) found that, although only roughly one in four of their
respondents had had a sexual relationship with another woman, the
overwhelming majority of both married and single women had their
deepest emotional relationship with a woman. The overwhelming
majority of them felt that it was far easier to talk to other women than to
most men – including their current male partner. Gouldner and Symons
Strong (1987) noted that amongst the women in their study the value of a

good friend went far beyond the pleasures of sociability. There was 'a great longing for friendship' (1987: 7), amongst these respondents, with the idea of a really close friend playing an important part in their imaginations. Indeed, the idealized descriptions of these friendships sound like descriptions of romantic relationships:

> This perfect friend was thought of as possessing, above all, the traits of trustworthiness and unswerving loyalty and the ability to keep confidences. She was a person, who was, at the same time, a good listener, an entertaining companion, someone with whom she could gossip and air serious problems. Ideally she would provide sympathy and opportunities for catharsis and self-insight along with distraction and fun.
>
> (Gouldner and Symons Strong, 1987: 105)

Typically in these studies (e.g. Gullestad, 1984; Oliker, 1989; Goodenow and Gaier, 1990), it is clear that the husband–wife relationship is ideologically dominant: most of the women in these studies would have preferred to have shared their victories and defeats, their routine activities and everyday experiences with their husbands rather than with their friends. Their common experience was that the men in their lives were simply not interested in these issues: hence potentially increasing the importance of their female friendships – if not their perception of their value. This implicitly raises the question of the basis on which the importance of friendship is being assessed: in terms of the emotional strength of the relationship; its cultural value; salience in the respondents' personal life and/or its effects – whether at an individual or societal level.

It is to a more detailed consideration of the latter that we now turn.

THE EFFECTS OF FRIENDSHIP: GENERAL ISSUES

Interest in the effects of friendship has until very recently mainly referred to the contribution it makes to the respondents' own individual well-being (particularly their mental health). Thus, a considerable body of research over the past twenty-five years has been concerned with the association between the existence of friends and various indicators of emotional well-being (psychiatric health, loneliness, self-esteem, etc.). Within this tradition there have been those who have argued in favour of an 'assets-benefiting hypothesis' (i.e. suggesting that friendships of a particular frequency or quality were associated with positive mental health in any situation); those who have adopted a 'stress-buffering approach' (i.e. looking at particular relational provisions, such as intimacy, and their impact on the respondents' mental health under various conditions such as divorce, death of spouse, unemployment, etc.); and those who have looked at the perceived existence of such support (i.e. in terms of relationships which were felt to be important in some way).

Work within all of these traditions has tended to look either at the number of friendships of various kinds that respondents have; at the supportive content of these relationships – either individually or in conjunction with other ties, or at the degree to which such relationships have positive effects on individual well-being. In general, researchers have found that those who have high levels of support (variously defined) are likely to have better physical health; they are likely to live longer; to be less prone to alcoholism, suicide and mental illness; to have higher levels of resistance to stress; to be better able to deal with transitions and reversals in life, such as unemployment, divorce, pregnancy, death, etc. (Walker *et al.*, 1977; Brown and Harris, 1978a, b; Duck, 1983; Cutrona, 1984; Fleming and Baum, 1986, Hobfoll and Stokes, 1988; O'Connor, 1991a). It has been recognized that it is difficult to argue that this relationship is causal (Thoits, 1982, 1983) – or indeed even to disentangle the extent to which positive outcomes are due to the direct positive effects of social support (the assets-benefits hypothesis), or to the fact that stress is more acute if social support does not mitigate its effects (the stress buffering hypothesis). Pierce *et al.* (1990) argued that perceptions of support were likely to have little causal relevance and might well simply reflect the individual's own self esteem and/or their sense of trust in others – constructs which were likely to be strongly associated with mental health. Nevertheless, Fleming and Baum (1986) concluded that it was fairly well established that having social support was beneficial during stress.

Work on social support generated an interest in the kinds of relationships which provided that support, as well as in the types of situations in which it was most important. Initially, much of this work was concerned with intimacy – particularly within the marital relationship, although more recently there has been a concern with the supportive potential of friendship relationships. Thus, for example, O'Connor (1991a) found that those who lacked a confidant relationship with a friend were just as likely as those who lacked that type of relationship with their husband to have poor psychiatric health. However, since much of the work on friendship has originated within and/or been stimulated by a concern with social support, it has tended to make simplistic assumptions that the existence of friendship could be equated with its supportive content. Thus, it is only now being recognized that it is not useful simply to assume that friendships are totally and inevitably helpful or supportive – even intimate ones: 'an emerging body of evidence finds that if one first elicits the membership in a social network and then asks which members provide various forms of support, only about half of these relationships are actively supportive' (Morgan, 1990: 194). For example, Ratcliff and Bogdan (1988) showed that potentially supportive relationships with friends were not supportive to unemployed women because these friends did not approve of them working in the first place. Work within the personal-relationships area has shown that emotional support or comforting from a friend may simply exacerbate feelings of helplessness. It may provide a short-term release (e.g. when a woman is depressed over a past event) but it may well not help her to 'solve' other problems (such as what to do about a violent marriage, where to look for a job, etc.). Furthermore Costanza *et al.* (1988) found that confiding in a female friend before a future anxiety-provoking event heightened a woman's anxiety and depression (and did so to a greater extent than either problem-solving talk or just unrelated chat).

There has also been an increasing awareness of the costs of maintaining friendships. The failure to recognize such costs before partly reflected a lack of interest in the processes operating in relationships, and a tendency to see intimate relationships as what Duck and Sants (1983) called 'the crock of gold at the end of the rainbow'. It also arguably reflected a failure to differentiate between the existence of relationships as mental constructs (i.e. the belief that they are important in their lives) and their interactional content (e.g. in terms of providing practical help, information, emotional support, intimate confiding, etc.). The latter interactional transactions inevitably bring costs: of time, energy and resources. It is easy to see the costs involved in minding a friend's children for an afternoon, or taking an afternoon off work to drive a friend to visit her husband in hospital. It is less usual to see listening and/or emotional support in these terms. However, on the basis of his review of research in the area, La Gaipa noted that

> Women with more intimate friends are liable to greater emotional strain
> than women with fewer. . . . The costs of friendship accelerate when the

number of friends goes beyond an optimal level. . . . To maintain an
extensive personal network requires engagement, time, and attention – in
short, it brings costs as well as rewards.

(1990: 126)

Such costs are, of course, particularly likely to be experienced by women
whose resources (time, money, etc.) are limited anyway, and on whom
there are considerable culturally legitimate and often competing demands.
There has been a failure to recognize this and a tendency to continue to
see the costs 'as virtually a personal luxury' (Allan, 1989: 78).

Work such as Larson and Bradney's (1988) and Argyle's (1987, 1990)
have suggested that the crucial importance of friendships lies in their
provision of positive and very enjoyable experiences: 'With friends our
attention becomes focused, distractions lessen, awareness of time dis-
appears: we emerge into a world in which the intimacy and joy shared
with others is the fundamental reality, and for a time the world becomes
a different place' (Larson and Bradney, 1988: 14). Larson and Bradney
(1988) found that in their studies, across all age groups, levels of
happiness and excitement were consistently high when their respondents
were with friends (although they were particularly high in old age).

Similar themes are mentioned by Argyle (1987, 1990), who noted that
amongst both his European and American respondents relationships with
friends were important sources of joy – this stemming from the easy,
relaxed nature of their interaction with each other. He sees social events
such as getting together with friends as 'the most common source of
positive emotions' (1987: 131). The reason for this is not clear, although
he sees it (1990) on the same continuum as festivals of song and dance
which are associated with co-operation in primitive society. Joy in
Argyle's term is one dimension of happiness (the others being satisfaction
and the absence of anxiety and depression). Indeed, it is one which has
tended to be neglected and to have, to our worldly ears, an untowardly
quaint flavour. This, indeed, is ironical in view of the fact that classical
theorists such as Simmel (1971) also recognized that 'emancipating and
saving exhilaration' of sociability (1971: 140) as peculiarly characteristic
of interaction with friends.

For the most part, little attempt has been made to look at friendship in
the context of a discussion of the way in which the class structure is
reproduced or the institution of marriage upheld. Yet, nowadays,
friendships (with marriage) are increasingly seen as one of the ways
through which 'closure' occurs; that is, the way in which a group or social

class maintains its own identity and separateness from other groups or classes: 'friendship relates to wider issues of status and stratification; whom you mix and associate with serves to locate you within a status hierarchy, in the process conveying images of character and social worth' (Allan, 1989: 62). Implicit in these ideas is the suggestion that friendship must be seen within the context of the wider social structure; that, in effect, it facilitates the maintenance of that structure of economic privilege and power:

> While in Britian, sociologists have hardly examined insider dealing or, say, the workings of masonic lodges or rotary clubs, there is at least *prima facie* support for the idea that friendships serviced through such institutions play some role in furthering economic and political interests.
>
> (Allan, 1990: 5).

A small number of studies have shown that friendship plays a part in shaping the flow of information especially amongst elites (e.g. Scott, 1982); while Morris' (1985) work showed that the density of male respondents' networks was associated with the type of jobs they heard about and the speed with which they acquired that information (i.e. dense networks acting quickly – albeit only providing access to short-term, irregular work, whereas dispersed networks, although more successful in providing regular employment, were often slow in providing that information). Indeed, Leyton (1975) argued that amongst the male elite in 'Aughnaboy', the endorsement of friendship rather than kinship as the dominant ideology was a way of minimizing obligations towards their kin, and in this way reinforcing their class interests. However, it is certainly true that, brutally realistically, relationships with women are unlikely to provide direct or indirect access to financial resources. This is reminiscent of one of Hite's respondents, who noted that: 'While women are good as friends, they generally don't have enough know-how of the world to give practical advice or offer "connections" – therefore women can't be taken as seriously' (Hite, 1987: 734). Few women have independent access to political, economic or legal power so that in this sense, the possibility of friendships between women either reproducing or indeed transforming the structure are limited. An attempt has been made to begin the latter through the institutionalization of women's business networks and women's political groupings. Such networks, of course, only benefit those women who are already privileged, and are only of importance to their occupational careers. A small number of studies (such as Cohen's, 1978, and Jerrome's, 1984) have explored the extent to which women's friendships are used to create and maintain a class position: such relationships being part of what Jerrome has called the 'politics of status maintenance' (1984: 714). In addition, Evetts' (1988) work shows how in schools female principals could by their management strategies and the supportive environment they created, facilitate their subordinates' domestic and teaching arrangements and so make an important contribution to the overall quality of their lives. Work such as this, however, is unusual. The preoccupation with women's close and/or intimate relationships has meant that relatively little attention has been paid to such topics.

Qualitative work such as Gullestad's (1984), Jerrome's (1984) and Oliker's (1989) has looked at the way in which friendships not only meet individual needs, but also create what they call 'a moral discourse between friends – one that combines a tolerance of individual liberty and a concern for family responsibility' (Oliker, 1989: 76). In Oliker's study child rearing, housework and household purchase, exchange of news, personal appearance, personal problems, dreams and hopes, as well as difficulties within marriage are all part of this discourse.

Oliker suggested that the friendships between the women in her study created a universe where women's personal identities could be validated within constraints imposed by the acceptance of the overall primacy of their family responsibilities. Furthermore, their friendships enabled them to tolerate the culturally generated contradiction between the vision of a companionate marital relationship and what she called the 'actuality of marriage' (1989: 156). Thus Oliker's work (like Gullestad's study of young Norwegian women, 1984) suggests that friendships between women maintain marital structures, while at the same time creating personal space and autonomy within them (see Chapter 3). Indeed, Jerrome's (1984) study of a group of elderly women suggests that these processes may well apply across the life cycle (see Chapter 5). Thus, at any rate, in both groups, although interaction reflected individual skills and preferences, it did not in any way undermine a commitment to marriage.

In essence, then, most of the work which has been done on the effects of friendship has focused on its positive effects on the individual's mental health (typically defined as the absence of psychiatric disorder, rather than the presence of joy). It has tended to equate the existence of a friendship, particularly an intimate one, with its supportive content, and has tended to ignore the costs of creating and maintaining such a relationship. Relatively little attention has been paid to the wider social implications of friendships – in particular, to the implications they have for the maintenance of the class structure and the nature of marital responsibilities and obligations.

Implicit in this critique is the notion that an understanding of friendships between women must be located within the context of an examination of women and their lives. This theme becomes even more explicit in the next chapter. Before moving on to this, it is necessary to begin to open up the whole question of the nature of friendship: the topic to which we turn in the next section.

THE NATURE OF FRIENDSHIP

Frequently, friendship is simply seen as an affectively significant relationship with people who are not socially defined as kin, namely anyone whom the respondent knows more than casually and does not dislike. However, Wright (1978) noted that, on further questioning, respondents found it difficult to distinguish between friendship and non-friendship. In an attempt to deal with this problem, studies in the network tradition asked respondents to identify 'close', 'very close' or 'best' friends (see Craven and Wellman, 1973; Shulman, 1975; Bell, 1981a; Wellman, 1982, 1985, 1988; O'Connor, 1987; Wellman and Wortley, 1989, 1991). However, this approach obviously begs many questions (e.g. what do people mean when they identify a relationship as 'close'? can one assume that such relationships are similar in content? that they encompass the universe of 'friendship' relationships?).

Different degrees of friendship have also been recognized. Thus Kurth (1970) differentiated in very broad terms between friendly and friendship relationships; La Gaipa (1977) identified five different levels of friendship: best friend, very close friend, close friend, social acquaintance and casual acquaintence; Fischer *et al.* (1977) distinguished between friendships of commitment and friendships of convenience; and Reisman (1981) differentiated between associative, reciprocal and receptive friendships (the latter type of friendship being one in which one partner was primarily the giver). In 1987 Rose and Serafica concluded that there was no agreement about levels of friendship or about how to define them, although Wright (1985) did note that friendship was less exclusive, less intense, more forgiving, less permanent and less regulated by norms than heterosexual relationships. Recently, there has been a tendency to abdicate any attempt to define the nature of friendship. Thus, Derlega and Winstead noted that 'when authors refer to friendship, they seem to rely on a consensual, but unspecified idea of what a friendship is' (1986: 2). Within Western culture, friendship is seen as being appropriately located within the private arena. Wellman (1990) argues that in the First World friendship is used mainly to meet either sociable and emotional needs or minor practical domestic ones. In contrast, in the Second World, he argues, friendship is used to short-circuit bureaucracy; while in the Third World it is used for basic survival. Most of the data presented in this book deals with American and British work, although work done in Canada, Holland, Norway and the Soviet Union is also referred to. It is argued that in these contexts friendship is best seen as a privatized, equal and voluntary relationship (Wright, 1978; Bell, 1981b; Aries and Johnson, 1983; Jerrome, 1984).

In one of the clearest statements on the nature of friendship, Wright has suggested that there are two essential elements in friendship: voluntary interaction, and what he calls a 'personalistic focus on the part of those involved in the relationship' (1978: 199). He suggests that the strength of friendship at any moment in time will depend on the extent to which the individuals involved react to each other as 'genuine, unique and irreplaceable individuals' (1978: 201); and the extent to which their plans and activities are voluntarily interwoven. Wright goes a step further in so far as he also suggests that friendships can also be differentiated in terms of the degree to which they provide stimulation, ego support, self-affirmation and what he calls utility value (i.e. being willing to use time or resources to help the other person meet his/her needs or goals). Implicit in Allan's (1979, 1989), Argyle and Henderson's (1985a, b), Davis and Todd's (1985) and O'Connor's (1987) work is a similar conception of the content of the friendship bond. Typically in such work, in addition to referring to its voluntary nature, reference is made to enjoyment, ego support, validation, stimulation, intimacy, trust, acceptance and companionship. Wright, however, implies that in so far as one has to identify a single characteristic of friendship, it is the extent to which it provides self-affirmation: 'Acting and reacting in ways that facilitate the subject's expression and recognition of his/her more important and highly valued self attributes' (1978: 201). It is possible to argue (although Wright does not do so), that in a society where women are systematically viewed as 'the Other' (de Beauvoir, 1972) the most important characteristic of their relationships will be the extent to which they provide ego support (i.e. relationships which are 'encouraging, supportive, non-threatening and in general capable of helping the subject maintain an impression of him/herself as a competent, worthwhile person' (Wright, 1978: 201). This line of thought raises the whole issue of the importance traditionally attributed to emotional depth and intimacy as properties of friendships. It also raises the question of the extent to which such conceptualizations in fact reflect and reinforce power relationships between men and women (topics to which we return in the next chapter). For Duck and Perlman (1985: 5), however, 'The single most important question for research is to discover how relationships are created, both subjectively and objectively, from strings of interactions and from the changing beliefs that individuals form about them' (1985: 5). Implicit in this is the idea that an adequate understanding of friendship cannot be derived simply from an examin-ation of its content. The subjective element has been referred to by Marris (1982), O'Connor (1987, 1990) and Willmott (1987) as felt attachment, solidarity and/or primary quality. These have been variously defined, although the essence of them appears to lie in the idea that exchange is not a crucial factor in the relationship, and that the relationship has an element of what Fortes (1970) called the 'axiom of prescriptive altruism' (i.e. the moral obligation to forgo self interest in favour of another).

The perceived willingness to provide help (what Weiss, 1974, called a 'sense of reliable alliance' and O'Connor, 1990, referred to as felt attachment) has been widely seen as an important characteristic of friendship. Some studies have gone so far as to use it as a definition of a close friend or best friend in surveys exploring variation in the number of such relationships. O'Connor (1987) has suggested that beliefs that the other person would always be there, would always be willing and able to help out, are by no means a universal property of friendships. There is also, in fact, little evidence to suggest that high levels of practical help are an inevitable characteristic of friendship (Allan, 1990; La Gaipa, 1990). Like intimacy, it is suggested that these properties typify particular types of relationship – but not ones which can in any way be regarded as synonymous with the whole arena of friendship relationships.

The rather complex relationship between objective and subjective reality is further illustrated by Duck *et al.*'s (1991) work, which showed that conversations between friends which were recalled as mundane in content were still seen as important in creating and maintaining their attachment to that person – leading Leatham and Duck to the conclusion that 'the content of a conversation may on occasion be less important than the attachment sensed through conversation' (1990: 6). Friendships are popularly seen as personal relationships which recognize the unique qualities of the other person. This suggests that the relationship has a closeness, an intensity and a 'we-feeling'. Traditionally, the concept of 'primary group' was used by sociologists to denote the existence of such qualities. Hoyt and Babchuk (1983) argued that sociologists have continued to rely too much on this concept, and have generally failed to operationalize it (more recently some attempts have been made to do this: e.g. O'Connor, 1987, 1990).

Reciprocity is also commonly identified as a characteristic of friendship. However, it is now recognized that it is almost impossible to explore empirically the real extent of reciprocity in a relationship since similar behaviours or goods will not always be exchanged. Furthermore, there is some evidence to suggest that the more long-standing the relationship, the less likely there is to be a move towards symmetry in the short term. Indeed, Jerrome (1990) noted that in long-established friendships an obligation to reciprocate might be waived, while Shea *et al.* (1988) found that, although new and old friendships differed little in terms of content, those in enduring relationships had a willingness to care for each other without regard to reciprocity.

Drawing on a range of multidimensional relational assessment procedures which were developed in the previous fifteen years, Davis and Todd (1985) put forward a prototypical model of friendship, that is, 'a list of features or attributes that are typical of the class but which do not constitute a set of necessary or sufficient conditions to define the category' (1985: 17). The elements they refer to include friends' participation as equals; enjoyment of each others' company; mutual trust; an inclination to provide each other with assistance and support and to feel that they can rely on each other in times of need; mutual acceptance, respect and understanding; the ability to be spontaneous (i.e. 'to be themselves' within the relationship); and finally, the ability to be intimate either in the sense of confiding in each other or through sharing experiences (i.e. by doing things together). Davis and Todd's formulation is interesting in so far as it implicitly suggests that friendships between different genders; at different stages of the life cycle and in different cultures may vary:

> The archetypal paradigm case is an unconstrained case – unconstrained either by personal limitations or by the facts of social structure. When these two constraints come into play, the friendships found in everyday life will vary from this ideal case not only in matters of degree, but also to the extent of literally not having one or more properties in the archetypal list.
>
> (Davis and Todd, 1985: 20)

It thus implicitly opens the way both for a discussion of variation in types of friendships, and for an attempt to explain variation in them.

SUMMARY

In this chapter, it has been argued that although there is a human need for attachment, the cultural forms through which that need is met differ considerably. The concept of friendship has been shown to vary both historically and cross-culturally. Its shape in Western society is opaque, although it is argued that it cannot be seen simply as an idiosyncratic, purely personal relationship. Davis and Todd's (1985) identification of an archetypal paradigm case of friendship seems particularly useful – encapsulating as it does both the commonly accepted elements in the friendship bond in Western society, while at the same time allowing for the identification of types of friendships.

In this chapter, it has also been noted that until relatively recently, little serious attention was paid to women's friendships – and that, in fact, there has been a clear tendency to trivialize them and/or to see them as 'suspect' (i.e. as lesbian relationships). In this context, it is difficult to provide a clear picture of their importance in women's lives in Western society. Nevertheless, even a cursory overview suggests that they are emotionally important – if for no other reason than that frequently the support and interest which is expected from a heterosexual relationship does not in fact emerge.

Such recent interest as has been shown in women's friendships has tended to be concerned with the similarities and differences in men's and women's friendships (a topic which is discussed in the next chapter) and/or with their effect on women's psychological well-being. Typically, work in the latter tradition has tended to equate the existence of friendships with their supportive content and has tended to ignore the costs of creating and maintaining such intimate friendships. A small – albeit very interesting – number of studies have been concerned with the wider effects of friendship, that is, on creating and maintaining class position and marital structures. These themes will continue to be explored in the next chapter, in the context both of a discussion of structural factors (such as class and gender) and of the relational processes operating within friendship (i.e. formation, maintenance and dissolution). It is to an examination of these issues that we now turn.

— 2 —

Towards a theory of friendship:
Identifying the elements

INTRODUCTION

Friendship is, as previously mentioned, both a personal attachment and a socially constructed and culturally articulated form of relationship. Hence, any attempt to understand it and to explain variation within it must draw on a number of streams of literature over and above those relating to theories of needs. Ironically, because of the tendency to see the existence of friendships in Western society simply as an indicator of popularity, relatively little work has been done at a theoretical level to highlight the wider structural and/or cultural context within which friendships are created and maintained. This is despite the fact that since the 1960s, there has been an increasing awareness of the importance of a structural analysis of various aspects of women's lives – taking into account both patriarchy and capitalism.

Friendship has typically been seen as the most idiosyncratic form of personal relationship. Hence, little attention has been paid to looking at either the social factors which are associated with its emergence, maintenance or demise. In fact, like other personal relationships, there has been a tendency to idealize it and to ignore the idea that it requires resources – such as time, money, etc. Furthermore, because it has tended to be seen as a purely personal relationship, there has been little interest in exploring the ways in which the discourses generated within friendship play their part in creating and maintaining social structures:

> Unfortunately, in much of the literature on friendship, notions like class, age and gender are treated simply as traits that a person has in some form, rather than being regarded as features of the social landscape that facilitate or discourage to differing degrees, in interaction with other aspects of social topography, the emergence of particular social patterns.
>
> (Allan, 1989: 34)

Finally, the work which has been done on friendship has tended to take for granted the idea that the concept as we know it in Western society, is a culturally specific one. Its shape is influenced not only by class and marital-role ideology, but also by the emergence of the sexual category of lesbian, and the sexualization of physical contact between women in the wake of the work of figures such as Freud and Havelock Ellis.

In this chapter, the elements which might be included in a theory of friendship will be outlined, drawing on work dealing with the processes operating within friendship, and on work which has highlighted the importance of particular aspects of women's position in understanding the nature of their friendships. Prior to doing this, however, the chapter will indicate the main foci of interest in women's friendships and will provide a brief overview of that theoretical work which has attempted to explain variation in friendship styles.

INTEREST IN WOMEN'S FRIENDSHIP: ITS FOCUS

Over the past twenty years there has been a very considerable increase in interest in friendship. This interest showed itself initially in a concern with establishing the number of close, very close or best friends and was mainly done within the tradition dealing with the association between social relationships and psychiatric state and/or in the American network tradition. Later work has been particularly concerned with describing and explaining differences in women's and men's friendships – focusing particularly on variations in intimacy.

Much of the work in the social-networks tradition was originally stimulated by qualitative work by Bott (1957, 1971) and Mitchell (1969). However, studies in the American network tradition have typically asked people to name their close, very close or best friends outside the household (e.g. Craven and Wellman, 1973; Shulman, 1975; Bell, 1981b; Wellman, 1982, 1985; O'Connor, 1987; Wellman and

Wortley, 1989, 1991). The average number of such friends identified has varied – partly depending on the British or American composition of the sample, the age, marital status, social-class position and life stage of those involved, and also depending on whether or not the question has focused on close or very close friendships. However, the picture across these various samples is broadly consistent with Argyle and Henderson's (1984) and Gouldner and Symons Strong's (1987) conclusions that most people have one or two particularly close friends although they may have up to five other close friends.

Over and over again it has been noted that male and female same-sex friendships vary systematically (Bell, 1981b; Caldwell and Peplau, 1982; Wright, 1982; Duck, 1983; Sherrod, 1989). Researchers have found that women are particularly likely to have intimate confidants (Komarovsky, 1967; Booth, 1972; Cozby, 1973; Powers and Bultena, 1976; Bell, 1981b; Wright, 1982; Aries and Johnson, 1983; Derlega and Winstead, 1986); that mutual helpfulness is most central to female friendships, whereas shared activities and similar interests are most central to males (Weiss and Lowenthal, 1975; Aukett *et al.*, 1988) and that females use more non-verbal expressions of affection (Rands and Levinger, 1979). Wright (1982), in reviewing this extensive literature, suggested that the essential difference in males' and females' friendships was that female friendships were 'face to face' whereas male friendships were 'side by side'. A similar view was put forward by Farrell (1986), and in Crawford's study (1977) these differences were obvious even at a definitional level: the most common elements in women's definitions were 'someone I can trust' and 'someone I can call on for help', whereas the most common elements in the men's definitions were 'someone whose company I enjoy' and 'someone I go out with'.

More recently, however, Wright (1988) has argued very strongly indeed against such 'dichotomous thinking' on the grounds that

> Virtually all close friendships involve shared interests and activities, various kinds of intimacy including self-disclosures and the sharing of confidences, emotional support, small talk, shop-talk and exchanges of tangible favours. . . . Rather we should think in terms of what qualities or characteristics are more typical on average of the friendships of women than of men and vice-versa.
>
> (Wright, 1988: 370).

A similar conclusion was reached by Helgeson *et al.* (1987) who noted that, overall, men's and women's experiences of intimacy were more similar than different, although, to the extent to which they existed, there was a tendency for men to emphasize proximity and women to emphasize communication. Helgeson *et al.* also raised the question of the appropriateness of equating self-disclosure with intimacy, arguing that it was not a necessary and sufficient feature of intimacy for either sex. They also argued that the concern with confiding *per se* was inaccurate if not actually misleading, the crucial thing being the extent to which it occurred within a context characterized by appreciation, affection and warmth.

The limitations of using intimacy as a defining characteristic of close friendships have also begun to be realized purely on a micro-level (Helgeson *et al.*, 1982; Ratcliff and Bogdan, 1988; O'Connor, 1991b). Thus recent work by Ratcliff and Bogdan (1988) showed that intimate relationships were frequently unhelpful when married women lost their job, because the people with whom they were intimate were basically opposed to them working in the first place. Quite clearly then, a high level of intimacy could well exist in a very unsupportive or even destructive relationship. Indeed, it is now being increasingly recognized that the most supportive relationships may well be those which provide support (without it being asked for) as part of the interactional dynamics of the relationship (Eckenrode and Wethington, 1990); and/or support which is offered in such a subtle way that no-one loses face or has to admit their need for help (e.g. the giving of advice through the telling of a story, Glidewell *et al.*, 1982). Yet, oddly enough, intimate relationships have until very recently, been seen by psychologists, social psychologists and sociologists alike as the ideal and the epitome of women's friendships.

Cancian (1986) has examined this issue, and implicit in her view is the idea that although 'feminine' styles may be seen as morally, or even psychologically, superior, they are incompatible with control. This is consistent with the fact that although a number of studies have shown that men were equally capable of intimate interaction, they preferred to interact intimately less often than women (Reis *et al.*, 1985); and preferred to disclose to women than to men (Hacker, 1981; Derlega *et al.*, 1985). Helgeson *et al.* (1987) argued that men's definitions of intimacy in terms of proximity and shared activities effectively protected them from situations of emotional vulnerability and potential loss of control. Intimacy for women, on the other hand, typically involves admitting dependency, sharing problems and being emotionally vulnerable. In fact, according to Cancian, the only area of personal experience that women confide less than men about is their victories and achievements (Cancian, 1986: 701). This latter type of intimate disclosure reflects and reinforces power rather than helplessness – something which Cancian argues sits uneasily with women's 'feminine' style of relating. Hence, rather than seeing disembodied intimacy as an indicator of a particularly close and highly desirable relationship, it is possible to see it as a reflection of a disempowering situation. In this context, talking about her situation may be the only alternative available to a woman.

Furthermore, in so far as women's relationships with each other are purely at a feeling level and exclude any discussion of ideas or involvement with the world, they abdicate any attempt to change that world (Raymond, 1986). Hence, the definition of friendship in terms of confiding does nothing whatsoever to challenge power relationships between men and women.

Finally, this concern with intimacy has recently been seen as endorsing what Fleming and Baum (1986: 210) called 'palliative coping', that is, manipulating one's emotional state rather than actually changing the situation. Philosophical reservations about this type of strategy have been further underlined by work which has shown that mobilization of resources under stress does not always have a positive effect on long-term mental health (Billings *et al.*, 1983).

To date, much of the theoretical work which has been done has tended to focus on confirming/disputing gender-differentiated patterns in friendship. This will be explored in the next section.

THEORETICAL EXPLANATIONS FOR FRIENDSHIP

As previously mentioned, by far the most common theoretical interest has been in the existence of gender differentiated patterns of friendship. Various types of explanations for this phenomenon have been put forward – although most of these have looked particularly at the early care-giver and/or socialization experiences. Very much less attention has been paid to different aspects of women's adult situation (such as their position of financial dependence) and/or the cultural valuation of female friendships. These will be briefly referred to in this section. However, the situation has not changed since 1986, when it was noted that 'A full-fledged theory of friendship does not yet exist. Instead we are confronted with a wide array of descriptive studies, sometimes guided by a hypothesis or an empirical generalization but more often interpreted with post-hoc theoretical analysis' (Farrell, 1986: 164). Theorists who attempt to explain gender-differentiated patterns of intimacy in friendship typically stress some aspect of the child's early socialization experiences in influencing the development of capacities for intimacy. They focus on the male/female identity of the early care giver (Chodorow, 1978; Rubin, 1983, 1985; Sherrod, 1989) and suggest that in this early relationship, the child is struggling both to develop a gender identity and to develop ego boundaries. Where the main care giver is a woman, the female child has little difficulty establishing a gender identity. She does find it more difficult to separate from her mother and to establish clear ego boundaries. In this experience, they argue, lie the seeds of women's greater involvement with other people; the greater importance of intimacy in their lives and their greater sense of empathy with other people. Farrell (1986) takes this a stage further by also seeing in this early experience the seeds of females' difficulties in dealing with conflict, decision making and leadership, and so their tendency to move towards dyadic intimate relationships which side-step these issues. (Male difficulties, he argues, are of the exact opposite kind, leading them to avoid intimate relationships.)

An alternative, albeit somewhat similar, theory might be erected on the basis of Bowlby's ideas and their later revision by both Bowlby himself (1971, 1975, 1979, 1980) and Rutter (1981). Thus, one might suggest that in a society where males are more highly valued than females and where interaction with male children has been shown to be more responsive and more extensive than with female children (Oakley, 1972) males will be more likely to be provided with a 'secure base'. Hence they will be less likely to continue to engage in 'attachment behaviours'. Thus, one might argue, males will be likely to move on more rapidly to interaction in larger groups than their female counterparts – a trend which has been continuously noted in children's and adolescent's friendships (Bell, 1981b; Rubin, 1985). This type of explanation has enjoyed very little popularity – arguably because implicit in it is the idea that one-to-one or intimate relationships are less highly valued than group or activity-based relationships.

Relatively few attempts have been made to explain differences in male–female friendships in terms of, for example, power relationships between the sexes. There is considerable potential for work in this area. Thus, drawing on Cancian's views (1986) one could suggest (as Cline Welch, 1989, does) that the maintenance of an intimate style of relating amongst females and a non-intimate one amongst males reflects and ultimately reinforces power relationships between the sexes. Rose (1985) suggests that

> men do not act as friends toward women in the same way they do toward men. A power/resource analysis seems to more easily explain this finding . . . women will tolerate less acceptance and intimacy from men friends in return for the increased status they might acquire by having male friends. Men, in turn can safely offer women less than thay might men.
>
> (Rose, 1985: 72)

This still leaves open the question of the bases of men's greater power and/or status. Sherrod (1989) considered – and rejected – a biological and economic/historical explanation for this phenomenon. Radical feminists and Marxists have reached very different conclusions, focusing on the importance of patriarchy and capitalism, respectively, in explaining the power relationships between men and women, while socialist feminists (such as Rubin, 1974; Hartmann, 1976; Young, 1981; Jaggar, 1983) have combined both elements within their theoretical explanations of women's position. Unfortunately, however, they have shown relatively little interest in theorizing about friendship.

It is clear, however, that in Western society friendships between women typically occur within a culture where marriage is highly valued and an important institutional structure. Romantic love is the ideological core underpinning the marital relationship but, in effect, the emotional primacy of that relationship has arguably become translated into sexual fidelity by a culture which does not wish to confront the effective primacy of occupational responsibilities in men's lives. Inevitably, then, the essence of the male–female relationship is seen as the sexual aspect. Hence, issues related to respectability, reputation, sexualization of all physical contact, the social construction of lesbianism and its stigmatization become part of the context within which friendships between women are located.

In addition, it is increasingly obvious that, despite women's rising participation in the labour force, they are very unlikely to be completely financially independent in Western society. This is vividly illustrated by the fact that although the proportion of women with some income increased dramatically over a twenty-year period in the United States (i.e. from 55 per cent in 1960 to 88 per cent in 1982) less than a quarter of the wives and female family heads in a random sample of US households could be considered to be completely economically independent over a five-year period (Acker, 1988: 483). It has also been very clearly documented that women are more likely to be at the bottom of the job hierarchy than men and are unlikely to be as well paid as men (Acker, 1988; Marshall *et al.*, 1989, Webb, 1989):

> At any given level of intelligence, education and occupation, women are less likely to be as well paid and to have as satisfactory work conditions as men and they are likely to have greater difficulty in obtaining those positions at any given educational level.
>
> (Marshall *et al.*, 1989: 138)

For most married women, a spouse contributes at least partially to their financial well-being, particularly during the early child-rearing period. At this stage, gender differentiated patterns of responsibility as regards child care, and lack of state-funded facilities for child care typically make financial independence very difficult for mothers.

Even for those who are not married, the institutional importance of marriage, buttressed by the ideology of romantic love and what Green *et al.* (1990) called the 'cultural sterotype of women as carers', has important repercussions. Thus, even the lives of single women (who are most likely to have resources to invest in friendship, and who are least likely to be constrained by caring responsibilities) are still limited by 'issues related to sexuality, respectability and social control' (Green *et al.*, 1990: 167). Thus, for example, ideologies of respectability and concern with their reputation effectively limit their freedom of movement and their access to public arenas. Equally (as will be argued in Chapter 6), the emergence of the social construction of lesbiansim, and the continued stigmatization of that identity, has inhibited the development and maintenance of friendships between women. It has effectively excluded intimate physical contact from the ambit of normal friendships. (Ironically, this very exclusion may well be associated with a rise in the value of friendship as fears about Aids and its transmission affect the cultural value attached to genital relationships.) Indeed, as Smith-Rosenberg (1975), Faderman (1981) and Ruehl (1983) have argued, there is considerably more inhibition about either physical or verbal expressions of affection between women today than there was in the nineteenth century.

In the meantime, however, in a society where relationships with men are status enhancing and where women are defined as 'the Other' (de Beauvoir, 1972) female friendships have a rather doubtful status – frequently being seen as 'going nowhere' and 'a waste of time'. The Women's Movement in the 1960s and 1970s went some way towards revaluing such friendships – even seeing them as part of an informal power base. This idea has been formalized in the establishment both of networks of women in community-development projects, as well as in networks of middle-class women in business, in education, etc. Outside such limited arenas, however, women's friendships with each other are still typically seen as providing little direct or indirect access to power or status. Furthermore, like all ties within stigmatized and oppressed categories, they remain vulnerable to the patriarchal definition of them as limited and ultimately stigmatizing (Bernard, 1976, 1981; Hacker, 1981).

As previously mentioned, the relationship between friendship and the wider structural and cultural setting has been virtually ignored by feminist theory (with the possible exception of radical feminism) and indeed also by Marxism. Within a structural–functionalist tradition, Hess (1972) did partly address this issue by identifying four possible types of connection between friendship and other roles: namely, complementarity, substitution, competition and fusion. (Three of these are discussed below: the fourth, fusion, is concerned with the similarities and dissimilarities in friendship and kinship relationships and is thus more appropriately explored in Chapter 6.) Hess' framework is important because it effectively indicates the context within which questions about friendships have been raised in the case of the married, the single and the elderly (the three groups on which attention is focused in Chapters 3, 4 and 5 respectively).

The perception of friendship in Hess' schema (1972) as complementary implicitly focuses on the marital situation. At its best, friendship in this situation is seen as 'propping up' the marriage by providing help with child care, emotional support in marital conflict and generally deflecting and mitigating the emotional and physical pressure within the marriage and ensuring that no attempt is made to change the structure (Bernard, 1981). In a gender differentiated society, it is argued, where women are primarily responsible for domestic activities and where family concerns are seen as primary elements in their identity, where occupational segregation exists, where men's primary identity is still seen in occupational terms and where men's and women's interests and activities are typically differentiated, men and women will feel more comfortable in same-sex relationships. Women's friendships, seen in this context, are a positive aspect of female culture (Bernard, 1981). Hess does not raise the issue of the extent to which such relationships may compete for emotional primacy: something which is just coming to the fore in work on married women's friendships. Nevertheless, it will be shown in Chapter 3 that the perception of such relationships as occurring within, and being predominantly shaped by, the marital relationship has set the parameters within which questions about married women's friendships have been asked.

Hess' (1972) second view of friendships as substituting for other socially institutionalized roles sits most easily with studies of the elderly. This view is echoed by Jerrome: 'Friendship thus assumes special importance at times of relative rolelessness. It serves as a means of social integration, and where the individual is in a state of transition to a new pattern of existence, assists in the process of socialization' (Jerrome, 1984: 698). It will be shown in Chapter 5 that some of the most insightful work has been done on friendship amongst this age group. Furthermore, this work has tackled issues related to variation in the form of friendship; as well as those related to the existence of different types of friendship and the personal and social effects of friendship.

Relatively little work has been done which has explicitly looked at friendship as a competitor of the marital relationship (i.e. in Hess', 1972, terms, substituting for it). Indeed, it will be shown in Chapter 4 that, although a good deal of work has been done on single women's friendships, the questions asked about such friendships have typically arisen from within a context dominated by an acceptance of the centrality of heterosexual relationships. Thus, this work has looked at issues such as the fluidity of friendships amongst the single; or has shown the extent to which such relationships are incapable of providing practical help to the divorced or separated.

Hess' (1972) framework is thus interesting in so far as it helps us to contextualize much of the work which has been done on friendship. However, it does not enable us to locate these issues structurally. Thus for example, it is not concerned with power at all. Female–female relationships could be seen as a potential power base, a micro-world where oppression did not exist. Friendships in this context would be inevitably political insofar as they involved a sharing both of personal feelings and of ideas about the world. They would give 'depth and spirit to a political vision of feminism' (Raymond, 1986: 29).

This type of perspective is typically characteristic of the radical feminists. The challenge for such feminists is to facilitate the emergence and development of relationships between women; to establish their legitimacy and to use them to develop women's awareness of their own oppression. Possibly because the existence of such friendships is the premise on which this perspective is based, it has stimulated little empirical work, (although Orbach and Eichenbaum's work (1987) does challenge its rather idealized view of female friendship).

In essence, then, much of the work on friendship has occurred within a framework which effectively takes for granted the social and cultural context within which it occurs. It raises questions within these parameters. Thus, it is not surprising that the most sophisticated theorizing has been concerned with the issue of gender-differentiated patterns of friendship. This has tended to assume implicitly that close intimate relationships are psychologically and morally superior (conveniently ignoring the fact that although women were more likely to have such relationships, they were also more likely to be mentally ill; Argyle, 1990).

In attempting to move towards a theory of friendship, it is necessary to address these cultural and structural issues, and to raise questions about friendship within this wider context. It is also, however, necessary to look at the social processes through which friendships are created and maintained. This is what we now turn to.

THE CHARACTERISTICS OF FRIENDS AND THE PROCESSES THROUGH WHICH FRIENDSHIPS ARE CREATED

Friendship, like love, is unlikely to occur randomly between those in different parts of the social structure:

> friendships in whatever form they take are relationships of equality. They are so in two different senses. Firstly there is a reciprocity and an equivalence of exchange within friendships. . . . Secondly, friendships are relationships of equality in that friends are accepted as being equal within the relationship. There is no hierarchy in friendship, no differentiation.
> (Allan, 1986: 45)

There has been a tendency to ignore the second point made by Allan in the above quotation, viz. that friends are accepted as being equal. On reflection, it is clear that it is almost impossible to have two friends who are exactly similar, although similarity tends to be sought in socially and/ or personally significant areas (typically, for example, those related to gender, social class, age, life stage, marital status, race, religious attitudes, interests, personality traits and intelligence; Hays, 1988).

At any rate, it is commonly accepted that friendship occurs not only amongst those with the same gender but also those of similar social attributes, that is, similar class positions (Allan, 1979, 1989; Bell, 1981b; Willmott, 1987), age (Willmott, 1987) and similar marital status. It has been suggested that this pattern of status homophily (Lazarsfeld and Merton, 1954) may occur because individuals who share social statuses tend to have similar values, attitudes and interests (Lea and Duck, 1982; Aries and Johnson, 1983) and/or because such similarity promotes liking and interaction (Lazarsfeld and Merton, 1954; Newcomb, 1961).

Baker and Hertz (1981) are unusual in so far as they go on to suggest formally that if age and sex are important elements in a structure, then friendships will be homogeneous on these dimensions; that if a community is geographically and socially stable, then friendships will tend to be life-long, etc. Hence, Baker and Hertz are effectively arguing that the form of the friendship which is institutionalized, as well as the identity of the participants who are considered as eligible for friendship, varies in different societies and/or at different points in time. Work such as this is, however, very rare.

Duck (1983) identified several stages in the initiation of friendships, and the skills involved at each stage. Very little attention has been paid to the question of the extent to which these models fit women's friendships – especially their same-sex relationships. At any rate, in discussing the first stage he stressed the importance of the ability to recognize situations suitable for the development of friendship, to recognize potential partners' desires for friendship, to have the ability to identify a suitable target group and to present oneself in a friendly manner with a sensitivity to verbal and non-verbal cues (Duck, 1983: 58). He saw the second stage as involving a movement towards intimacy and the development of shared patterns of activity, communication and exchange (1983: 75, 87). However, his main concern was with heterosexual couples and so he then moved on to issues related specially to that area, that is, to the stage concerned with the decision to cohabit and then to have children. This is, in fact, a common pattern and has been noted by Perlman and Fehr (1986) and Winstead (1988). It is arguable that it implicitly reflects and reinforces the view that friendship relationships are only transitional stages on the road to heterosexual fulfilment.

Gouldner and Symons Strong (1987) are critical of the typical focus in this work on 'choice' and 'selection' of friends:

> An emphasis on this kind of decision making has created an image of shopping in a department store where all the items for sale have been put on display so that each piece of merchandize can be pulled off the rack and tried on for size and style. But . . . the process would be more accurately described as easing into friendship, rather than choosing or selecting friends.
>
> (Gouldner and Symons Strong, 1987: 57)

Gouldner and Symons Strong suggest that there are four important elements involved in the process of making friends: namely, disliking criteria; disregarding criteria; liking criteria and what they call 'individual budgets of friendship' (i.e. the number of friends an individual wants and/or feels they can maintain, given their time, resources and need for friends). Like Duck (1981) and Miell and Duck (1986), they highlight the tentativeness and ambiguity of the relationship, and the delicacy of the process involved in moving the friendship forward.

Gouldner and Symons Strong argue that the similarities apparent in friends arises from the application of criteria for disregarding various categories of 'others' as prospects for further acquaintanceship: 'as a general rule, they consisted of differences in race, educational attainment or cultural background, social position, economic status, intelligence, age, and mode of dress and grooming' (Gouldner and Symons Strong, 1987: 33). Hence one can see these as almost socially constructed 'blinkers'. Under certain conditions (e.g. a prolonged period of desperate loneliness) they suggest that these criteria are modified. Nevertheless, they note that in practice this rarely occurred.

In their own model they focus particularly on the existence of a 'pool of eligibiles' with whom friendships will be formed depending on the individual's need for affiliation (viz. sociability and/or intimacy); the amount of time and energy they have as well as the level of social skills they possess to develop and maintain relationships. They suggest that this 'budget' will vary over the life cycle: 'In the end it appeared as if there were some natural forces operating to limit the first-tier friends to one or two persons, while the second-tier friends numbered about four or five, and so on to larger numbers as involvement tapered off (Gouldner and

Symons Strong, 1987: 43). They noted that good friends were typically likely to meet in settings where they both enjoyed spending time, and where the friendship could be pursued. In this way, the development of the friendship was easily integrated within their life style and was less costly in terms of time and resources. Their model, however, pays little attention to either the social contruction of similar others or the structural factors involved in the creation and/or maintenance of friendships – topics which are taken up in the next two sections.

THE IDENTIFICATION OF 'SIMILAR' OTHERS: AN UNAMBIGUOUS ISSUE?

Although there has been widespread agreement that similarity is an important element in friendship, less attention has been paid to the social construction of that similarity. Thus for example Rose and Roades (1987) suggested that amongst the heterosexuals in their sample, friendships with women of a different generation were more common amongst feminists than non-feminists. The implications of this as regards the differential salience of the identity of woman, and as regards age-similarity as a defining characteristic of friendship have not been explored. Indeed, it is arguable that women's friendships provide a crucial insight into those aspects of their social situations which they see as most central, and hence into those social characteristics which they seek in friends. Thus, although it is clear that similarity in gender and marital status are perceived as important elements in the identification of similar others, there is a good deal of ambiguity surrounding other aspects of the position of women. Bell's work (1981b) ignored the very real differences which can occur between married women on the basis of their life stage and their participation in the labour force, etc. It also ignored the fact that women's lives are not static and that status transitions (whether to parenthood, participation in the labour force or attendance at college) are likely to affect friendships. Most centrally, perhaps, it ignored the ambiguities surrounding women's position in the class structure, and hence the extent to which their friendships were likely to reflect their husbands'/fathers' position in the class structure as opposed to some aspect of their own position (as indicated by their education, occupation before marriage, current occupation, etc.).

Discussions of class position and ways of measuring class can appear totally unrelated to discussions of friendship. They cease to be so, however, within a context where one is concerned with identifying the characteristics of those who are perceived as socially similar (e.g. whom does a divorced woman, currently working as a waitress, but whose ex-husband was a managing director, consider eligible for friendship: her colleagues at work and/or those whose class position was similar to her 'borrowed' one, i.e. her ex-husband's?).

Unfortunately, this type of issue has barely begun to be discussed. Typically, married women are still classified in terms of their husbands' occupation. This ignores the fact that a woman's class position is thus implicitly dependent on her continuing relationship with her husband. It also ignores the fact that women's life style (particularly amongst the very poor – see Stack, 1974) may be crucially affected not by this indirect relationship with the labour force, but by relationships with kin and friends. Furthermore, treating women who are not in paid employment as if their class membership was the same as their husbands', sits uneasily with a definition of class position in terms of participation in the labour force (Delphy, 1984; Acker, 1988).

Since the early 1980s there has been increasing unease as regards classifying women in terms of their husbands' occupations (Murgatroyd, 1982, 1984; Stanworth, 1984; Erikson and Goldthorpe, 1988; Leiulfsrud and Woodward, 1988). Nevertheless, no entirely satisfactory alternative system for classifying occupations has emerged. Crompton and Mann (1986) identified various types of strategies: rejecting the household as the unit of class analysis and classifying each individual separately (originally suggested by Stanworth, 1984); taking the woman's paid employment into account in an overall cross-class description of the family (Britten and Heath, 1983; McRae, 1986); abandoning the categories 'women', 'men' and 'gender' altogether (Siltanen, 1986); defining housewives as a class – so that married women participating in wage labour would have a dual class position (i.e. deriving from their own paid work and from their position as housewives; Walby, 1986); and constructing new occupational scales based on respondents' friendship choices (Stewart *et al.*, 1980).

Such technical decisions can appear to be completely irrelevant to any discussion of friendships between women. They cease to be so if one is interested in looking at class similarities/dissimilarities in friendships or indeed the effect on them of divorce and/or return to college. Indeed, it is obvious from Suitor's (1987) work that the husband's class position is not sufficient to explain the friendship choices of a small sample of married women who returned to college. Thus she found that by the end of their first year at college, those who were full-time students had increased their closeness with friends who had attended college themselves, and had reduced it with those who had not done so. She suggested that her full-time students were basically reducing their closeness with those people to whom (despite similarity in ascribed class position) they no longer felt similar, and intensifying their relationships with those to whom they now felt similar. (The complexity of the situation was, however, illustrated by the fact that the part-time mature students – possibly in an attempt to maintain support for the priority they were giving to family life – adopted a different strategy; that is, they maintained their relationships with their less educated friends and diminished their involvement with their more educated friends.)

Very similar issues arise as regards friendships between women who are in paid employment and those who are full-time housewives. As will be shown in the next section, these difficulties have tended to be interpreted in terms of the rather different timetables of the two groups and their differential access to resources. It is equally possible, however that these friendships are inhibited by a lack of perceived social similarity between the two groups.

It is also obvious that in many situations a structural shortage of 'similar' others may necessitate the creation of equal relationships out of those which are socially unequal. In Chapter 4, for example, it will be argued that in Western society, single never-married women in their thirties or forties may, because of their statistically deviant situation, effectively have to choose as friends either married women, who are similar in status and age, or single never-married women from a different age or class position. The strategies used in 'creating' similarity in such situations have not been explored, although Blumstein and Kollock (1988) have suggested that they could include affirmation of the lower-status person's contribution to the relationship; devaluation of what the higher-status person has to offer and symbolic reduction of the higher-status person's position. Other possible strategies include the restriction of interaction topics or venues to those where status disparity is not visible restriction of interaction to the dyadic level, etc. Such strategies may play a very important part in maintaining the appearance of equality in such friendships and could provide a very useful insight into the nature of the friendship tie. Indeed, one might go on to explore the extent to which the possession of certain objective status resources could be 'traded' against relational 'work' within a friendship; as well as looking at the conditions under which such an arrangement breaks down.

Ironically, these issues, which have been ignored by those who have adopted a traditional undifferentiated view of women have also been ignored by radical feminists, such as Rich (1976), Millett (1977), Firestone (1979), Bunch (1981), Dworkin (1983) and Raymond (1986, 1990). These theorists argue that it is impossible to understand women's experiences outside the context of the hierarchy of relationships and institutions by which men dominate women. In this situation, friendships between women are an essential basis of solidarity and part of a strategy to challenge the system. They argue that the single most important aspect of women's situation is their oppression. In this context women are natural allies – regardless of their age, class or life stage. They argue that women's oppression is more or less constant in various societies although its form may vary:

> whatever my status or situation, my derived economic class, or my sexual preference, I live under the power of the fathers, and I have access only to so much of privilege or influence as the patriarchy is willing to accede to me, and only for so long as I will pay the price for male approval.
>
> (Rich, 1976: 57–8)

Baker Miller (1986) has taken this a stage further by arguing that the experience of oppression has created particular strengths in women, viz. their 'greater sense of the emotional components of all human activity' (1986: 39). This view has been very strongly criticized by others (e.g. Ringelheim, 1985; Guillaumin, 1987) who have seen it as no more and no less than an attempt to obscure women's awareness of their own subordinate position, and in a sense to validate their oppression. For others, women's friendships are linked with both their personality traits and an alternative set of values and life styles: one which they see as potentially culturally radical, 'we [i.e. women] support an ethic of sharing, cooperation and collective involvement that stands in clear opposition to an ethic based on individualism, competition, and private profit' (Ferguson and Folbre, 1981: 329). In each of these perspectives, however, class and racial differences between women have implicitly been ignored, so that, in a sense, one ends up endorsing an undifferentiated view of women (Dhavernas, 1987). This view is increasingly criticized: 'Now that gender divisions between women and men have been so clearly delineated within feminist theory the issue of differences among women deserves far greater attention' (Beechey, 1986: 7). The implications of this view for the identification of socially similar friends has barely begun to be explored.

SITUATIONAL FACTORS FACILITATING AND/OR INHIBITING THE DEVELOPMENT OF WOMEN'S FRIENDSHIPS

> Sociologists have come to realise that communities are ultimately social networks rather than neighbourhood or kinship solidarities; that paid work is a set of social class relations and not an occupational status; and that domestic work, too, is a set of work relations and not an occupational status.
>
> (Wellman, 1985: 159).

Implicit in applications of such an approach to women's friendships is a recognition of the situational factors that influence the initiation, maintenance and termination of such relationships. Concepts such as the immediate social environment (Bott, 1957; Milardo, 1986), personal space (Deem, 1982; Allan, 1989), personal resources and situational constraints (Wellman, 1985; and Allan, 1989) have been used to identify the kinds of factors which are important.

Gouldner and Symons Strong recognized that: 'some social settings discouraged the likelihood of making friends, regardless of the psychological attributes of the women who lived in them' (1987: 20). However, they effectively ignored this issue in their own model. A concrete, but important inhibitor of women's friendships within a patriarchal society arises from the scarcity of public places where women can meet and mingle and form and maintain friendships. This situation is particularly noticeable in Britian:

> Whether the focus is on formal organizations like political parties or trade unions, less formal associations like sporting clubs or other recreational and interest-based clubs, or on explicitly sociable facilities like pubs or social clubs, the majority are distinctly male-oriented. There are comparatively few such organizations which are specifically aimed at women, though the number is undoubtedly growing.
>
> (Allan, 1989: 39)

Whitehead (1976), Allan (1979), Imray and Middleton (1983), Hey (1986) and Green *et al.* (1990) have graphically argued that there are clear social pressures excluding women from public arenas: 'Male social control of public spaces, including leisure venues, can take a number of forms, ranging from silent disapproval, joking or ridiculing behaviour and sexual innuendo, through to open hostility' (Green *et al.*, 1990: 131). On the basis of their own ethnographic study of pub life, Hunt and Satterlee concluded that: 'women to a large extent entered the pub as appendages of men. They came into the pub as sisters, wives, daughters, nieces and girl friends, but hardly ever only as women. The single female drinker was still largely unacceptable' (Hunt and Satterlee, 1987: 591). Hunt and Satterlee do note that for the working-class women in the village they studied, the all-female darts team both enabled the women to gain access (without a male escort) to the pub on a Monday night and gave them the opportunity to attempt to exert some control within the pub on that night by teasing and joking the men who were there. Nevertheless, Hunt and Satterlee suggest that continuing male control was indicated by the fact that on the women's nights, other activities in the pub continued, whereas when the men played darts, such activities were curtailed. Women were even more clearly assigned to marginal or guest status on other nights. In this way 'any possible threat to their [i.e. men's] general perceived solidarity was negated' (1987: 596).

Hunt and Satterlee suggested that this had greater implications for the social life of the working-class women, because they were less likely to be able to go outside the village, and home entertaining was much less a part of their life style. It is worth noting that bingo was not available in that village, and it is seen, at least in other studies, as an acceptable locus for female interaction: 'When you get in there its sort of like going to a meeting you know . . . you can drink and you can have a laugh, and you're safe from anyone coming up and pestering you, not like if you go into a pub, especially around here' (Dixey and Talbot, 1982: 78). This theme was not unusual, with the overwhelming majority of those interviewed in Green *et al.*'s British survey also feeling uncomfortable about going into a pub or a wine bar on their own. Indeed, Whitehead (1976) and Hunt and Satterlee (1986, 1987) have noted that the attempted utilization of public spaces by females, either singly or in groups, tends to be inhibited by the dominant perception of such behaviour as an attempt to initiate contact with a male.

In modern Western society, the communal wash-room, or even the local laundrette is not a common venue for female interaction. The church, in traditional societies, was a potential public focus for such interaction – but increasingly this too has limited appeal. Greater health awareness has provided alternative venues which appear attractive to married women in their twenties and thirties at least (e.g. aerobics classes, leisure centres, figure clinics). These seem to be particularly attractive to middle-class women, although, in fact available British National Data from the General Household Survey (1985) shows that, overall, women are very much less likely than men to engage in sport or to go out for a drink. Assertiveness courses and consciousness-raising groups provide venues for the radically aware while flower arranging, coffee mornings and evening classes cater for others. Such venues, however, appear fragile, middle class and highly self-conscious by comparison with the male-dominated worlds of the pub, darts and pool clubs, outdoor sporting venues, etc. Furthermore, the implications of the absence of public venues for friendships between minorities of women, including those who are homeless and/or in bed-and-breakfast accommodation, have not begun to be discussed (Allan, 1990).

Friendships, as well as being located in a physical setting, are also located within a social setting. Milardo (1986) and Wiseman (1986) suggested that friendships could be initiated and maintained by the networks in which they were embedded. Milardo (1986) argued that where such friendships were embedded within dense networks they were more likely to be stable and enduring (1986: 159–60). Such relationships were likely to be diverse in content; and to be more intense than those in loosely knit networks – partly because one simply got to know more about one's friends in such networks, one was more likely to meet them in various settings and to discuss them with other people. The possibility of receiving help without actually asking for it was also greater within such networks because of the greater visibility of the situation (although it is important to recognize that a dense, highly connected network may be very well aware of, for example, a woman's need for physical protection from a violent husband, but may not either approve of intervening, or may not see it as their job to do so: Eckenrode and Wethington, 1990). Milardo also recognized that 'Paradoxically, however, association within dense clusters may be high in conflict as well as closeness simply by virtue of the intensity and breadth of the structural interdependency' (Milardo, 1986: 162). In some cases, networks may stimulate friendships directly (by providing introductions), while in other cases it may be simply that the presence of a local network acts as a 'secure base' from which the respondent can easily move forward to form friendships (O'Connor and Brown, 1984). In an increasingly geographically mobile society, where men are still seen as the main wage earners, women's experience of – often involuntary – geographical mobility will have implications for their friendships. In this situation, it will be difficult for women to maintain contact with childhood, school or premarital work or socially based friendships. These relationships may continue to exist 'in their mind', as sources of attachment, but not as viable sources of interaction, intimacy, etc. In this situation the development of new friendships presupposes the existence of accessible similar others. It also typically requires considerable time, energy and social skills. Working-class women have traditionally been seen as less likely to have these social skills (Gavron, 1966) – although it may also, of course, be that they simply have fewer resources to initiate such relationships.

The ability to create and maintain non-local friendships is ever more clearly related to the availability of resources such as time, money and transport: resources which are more likely to be available to middle-class than working-class respondents. Various studies have found that involvement with friends outside the neighbourhood was likely to be greatest amongst middle-class respondents. This is arguably not unrelated to the fact that women – especially working-class women – are less likely either to have a driving licence or to have access to a car (Deem, 1986; Allan, 1989). Inevitably, then, their movements – both by day and by night – are more restricted (fears of sexual harassment in public places and of walking alone, especially at night, further exacerbating the situation). In this situation in the absence of socially similar others within the neighbourhood, their friendship options are very severely limited indeed.

Many forms of routine sociability require some level of resources. Indeed, Cheal (1987) has argued that the construction of social ties is interwoven with the issue of resources. He argued that buying and giving gifts was seen as predominantly the woman's responsibility (1987: 153) at all levels of the class structure. However, the actual expenditure of family resources on the maintenance of the women's own personal friends (as opposed to joint friends or relatives) is arguably likely to be a contentious issue.

Oliker (1989) suggested that women are unlikely to have material resources of their own to dispose of and can often have little to offer other than themselves. Certainly, Green *et al.* (1990) concluded that in their study of roughly 700 women there was little free time (especially uninterrupted time) available for the women's own leisure activities, because of the women's domestic and family caring responsibilities. In that study the women's leisure expenditure also typically had a low priority in the household budget and they were expected to choose from a limited range of inexpensive home-based, 'respectable' leisure activities. In this context 'going out for a laugh with the girls' was very much a highlight, but one which had to be carefully planned and negotiated, with the more-or-less explicit understanding that it should not become too regular. Middle- and upper-class white women are, of course, likely to have more extensive resources to spend on friendship (although Green *et al.*, 1990, suggested that they rarely feel free to exercise their right to them). The implications of this for their friendships have only begun to be explored.

Paradoxically, Stack's (1974) and Nelson's (1978) studies of poor socially marginalized women did suggest that in these extreme situations, women's relationships with each other were strong despite, indeed because of, their very limited resources. O'Connor (1990) and McKee and Bell (1986) suggested that less extreme situations of social marginality (e.g. where the husband was unemployed) were associated with the absence of a close confidant relationship. This situation arose partly because of the absence of financial resources to maintain patterns of routine sociability, and partly because the husband's unemployment restricted the wife's own social space, so that she became in McKee and Bell's terms, 'doubly isolated' (i.e. because friends were less willing to visit during the day or evening, seeing it as an intrusion into their couple-based life; and because the very visibility of her interaction with friends during the day highlighted her husband's own social isolation and so provoked his attempts to control or limit her activities). In this situation, it is obvious that the lack of financial resources and of public interaction venues, as well as the construction of the home as a site for couple-based interaction inhibits the development of female friendships.

It is clear, then, that for the most part the situational conditions operating in our society do not encourage the development of female friendships – but to a greater or lesser degree can be seen as inhibiting them. Little attempt has been made to theorize about these phenomena, or indeed to integrate these insights into a more structural analysis of the position of women in society. Allan (1989, 1990) has argued for a wider view of class (encompassing employment, housing and geographical mobility) and for a conception of gender transcending the categorical and taking into account its implications as regards personal and public space, caring responsibilities and the availability of resources such as time, money, etc. Issues related to the stereotype of women as carers, to the ideological definition of femininity and of respectability and sexuality are all arguably related to the situational limitations on the creation of friendships between women. Typically, however, these issues have not been tackled at a theoretical level.

MAINTAINING AND ENDING FRIENDSHIPS

Up to the mid-1970s much of the work on relationships was concerned with initial attraction, and hence issues related to the maintenance or termination of friendships were virtually unexplored. A number of models of relational development were available, for example, reinforcement theories, including both exchange and equity theories (e.g. Homans, 1961; Blau, 1964; see also Robeito, 1989), penetration theories (e.g. Altman and Taylor, 1973) and stage theories, that is, those which focused on the interaction processes at each stage and on the factors affecting movement from one stage to another (e.g. Levinger and Snoek, 1972; Levinger, 1980). Within the past few years there has been increasing disenchantment with these theories in general terms, but more particularly as a way of understanding friendships (see e.g. Duck and Perlman, 1985; Perlman and Fehr, 1986). Since that time a number of advances have been made at the level of identifying the issues involved in maintaining and terminating friendships: for example, managing dissimilarity, reclassifying friendships, balancing autonomy and connection, openness and closedness, and predictability and novelty. Once again, however, relatively little empirical work has been done in this area.

Duck (1988) suggested that several very different concerns were implicit in the idea of maintaining a relationship: namely, ensuring that it did not atrophy; that it remained at its present level of commitment and intimacy; and that conflict was dealt with in such a way as to avoid the termination of the relationship. Part of the problem involved in looking at the maintenance of relationships arises from the difficulty of knowing when a relationship exists. Thus, for example, there may be almost no interaction between friends for years (because of situational factors such as geographical inaccessability) and yet the friendship may be felt to exist, and may indeed provide an important source of identity validation. It is not unusual (see e.g. Pahl and Pahl, 1971; O'Connor and Brown, 1984) for respondents to include those whom they have not seen for several years amongst their close friends. (Indeed, such people are frequently described by respondents as their 'best' friends.) Such friendships may be maintained by no more than a Christmas card or a holiday postcard. Indeed, it is difficult to know whether or not such relationships are merely mental constructs. However they may be very important to isolated women, who cling to some concept of self which transcends, and possibly predates, their current identities. There is evidence to suggest that those who have no other friendships may well be simply indicating their own anxiety and/or search for attachment by referring to these friendships as 'close' (O'Connor and Brown, 1984).

At the very opposite end of the continuum, Duck (1988) suggested that embeddedness in the routines of daily living may play an important part in maintaining friendships: 'One way of looking at it is to recognize that the sharing of close relationships involves the sharing of our lives, not just our feelings, and that our lives are made up of all that humans think, feel, experience, and do' (Duck, 1988: 8). Individual work (e.g. making plans, writing letters, making phone calls, buying presents, giving surprises and providing meals) all play a part in maintaining the relationship. Ayres (1983) suggested that such relational work becomes particularly important in maintaining the relationship when one partner wants to withdraw and the other wants to maintain the status quo. There has also been a recognition that relationships may be sustained by the exchange of gifts (Caplow, 1982; Cheal,1986) and/or the development of a dyadic culture, with its own rituals, pet names, etc. (Baxter, 1987; Duck, 1990b).

Duck and Pond (1989) argue that people think about their interactions and discuss their interpretations of them, and that this may, in certain circumstances, lead them to modify their view of a relationship and/or their own behaviours in it.

> In many cases, talk and accounts to friends serve to assess and create or modify the 'digestive juices' for prior or subsequent interaction. Questions such as 'Was I right?', 'Do you think I was silly?' 'What should I do to change this state of affairs' can lead to talk that changes one's views of a relationship.
>
> (Duck and Pond, 1989: 22)

It is indeed plausible to suggest that this type of process is very common in friendship and that it both reflects and maintains the relationship. A small number of qualitative studies (Gullestad, 1984; Jerrome, 1984; Oliker, 1989; Morgan, 1990) have looked at 'talk' in these contexts within women's friendships. This work (which will be described in more detail in subsequent chapters) is very revealing, raising as it does the whole question of the relationship between the form and content of friendships, as well as the relationship between micro-level and macro-level processes.

Baxter's work (1990) on the dialectical tensions between autonomy and connection, between openness and closedness, and between predictability and novelty in romantic relationships has interesting possibilities as regards providing an insight into the processes maintaining friendships. So far, most attention has been paid to the intimacy dimension (see Reis and Shaver, 1988), the suggestion being that confiding offers the partner the possibility of moving the relationship to a point of greater intimacy – or alternatively (by ignoring this opportunity) of maintaining it at the existing level. Less attention has been paid to the processes operating at the other two levels, although both appear highly applicable to friendship. Certainly, interactional manoeuvres to establish a satisfactory balance between autonomy and connection are part of the friendship process. This balance will often change as the respondents' family situation or personal needs change. There are considerable possibilities for error in friendship in this area, for example, in the sense of being overintrusive or uninvolved. Indeed, La Gaipa (1990) sees this as one of the dialectical points of tension in relationships. It featured as an important source of grievance amongst Gouldner and Symons Strong's (1987) respondents in exploring the break-up of their close female friendships. It has also been implicitly endorsed by Argyle and Henderson's work (1985a), which, from a very different perspective, highlighted the importance of successfully negotiating this tension by noting that respecting the other's privacy was one of the universal rules in the twenty-two types of relationships they studied (the limits of that private area arguably reflecting the balance achieved at any one point between autonomy and connection).

The third tension, between predictability and novelty, has been the subject of even less interest although Duck and Miell (1986) and Duck (1988) noted the importance of the process of uncertainty reduction in relationships. Hence one would expect that strategies to create predictability in relationships would be important. Equally of course, since at least certain types of friendships are essentially 'fun' relationships, one would expect them to include components of novelty. Hence, in friendship (as indeed in marriage) there is a tension between the elements of predictability and novelty.

Furthermore it is recognized that, over time, dissimilarities may occur in the characteristics of friends (e.g. in the wake of widowhood, divorce, return to paid employment or to college). Many friendships do wane in this situation, although others devise ways of managing such dissimilarity, and so continuing the relationship. The creation of similarity and equality out of dissimilarity is thus a process which continues during the life of the friendship. Work on strategies has only just begun, and to date much of it has either continued to deal with the marital dyad (Dindia and Baxter, 1987) or tended simply to report the use of very general mechanisms (e.g. Rose, 1985, who noted that same-sex friendships were maintained by acceptance, communication, common interests and effort).

Duck (1982) identified stages in the dissolution of relationships: beginning with dissatisfaction with the relationship, progressing to dissatisfaction with the partner, confrontation with the partner, publication of relationship distress and then what Duck called the 'grave-dressing stage', that is, getting over it all and tidying it up. At each stage he identified the concerns of those involved in the relationship, and the type of reparative intervention necessary. His model appears to show considerable promise as regards understanding the tension and conflict operating not only in courtship but also in friendship relationships, although few of these ideas have been specifically used in the study of women's friendships.

Wiseman (1986, 1990), unlike much of the other work, drew attention to the structural features of friendship and the implications these have as regards the process of termination. Thus, for example, she noted that, unlike marriage, friendship is buttressed by neither legal nor social supports; it involves the acquisition of no 'side bets', such as children, joint financial interests, etc. There are no rituals indicating when one has moved across a particular threshold of friendship (e.g. from being a casual friend to a work colleague, a special activity friend; good friend or a 'bosom buddy'; Wiseman, 1990). In fact she argued that it is possible for friends to be 'regraded' without discussion or negotiation, and often without even knowing that it has occurred: a strategy she suggests that is widely used to deal with problems in the relationship.

Most other studies (e.g. Rose, 1984; Gouldner and Symons Strong, 1987; Helgeson *et al.*, 1987) have found a similar pattern of avoidance of conflict in friendship (Wright's 1982 study is an exception in this respect). These implicitly suggest that the process of dissolution in friendship may be rather different from the general model of relationship dissolution proposed by Duck (1982). The sources of dissatisfaction identified in these studies as leading to partial or total withdrawal do, however, suggest the existence of what Wiseman (1986) calls unwritten contracts of friendship: contracts which, incidentally, it is not acceptable to discuss or clarify (a topic to which we return in Chapter 6).

Work by Weber *et al.* (1983) and Harvey *et al.* (1986, 1989) has begun to look at the types of accounts developed to explain the demise of relationships, that is, 'story-like explanations of past actions and events which include characterizations of self and significant others' (Harvey *et al.*, 1989: 40). Very little empirical work has been done on the extent to which such accounts are developed about the end of women's friendships although this seems likely to occur. Gouldner and Symons Strong (1987) noted that where women belonged to close-knit networks of friends, such networks occasionally volunteered or were asked to help ease the strain between friends. It is not at all clear, however, to what extent female friends actually involve their networks in developing publicly negotiable accounts of the history and demise of their friendships (as was implied by Duck's general model, 1982, of relationship dissolution).

In the general context of ending relationships, work in the wider personal-relationships area has highlighted issues related to the availability of more attractive partners, the perceived cost of leaving a relationship and the equitability of the 'returns' got relative to a partners' (i.e. exchange and equity theories). Duck (1988) has rather wittily criticized such approaches on the grounds that they assume that people have little else to do in their lives other than work out audits on their relationships. Indeed there is an increasing recognition that theories focusing on simple exchange processes are far too crude to explain satisfactorily the maintenance or ending of friendships. Equally, there is disillusionment with a simple concern with social skills:

> Relationships are sustained not merely by people's feelings for one another but also by people's routines, their trivial interconnections and presence in one another's spheres of life; by their strategic behaviour intended to sustain the relationship and also by the actions and communications of other friends, mutual acquaintances or colleagues.
>
> (Duck, 1988: 100)

It is clear that very little empirical work has been done on the processes involved in maintaining friendship relationships. Nevertheless key issues have been identified and work in this area seems likely to become increasingly important in the 1990s.

ISSUES ARISING FROM THIS WORK

The importance of a theoretical analysis has frequently been underlined (Hess, 1972; Bulmer, 1985). Attempts to theorize about friendship may arise at many different levels. In so far as one regards friendship simply as a human condition, then it is appropriate to look at it within the context of a theory of needs, a typology of love and/or an examination of relational provisions. As argued in the previous chapter, it seems necessary to go beyond this. Typically, the theoretical work which has been done so far has mainly focused on gender-differentiated patterns of friendship and has attempted to explain them: an exercise which appears to have doubtful validity not least because of the increasing tendency to stress similarities rather than differences in such relationships. Early functionalist attempts (Hess, 1972) to look at the extent to which friendship complemented, substituted for or competed with the marital relationship have arguably produced few theoretical insights, while radical feminists, although extolling their importance, have been disinclined to move beyond this.

A number of issues were raised in this chapter. Firstly, it was argued that there was a need to test and develop theories about the processes through which friendships are created, maintained and ended. Furthermore, it was suggested that such work should, where possible, attempt to build on those insights derived from descriptive studies of the characteristics of friends, and from a broader understanding of the social and cultural milieu within which such friendships are located. Thus for example, it was noted that although it has long been recognized that friends tend to have similar social characteristics, scant attention has been paid to the way in which such similarity is socially constructed and reflected in what Gouldner and Symons Strong (1987) called 'disregarding criteria'. Hence an important opportunity to identify what are regarded as the crucial dimensions of the social structure has been lost (e.g. ideas about relative importance of age as opposed to ascribed class position amongst married women, and of age versus marital status in the case of single women in their thirties and forties).

Equally, in theorizing about the initiation of friendships, greater attention needs to be paid to wider issues related to the position of women, such as the cultural valuation of friendships between women, sexualization of physical contact, the notion of respectability; the absence/presence of public interaction venues which are conducive to the initiation of friendship relationships, as well as the availability of personal resources (such as time, money, freedom from other responsibilities) to create and/or maintain friendships.

Work on friendship which has theorized about processes has tended to be located within a social psychological perspective. Inevitably perhaps then, it has paid little attention to the way that 'talk' in friendships may generate and maintain what Morgan (1990) called 'shared understandings' or 'shared knowledge structures'. Although within general sociology it is common to note that class structures are reproduced through kin and friendship relationships, the ways in which this occurs through friendship relationships tends to have been ignored by personal relationship theorists and sociologists alike.

Finally, the fluidity of the friendship relationship and its lack of institutional supports has implications for our understanding of the process of friendship termination – and especially the possibility of emotionally withdrawing from and reclassifying friendships without even the other person necessarily realizing this.

In this chapter an attempt has been made to identify the elements which would need to be included in a theoretical understanding of friendship between women. These issues will be returned to in the final chapter. Arguably, however, in order to move forward it is necessary to identify different types of friendship between women since one can no longer assume that the only or most important type of relationship is that characterised by intimate confiding – a focus which has implicitly dominated both the early functionalist theorizing and that relating to gender-differentiated friendship styles. This task is begun in the next chapter.

— 3 —

Married women and their friendships

INTRODUCTION

One of the strange paradoxes of Western society is that gender role stereotyping coexists with a strong commitment to the primacy of marriage and a heterosexual couple-based ideology. Implicit in this position is both the recognition and devaluing of 'women's worlds' and the imposition of culturally unrealistic demands on the marital relationship. The acceptable role for women's friendships in this scenario is complementing the marital relationship, that is, providing practical and emotional resources which, for various reasons, are not or cannot be provided by the marital relationship. In this context, friendships involving married women are potentially fraught with difficulty since the very closeness of a woman's ties with her female friends may well compete with the marital relationship, and so may generate feelings of jealousy and conflicting commitments. They will in any case generate and reinforce various aspects of the woman's identity which in themselves may create difficulties within the marriage.

Hence, although married women's friendships characterized by practical help and/or intimacy potentially ease the demands made on a spouse, their unintended effects may be feared. Traditional strategies for dealing with these possibilities have included devaluing these friendships, clearly limiting their importance and highlighting the primacy of the marital relationship (e.g. by discouraging visiting between female married friends at 'prime couple time' (i.e. during the evening and at weekends).

Friendships between married women which are rooted in the pure sociability and fun of recreational activities at first glance seem to pose no challenge to the emotional primacy of the marital relationship. In fact, however, the commingling of images of leisure with sexuality, and the tension between this and the stress on sacrifice and service in the stereotypes of 'good mothers and wives' generates considerable ambivalence about such activities and relationships.

As outlined in the previous chapter, the creation and maintenance of all women's friendships is affected by what Green *et al.* (1990) called 'ideologies of respectability' ('reputation' in Heidensohn's, 1985, terms), by their limited access to public arenas, especially those which, by their nature, are conducive to fun 'activities', by the ideology that public areas are 'dangerous' for lone females, and by their limited access to personal resources (including time, money and transport). These constraints are arguably widely experienced by women (Green *et al.*, 1990), regardless of their marital status. They are, however, likely to be particularly acute in the case of married women, although one might expect that their importance amongst this group might vary, depending, for example, on their own participation in the labour force, their stage of family cycle, their husband's class position and/or his attitude to their female friendships.

It is, however, far too crude to see the pressures operating on women's friendships as simply lying outside the women themselves. Rather, the shape of these friendships may reflect what Oliker (1989: 120) referred to as 'prudence regarding the higher commitments of marriage and family'. In fact, the processes operating in them may well reflect and reinforce ideas about the primacy of such responsibilities – so that they may be what Green *et al.* (1990: 135) called 'powerful reinforcers of the system of patriarchal control'. In that situation, what women see as their 'real' friendships may become simply mental constructs, starved of the resources necessary to undertake the solidary or 'love labour' (Lynch, 1989) to maintain them. They may retain an important subjective reality, and may well embody a salient self-definition, but still be devoid of interactional reality. In a sense then, the only threat they pose is at an ideological level – paralleling and potentially challenging the emotional primacy of romantic love.

In this chapter an attempt will first be made to explore the kinds of friends married women have (both drawing on a range of literature and providing in-depth vignettes illustrating these various kinds of friendship). Secondly, the chapter will explore the extent to which marriage and friendship complement and/or potentially substitute for each other – or indeed are perceived as doing so. Thirdly, it will look at the factors which influence the creation or development of particular kinds of friendships amongst married women. Finally, it will look at the effects of friendship both at an individual level and at a wider socio-cultural level, that is, in terms of creating and maintaining social realities – in particular, those related to the class structure and the identity of the couple as a unit. Underlying these specific foci is the idea that although at one level friendships between women are constrained in various ways, the cultural reality of many of these friendships – particularly, indeed, intimate relationships – is that they reflect and reinforce the constraints in their own situation.

WHAT KINDS OF FRIENDSHIPS DO MARRIED WOMEN HAVE?

Typically, there have been three kinds of approaches to this topic. Firstly, studies have asked married women if they have someone to whom they feel close or very close, and have then just noted the number of such relationships that exist. Secondly, studies have identified what are seen to be crucial properties (e.g. frequency of contact, intimacy) and have explored the extent to which they have relationships with these properties. Thirdly, studies have identified various types of friendships and have looked at the extent to which they exist within married women's lives. This section will present work drawn from each of these three streams.

A good deal of work has been done on the first topic – especially within the American network tradition. Typically this work has simply asked respondents to identify those who are identified as 'close', 'very close' or 'best' friends. One of the difficulties of this approach is that it is difficult to know to what extent the figures are comparable (e.g. does the identification of a 'best friend' imply that the relationship has a special quality, or does it simply indicate that it is the best of those relationships currently available to the respondent?). The situation is further complicated by the fact that some studies have not excluded kin ties from those identified as very close. Furthermore, others have asked their respondents to focus on those close friends 'living locally' or 'seen socially' – thereby making comparisons even more invidious. Argyle and Henderson (1985b) suggested that in fact, there is a tendency for people to have only one or two 'best' friends, whereas they may say they have up to five close friends. In fact, however, quite a good deal of variation emerges as regards the number of friends identified.

There is also considerable variation in the proportion of respondents who have no close or best friends. Thus, for example, roughly one in six of Strain and Chappell's (1982) married respondents in their Winnipeg sample had no confidant. A very similar proportion (i.e. one in five) of O'Connor's (1987) lower-middle-class London sample of married women said they had no very close friends. On the other hand, however, roughly half of the married female college alumnae in Goodenow and Gaier's (1990) study did not have a close reciprocal best friendship (defined as a friendship with a high level of intimacy, attachment and equality).

There was also some evidence to suggest that middle-class respondents were more likely than their working-class counterparts to have close friends; for example, less than one in ten of Bell's middle-class sample (1968) and one in twenty of Allan's (1979) middle-class sample having no best or close friend; as compared with one in four of Allan's (1979) working-class respondents and two-thirds of Mogey's (1956) working-class sample.

The picture as regards the number of close or best relationships identified is equally complex – again reflecting the nature of the samples and the definition of closeness implicitly or explicitly used. Thus, for example, Weiss and Lowenthal's (1975) mid-life sample identified 4.7 friends. Fischer (1982b) found that in his large north Californian sample a very similar number of friends were identified (i.e. 4.9). Wellman (1979) analysed the networks of a large sample in Toronto, and found that on average they had two to three unrelated intimates. Wellman also noted that typically one to three network members were identified as what he called 'socially close confidants . . . to whom people pour out their hearts' (1990: 202) – although only roughly half of these were friends. Indeed, broadly similar trends emerged in O'Connor's (1987) study of London married women who identified (on average) 1.9 very close relationships – with roughly half of these again being friends.

Apart from indicating that close ties exist outside the family, it is hard to know what can be made of these trends. Typically they have been 'mapped' in an atheoretical way in the American network tradition. In an attempt to move beyond the impasse, some work has attempted to map the supportive provisions of these relationships in more detail – usually looking at frequency and quality of interaction, intimacy, practical help, identity enhancement, perceived attachment and solidarity. Implicit in this work is the idea that certain types of experiences are supportive, and hence there is an interest in exploring the degree to which such supportive experiences are provided by friendship, and/or an attempt to explore what Davis and Todd (1985) called the 'essential relational attributes' of friendship.

Frequency of face-to-face contact has been widely used in these detailed studies of friendship provisions (Bell, 1968; Allan, 1979; O'Connor, 1987; Willmott, 1987). Thus, for example, O'Connor (1987) found that roughly two-thirds of those friends who were identified as very close in her study were seen at least every two to three weeks. Similarly, Wellman (1990), on the basis of a follow-up study of a small sample of those initially interviewed in 1977, concluded that companionship, both in the sense of discussing ideas and doing things together, was so typical of friendships that he concluded that without it there would be little reason for many friendships to exist.

However, the validity of frequency of contact as an indicator of the closeness of such relationships is questionable. Thus Pahl and Pahl (1971), Wellman (1982), O'Connor and Brown (1984) and Gouldner and Symons Strong (1987) found that people who were rarely seen were also sometimes identified as close friends. In part, this seemed to reflect the fact that the longer the friendship, the greater the likelihood that friends would not be living near each other, and hence the less frequent their contact. Indeed Rubin (1985) argued that frequency of contact could well be completely irrelevant, since the designation of someone as a friend might simply be a statement of attachment: 'These old friends can remain significant features in our internal lives – people to whom we made attachments, with whom we identified and who, therefore, played some part in our growth and development' (Rubin, 1985: 35). O'Connor and Brown (1984) found that roughly one in five of the women in that study who were identified as very close were of this kind. Frequently, these relationships were characterized by togetherness and a history of shared experiences. O'Connor (1987) suggested that such feelings, together with complete acceptance and the felt ability to confide, could be regarded as indicative of solidarity or 'primary quality' in a relationship. In that study, 70 per cent of the very close friendships identified by the respondents were characterized by a high level of this quality. In some cases, these feelings were clearly underpinned by high levels of face-to-face interaction. In other cases, however, it was clear that these feelings existed very much in a situational vacuum and reflected more the respondents' need for such a relationship than its actual supportiveness (O'Connor and Brown, 1984).

A vignette from O'Connor's study (1987) illustrates the existence of this property. Kay Holland describes her relationship with her friend Pam whom she had known since childhood, as 'strong – a lasting friendship'. She feels that Pam really knows and understands her. 'She knows what I'm thinking'; 'It's the same as her with me. I've often known what she's thinking after she's said a couple of words – you know – I know how she feels from the way she is speaking.' She does not think Pam would think badly of her for any reason and this unconditional acceptance means that 'we can talk about anything'. 'You don't have to worry about what you say.'

Kay would tell her things that she would not tell anyone else and she sees this as a natural continuation of the fact that: 'when we were at school, we had secrets and you know, you sort of follow it through.' The content of their confiding has changed over the years but the closeness has remained the same. The shared experience of the past is an important element in the relationship 'we can talk about old school friends . . . we can have a laugh.' She feels that they would still keep in contact even if Pam moved to the North, and does not feel they would drift apart in that situation. The relationship has become a fictive kin relationship. 'She calls them [Kay's parents] her second Mum you know and second Dad, so she's just like the family to us.' Kay Holland says that they think alike, have the same ideas and views and are so alike, 'So much like sisters that we might actually be twins.'

O'Connor (1987, 1990) differentiated between such feelings and what she called the existence of felt attachment or security. In that study the existence of such an attachment was indicated by the others' perceived willingness to help out in any situation, and in general to be a security figure in the respondents' life. Such a perception, of course, may or may not be associated with the level of help provided by the relationship on a day-to-day basis. Thus, for example, O'Connor (1987) found that in her sample only a tiny minority of the very close friendships actually provided high levels of practical help, while more than two-fifths were assessed as providing a high level of felt security. It was noticeable that a high level of such feelings did not exist where a friend was young, inexperienced or was seen as emotionally unstable, since in these circumstances they were not credible security figures. Similarly, recently acquired friends were not typically seen as sources of security either. O'Connor (1987) illustrates this property through the use of case material such as Rita Jackson's.

Rita says that it is important to her that her very close friend Vera is there. She says that 'if a bad sickness or something really terrible happened to me and she wasn't around, I would be lost. She knows my

parents and if anything happened to me, she can sort things out in a way.'
Rita does worry about her not being there: 'I do worry because, putting
my husband aside she's the only one that knows my family back home.'
When asked if she would feel lost if she was not there, she says: 'empty in
a way.' She sees Vera as willing to help her out in any situations: 'to put
herself out if she had to 'cause I would do it for her'. In fact, however, she
does not actually provide her with practical help on an ongoing basis.
Nevertheless, it is obvious that the relationship provides a high level of
felt security and so, in this sense, it is characterized by a high level of felt
attachment. O'Connor (1987) found that there was a strong association
between the felt security provided by the relationship, and the primary
quality of that relationship – both, in fact, indicated a relationship which
had little social reality although it was of considerable psychological
importance.

Intimacy has been widely used as an indicator of closeness in
friendship. This tradition goes back to Komarovsky (1967), who
suggested that:

> A person is said to have a confidant if he shares with the other such matters
> as suspicion of his spouse's infidelity; his own unfaithfulness; pleasant or
> unpleasant facts about his sexual life; regrets about marriage; details of
> serious quarrels; some of his deeper disappointments in himself – disap-
> pointments about the spouse's ambitions, intelligence or other traits; and
> confidences about the spouse's relationships with relatives and in-laws.
>
> (1967: 207)

Sometimes, however, there has been a failure to differentiate between
actual confiding in a friend and the feeling that one could confide in
them. Thus Bell noted that 'I found after probing that some women who
say they would reveal anything to a best friend often do not completely
do so' (Bell, 1981b: 65). Three-fifths of the women in Bell's study
(1981b) said that they would and did confide in at least one of their close
friends. Other studies have been less assiduous and this may partly
account for variation in the trends as regards intimate confiding in close
friendships. At any rate, Willmott (1987) found that four-fifths of the
married women in his study discussed such personal matters with
someone other than their spouse (1987: 52), a trend which led him to
conclude that 'friends generally – not just local ones – emerge in the role
of confidants' (Willmott, 1987: 65). In her small American study, Oliker
(1989) found that the overwhelming majority of women talked to friends

about their marital problems (even occasionally discussing marital issues with them before raising them with their partner). They preferred to talk to close friends (rather than their husband) about their children, news and gossip – although money problems, marital sex and conflict between friends were not seen as appropriate for discussion with friends in that study. In O'Connor's (1987) study just over half of the very close friendships were characterized by a high level of intimate confiding – and there did not seem to be any constraints in this area other than as regards talking about the details of the marital sexual relationship.

Thus, for example, Tessie Halpin's relationship with her close friend Brenda in that study was assessed as high in intimate confiding. She says of her: 'She is good [to talk things over with]. It's only Brenda really that I discuss my worries with.' She has talked to her about her money worries – trying to make ends meet now that her husband is out of work and four children have to be fed out of Social Security. Two of her children have had problems at school and she has talked to her about this. Her marriage has been turbulent and she has left her husband once and is considering leaving him again (at least for a trial period) and she has talked to her about this. However she feels that 'she can't know the bed side of marriage. I mean I've never discussed that with her – we've never made it a subject. I don't know why. We've never really spoke over our sex problems or anything like that. Now and again it might come up, but not really a conversation as such.' Nevertheless, when she was upset about her relatives' suspicion that she was having an affair with her husband's brother, she did confide in Brenda. She also talked to her before she had her recent sterilization operation ('get him done', she said). In addition to confiding in her about these major issues and rather personal topics, Tessie Halpin also confides in her about her day-to-day ups and downs: 'if I'm fed up and just generally had enough of everything'.

It is only since the early 1980s that this preoccupation with intimacy as an indicator of friendship has been challenged. Prior to this, it had almost become unthinkable that friendships between women could be defined in other terms. Since then, however, there has been an increasing awareness that relationships based on shared activities and/or enjoyable interaction could well make an important contribution to women's life style even if they were not characterized by high levels of intimacy. The importance of this type of purely sociable interaction was graphically outlined by Simmel, who spoke of 'the impulse of sociability . . . which distils as it were, out of the realities of social life the pure essence of association' (1971: 129). Very little interest has been shown in this aspect of life –

particularly in the context of friendships between women: although Rosencrance (1986) depicted it in his study of male relationships within a racing-track context.

O'Connor (1987) did look at the positive/negative quality of interaction with those who were identified as very close (i.e. taking into account the extent to which interaction was vibrant, humdrum, conflictful, etc.). She found that almost four-fifths of those friends who were identified as very close had interaction which was highly positive in quality. Henrietta Smith's friendship with her very close friend Ann illustrates this highly positive interaction. Henrietta meets Ann regularly once a week at keep-fit class and they have a drink together afterwards. She also plays tennis with Ann and goes out with her to other places from time to time. She says that 'it's a riot' when they are together and looks forward to seeing her friend: 'She's sort of good fun to be with. She's always laughing. She sort of cheers me up, you know. I just enjoy her company.' As Henrietta Smith remarks herself: 'There's some people who are your friends and all they talk about is their worries. It brings you down.' She stresses that 'we don't sort of bring each other down. I don't think I've ever known her to be in a bad mood or miserable really.' Because of the preoccupation with intimacy as the defining characteristic of 'real' friendship, relatively little interest has been shown in these sorts of friendships, although Gouldner and Symons Strong (1987) did note that in their study there was a small number of women whose friendships revolved around doing things together (such as recreational activities, hobbies, etc.).

What can broadly be regarded as nurturance has also, although very much more rarely, been used as an indicator in studies of friendship. At its simplest level, this can be conceptualized as the giving of practical help: something which has been seen as an ambiguous indicator of friendship. Thus, on the one hand, Baker and Hertz (1981: 279) have seen material exchange and assistance as a 'nearly ubiquitous role of friendship'. On the other hand, in O'Connor's study (1987) only a tiny minority of the very close friendships provided a high level of practical help. Indeed, Allan (1989) argued that such help, particularly if it was unilateral and long term, was incompatible with the nature of friendship. Willmott's (1987) study provided a fuller and considerably more complex picture in so far as it suggested that friends were seen as a main source of either babysitting or financial loans by only one in five of the respondents, although one-third saw them as a main source of help if a child was ill; and more than half saw them as a main source of help with shopping and house maintenance. Thus it may well be that it was the failure to differentiate more sharply between types of help which has been associated with the absence of clear trends in this area.

It is also possible, however, that some of the confusion in this area reflects the fact that, while some questions have tapped the level of help actually provided, others have been more concerned with the other person's perceived willingness to provide help – something which, as previously mentioned, can be regarded as an indicator of the felt security provided by the relationship. Weiss' (1974) and Wright's (1978) theoretical work has directed attention to what appears to be a more universal aspect of nurturance, namely, the validation and/or identity enhancement provided by the relationship. This aspect of friendship is in fact seen by Wright (1978), Rubin (1985) and Willmott (1987) as crucial. Thus, for example, Rubin argued that 'Although close personal friendships may be important to a man for other reasons, traditionally he has not needed them to affirm self in quite the same way a woman does, because marriage doesn't strip him so profoundly of a personal identity' (Rubin, 1985: 134). A similar argument was put forward by the Hite Report (1987). It found that three quarters of the American married women in that study had a strong sense of themselves 'as someone above and beyond the family unit' (1987: 109) – a phenomenon which they attributed at least partly to the validation provided by friendship relationships.

Surprisingly little empirical attention has been paid to this dimension in 'static' studies of friendship. It is, however, implicit in Oliker's (1989) and Gullestad's (1984) suggestion that, through their conversations, women friends create and/or validate identities – as wives, mothers, etc. In Gullestad's study, much of the conversation of the women revolved around the development of standards of sexual morality, and their attempts to deal with the tension between the values of monogamous love and faithfulness and their desire for novelty and excitement. There was a strong theme of moral responsibility in this talk: a theme which in Oliker's study (1989) found a particular expression in the validation of their identities as mothers. In fact, Oliker suggested that discussing their children created unique bonds between close friends; the validation they provided for each other in this area being one which was typically not available either from their husbands or indeed the wider society.

O'Connor's (1987) approach was in some ways more static in so far as it simply looked at the extent to which the respondents experienced their very close friendships as identity enhancing/destructive. This dimension took into account their perceived evaluation of their friends' performance in various roles and their general positive/negative evaluation of them as people (O'Connor, 1987, 1990). She found that roughly one-third of her respondents' friendships were characterized by a high level of identity enhancement. She also noted that amongst these very close friends it was frequently the perceived ability to cope with problems – both big and small – which was the main source of positive evaluation. (Thus, for example, Brenda, Tessie Halpin's highly intimate friend said: 'you always done your share.' 'I don't know how you've stuck him for so long.') Indeed, a high level of intimate confiding was almost a necessary precondition for a high level of identity enhancement in such friendship relationships.

These various studies suggest that, even within relatively homogeneous samples, married women's friendships vary considerably in terms of frequency and quality of contact, intimacy, nurturance, felt attachment and primary quality. This type of description, however, is not very helpful in providing one with a clear picture of the kinds of friendships married women have. In attempting to do this, some studies have identified various types of friendship. Thus, for example, Gouldner and Symons Strong (1987) differentiated between what they called 'extraordinary relationships' (characterized by 'shared experiences, loyalty, trust, enjoyment, and especially, revealed intimacies' (1987: 20)); less intimate relationships of convenience (both talking ones between neighbours, and activity-based sociable relationships, for example between tennis partners or bingo companions); friends made as byproducts of paid employment and characterized more by admiration than intimacy; and friendships between those sharing a similar intellectual world view which found expression in their mutual involvement in some voluntary organization and/or political movement.

O'Connor (1987) also put forward a typology of married women's friendships, which, although less comprehensive, is more fully developed. She identified four main types of very close relationships: confidant relationships (characterized by a high level of intimate confiding and seen at least every two to three weeks); nurturant relationships (characterized by a high level of either practical help and/or identity enhancement and seen at least every two to three weeks); purely companionable relationships (friends whose supportive potential was solely in the fact that they were seen every two to three weeks and so provided companionship); and latent relationships (those which were felt to be very close and were characterized by high levels of felt attachment and/or a deep feeling of specialness or 'we-ness', i.e. primary quality, although they were seen infrequently). Of the very close friendships which were identified in that study, just under two-fifths were confidant; a similar proportion were latent and just over one-fifth were companionable. These types will be described in detail in the next section. (The purely nurturant type was very much a minority phenomenon and thus is not described in detail.) Obviously pseudonyms are used to preserve anonymity.

DETAILED VIGNETTES

Helen Barker was born in Walthamstow and has lived in her present neighbourhood for more than thirteen years. Her mother and father and her sisters, Joan and Polly, are living within the immediate neighbourhood and she sees a great deal of them, though she does not mention any of them as very close. Helen Barker is twenty-nine years old with two children aged seven and six. She has been married for nine years to an undermanager of a dry-cleaning shop. For the past four years she has worked as a machine operator on a knife machine with four women under her. She works just over twenty-two hours per week, 5.30–10 p.m., five days per week.

Helen Barker identified just one person, Molly, as very close. She has known Molly for five years and 'liked her from the first time we met'. Molly is six years older than she, and is described by her as 'sort of like a guardian angel'. She sees Molly every day when they go to and from work together and they also see each other there. 'My real friend is Molly; she is somebody who is like me in a lot of ways. I think she is somebody you can rely on; you can talk to her and she'll listen to you without passing too many comments. She'll never interfere with anything. She takes you exactly as you are, and you have to accept what she is.' She feels the best thing about the relationship is that: 'I can talk to her and know that she would never say anything. She is so easy to get on well with – so friendly to everyone.' She feels that they understand each other and can see at a glance if something is worrying the other or getting her down. Molly lives in the immediate neighbourhood but she feels that even if they lived further away they would not drift apart. They feel free to call in on each other without notice, and can talk to each other about personal things – particularly 'woman-things': 'I mean, I don't have to keep saying to Timothy [husband] the pains I have every time I have a period.'

Molly was the first person Helen Barker told when she got into trouble, ostensibly trying to protect her younger sister and in the process getting herself arrested for shoplifting. 'Straight away she listened, and straight away she dished out sympathy. She says to me "What can I do? I'll come to Court with you." She's really good. She said, "The only thing you can do is tell them you are sorry. I'm sure the magistrate would have done the same thing if he'd been in your place." '

She has talked to Molly about other recent family crises, in addition to talking with her about day-to-day irritations with the children, with housework and the like. 'She knows how I feel. I can say it to her, and she'll say "I know, it drives me up the wall." ' Helen told her when she was worried about a man at work whom she felt had a bad influence on her husband. 'Molly said "It's nothing to do with me, but if I was you, what I'd do, I'd tell him where to get off".' Molly stands up for her even against her own family. When her sister was 'having a go at her', Molly said to the sister 'now look, don't you ever let me hear you talk about her like that again – she may be your sister, but she's my friend.' She feels she would never let her down. She would not feel very happy if she was not there: 'There would be something missing. She is a support – she sort of backs you up.'

There is some symmetry in the relationship, although Molly seems to confide in and depend on Helen Barker less than Helen Barker does on her. Nevertheless, Molly has often said to her ' "I know I can rely on you." Probably because she knows I'd never let her down.' She tells her that she is a 'smashing friend'. Molly has talked to her about arguments with her husband and asked her what she thought. 'She is not very sexually interested, and she tells me about that a lot. She can't even tell Jimmy' (her husband).

Helen Barker's husband, Timothy, likes Molly. The two couples go out together for a drink on a Saturday every fortnight or so. However, Helen prefers seeing Molly on her own ('We have more of a laugh when we are on our own'), and is much closer to her than her husband is. She never talks to her husband about Molly's marriage. 'It is not really to do with him.' Timothy regards Molly as a kind of custodian of his wife's sexual morality when they go to the club together after work. 'He says "It may not be you, but it's the others. You might not do it [i.e. get involved with another man] but others tend to push you into doing it." But if he knows I'm with Molly, its okay.' He always makes her welcome: 'Oh yeah, I'll say me and Molly didn't half have a laugh tonight. He'll say "It shows." I haven't really got to tell him.'

Helen Barker feels that she and Molly are alike, in that they 'don't talk about anybody. If I have something to say, I'll say it to that person, and

Molly is like that, she is the same as me.' She's also like her in 'the family aspect: to her, her family is most important.' Helen Barker's relationship with Molly was assessed as having a high level of identity enhancement. According to Helen, Molly sees her as a good wife: 'Oh, you're like me, she says, you like the place clean, you like Timothy to come home to a dinner and everything.' Helen likes to think of herself as a good wife, and Molly says 'Oh you are.' She feels that Molly thinks highly of her and knows that, although they go to dances and social evenings without their husbands, 'She knows I'd never get off with anybody.' Molly sees her as sympathetic, dependable and trustworthy: 'she'll always say, "I can always rely on you".' 'She knows I'll never let her down.' Molly sees her as a good friend: 'she always says "you're a smashing friend".'

They both feel that 'If you are married, you are married, and you should build your life around that person and your family.' Helen Barker feels some loyalty to Molly in the sense that she would not tell her husband if Molly hurt or upset her ('I'd tell her'). The place the friendship occupies in both their lives is none the less a limited one. As Helen Barker says herself, 'I think I'm a pretty good friend in how I could be, like the way I'm permitted to be. I mean, naturally there are a lot of things I would like to do, but you are sort of tied. You got your family, the same as she has.'

Helen Barker's relationship with Molly is clearly a confidant relationship since it is characterized by a high level of both interaction and intimate confiding. The relationship is also identity enhancing and characterized by highly positive interaction. There is some attempt to include the husband in the social aspects of the relationship, but Timothy is not at all as close to Molly as Helen Barker herself. Nevertheless, there is no evidence of jealousy on the husband's part. (This is typical of the situation where the existence of a confidant is associated with a low level of dependence within the marital relationship.) In fact, it is clear that Timothy sees Molly as a steadying influence on his slightly flighty wife. Helen Barker herself is typical of those in O'Connor's (1987) study who have this type of very close relationship in that she has experienced considerable geographical stability – having been born in her present neighbourhood.

Traditionally, the defining characteristics of close or best friendships has been intimacy: the revealing of private and potentially damaging information about the self. More recently, however, this perception of real or close friendship has been questioned. Work such as Wright's (1978, 1988) on the importance of the validation provided by friendship implicitly raises the possibility that important aspects of the self might be supported in non-intimate relationships. In addition, work such as Cancian's (1986) has directed attention to the fact that intimacy is negatively associated with control, and that hence women's intimate styles of relating may perpetuate rather than challenge a patriarchal system: it may, in Raymond's sense (1986), confine women to 'therapism'.

In O'Connor's (1987) lower-middle-class sample roughly three-quarters of the very close friendships which were highly identity enhancing were also intimate. Those, like Helen Barker's relationship with Molly, which were highly identity enhancing were in the majority of cases also characterized by highly positive and frequent interaction. They thus can be regarded as representing the most enjoyable and supportive friendships possessed by the respondents.

Potentially, such a relationship constitutes a threat to the marital relationship, but in fact in Helen Barker's case it does not do so. A broadly similar relationship, such as Tessie Halpin's with her friend Brenda, is felt to be such a threat – possibly because in that situation the husband is unemployed and highly dependent on his wife. The women's interaction is highly visible to him. He resents her intimacy with Brenda (frequently being driven to expostulate 'your bloody mate Brenda'). Further research could well be done on the conditions associated with such jealousy.

As previously mentioned, research on men has highlighted the fact that relationships which are non-intimate can play an important part in their lives. Such relationships are characterized as 'associative' rather than 'reciprocal' (Reisman, 1981); 'side by side' rather than 'face to face' (Wright, 1988). Relatively little attention has been paid to such relationships between women.

Ethel Freeman's friendship with Denise is an example of such a companionable – albeit non-group-based – friendship (O'Connor, 1987). She is forty years old, married for eleven years, and with two children aged nine and five. Ethel is a professionally qualified nurse and works three nights a week (a total of thirty hours) in an intensive care unit. Her husband is a welder. They own their own home and have both a car and a phone. Ethel was born outside London and has no relatives at all in London.

She identifies two people as very close. Her closest relationship is with Denise, a friend who lives in the local area. It is a purely companionable friendship. She sees her almost every day at the school and most days they go for a coffee to each other's house: 'If I haven't got a bit of cleaning or working to do, we'll go walking round the shops.' Ethel enjoys doing this and describes it as a break from the house. She talks to Denise about 'womanly things' – things that concern women alone – like pregnancy, and 'the usual things' – children and home. She does not talk to her about either things that are worrying or upsetting her, or about more intimate things such as serious arguments with her husband or relatives. Their relationship is easy and companionable: 'from the first time, we just hit it off more or less.' It is undemanding and obviously is a salient, if emotionally limited, element in her life which offers no threat whatsoever to her marital relationship.

The third common type of relationship amongst friends which was identified by O'Connor (1987) is a latent one, that is, one characterized by low levels of face-to-face interaction with high levels of primary quality and/or felt attachment. Ruby Benedict's relationship with Mary, her only very close friend, illustrates this kind of relationship. Ruth is a 25-year-old childless married woman. Her relationship with her husband, although highly intimate, is one in which she is effectively powerless and highly dependent on him. Her husband is a fireman who works 'shifts'. He is often around the house during the day, and this, if anything, increases her dependence on him, since he does not encourage her friends. He was opposed to her working as an animal nurse, a job which she thoroughly enjoyed and for which she had studied at night. Ruby felt that she had to choose between her job and her marriage. She chose her marriage and now works part-time in a poorly paid job in a local supermarket, a job which she dislikes but of which her husband does not disapprove. Ruby and Mary see each other about once a month now – a pattern which contrasts markedly with the situation which existed when they worked together. At that time, they saw each other every day and confided in each other a good deal. In the past year Ruby has stopped work and Mary has had a baby and the pattern of the relationship had changed considerably. Mary now lives outside London and it is expensive to keep in contact, particularly as Ruby and her husband are now less well off than they were and have been forced to sell their car. Ruby and Mary keep in touch and talk on the phone every other week – but the calls are brief and to the point. The relationship in this latent state poses little threat to the marital relationship. In fact, it is arguable that it is little more than a mental construct now. Certainly, it requires little time or resources to maintain it.

This classification is not exhaustive. It does illustrate both the variety of types of relationships which are concealed within the concept 'friend' – although it remains simply at the level of exploring what such relationships 'do' at a personal level.

MARRIAGE AND FRIENDSHIP: ALTERNATIVE SOURCES OF INTIMACY?

Implicit in this question is the idea that relationships are potentially substitutable for one another. Furthermore, there is also the suggestion that people have a limited and stable need for intimacy and other socio-emotional resources, and that in so far as this is met by the marital relationship there is little need for other relationships. Weiss (1969, 1974) was amongst the first to put forward the latter idea in his concept of a 'fund of sociability' (subsequently reformulated by Farrell and Rosenberg 1981, into a 'limited fund of intimacy paradigm'). On the basis of his research on lone parents, Weiss suggested that such substitution could occur within certain categories of relationship, but not, Bulmer (1987) argued, between marriage and friendship: 'Marriage and friendship are both close, face to face, primary relationships, yet what they provide is distinct and the two are not alternatives' (Bulmer, 1987: 144). At any rate, it is possible to argue that, partly because of cultural factors, and partly because of the social structure, the majority of men and women in Western society effectively occupy separate worlds, and have different values and beliefs. Rubin (1985) sees the source of this in the early child-rearing situation which creates a fear of intimacy in men. Bernard (1981) and Hite (1987) go further and see its ultimate roots in a patriarchal culture which not only devalues emotional vulnerability but also values competitiveness, financial rewards, hierarchical considerations and men's egocentricity and control over women. In Western society, love or attachment are legitimate female values; whereas jobs, careers and power remain important elements in male ideology. Inevitably perhaps, then, married men and women have different priorities and pressures, which make it difficult for them to understand, validate and support each other.

These pressures are exacerbated by a tendency to define housework and child care as non-work and/or low-status activities. Furthermore, there is widespread research evidence that 'wives still do the great majority of housework and child care' (Coverman, 1989: 362). Qualitative work by Oakley (1974, 1980), Boulton (1983) and Brannen and Moss (1988) initially suggested that this was the case and this picture has been subsequently validated by extensive time-budget studies of the participation of husband and wives in housework and child care in families where both, neither or only one participate in the labour force (Gershuny and Thomas, 1980; Thomas and Shannon, 1982; Pleck, 1983; Berhide, 1984; Coverman and Shelly, 1986).

In this situation it can be seen that there are structural and cultural barriers which inhibit understanding between men and women. Women still say that they continue to confide in their husbands but Brown *et al.*'s work (1986) and O'Connor's (1991a) suggest that such statements give no indication of the real level of either emotional support in or the potential helpfulness of their marital relationships. Indeed Gouldner and Symons Strong (1987) found that in their American middle-class sample, partners typically engaged in little conversation and husbands were seen as listening very little to their wives. Very different patterns emerged in female friendships, where Gouldner and Symons Strong noted that the women both perceived each other as giving greater attention, and as operating an 'equal time' (1987: 71) arrangement. Nevertheless, the strong cultural expectation is that women's needs for intimacy will be met within the marital relationship: 'It is ironic that the place women are going for love, to get love, is the very place from which getting it is hardest, according to women – because of the way men in this culture are conditioned, what "masculinity" means' (Hite, 1987: 132). In this situation it appears that married women continue to confide in their husband, although they also yearn for relationships which provide them with the understanding and acceptance that they expect but do not always receive within marriage. In this situation, some establish and maintain what Gouldner and Symons Strong (1987) called 'extraordinary relationships' and O'Connor (1991a) referred to as 'confidant relationships' with other women. One-third of the women in O'Connor's study (1991a) had these sorts of relationships (half of these being with friends). For Gouldner and Symons Strong's respondents such relationships were a source of 'almost childlike pleasure' (1987: 117).

Typically, according to both O'Connor (1987, 1991a) and Oliker (1989), these friends were rarely, if ever, acquired through their husband. In O'Connor's study only roughly one in three were even subsequently shared with him. (This was assessed on the basis of whether their husband was as close to them as they were; whether they talked about their friend to him or even told him things that their friend had told them in confidence; as well as whether or not they socialized together; O'Connor, 1987, 1991a.) This was quite low by comparison with other studies. Thus, for example, even in Oliker's study (1989) roughly half of those who were identified as best friends were shared with the husband in the sense that they associated as couples. The pattern in O'Connor's work can, however, be explained partly by the fact that the main focus was on the woman's own very close friendships, and partly by the fact that a rather subtle measure of shared friendship was used. Typically in that study, these friendships had been formed after marriage – although a small minority stemmed from childhood or premarital work experiences.

The husbands were typically intrigued, puzzled and somewhat threatened by these relationships which they perceived as a competing source of loyalty and intimacy. Yet O'Connor (1991a) found that there was no association between the existence of friends who were confidants and the respondents' level of confiding in their husbands. Indeed, Tschann (1988) suggested that the high value women attach to friendship leads them to continue creating and/or maintaining intimate friendships 'even when basic intimacy needs are being met by a spouse' (1988: 79). However, Whitehead (1976), Hey (1986) and Green *et al.*'s (1990) studies suggested that even where intimacy between women did not exist the men were hostile to any kind of female solidarity – especially those which they saw as providing the women with an opportunity for contact with other men.

Married women typically face considerable constraints in developing and maintaining friendships. A wide variety of studies have shown that married women typically have very much less financial resources, time and personal space than their husbands (Edgell, 1980; Pahl, 1984; Allan, 1985, 1989; Green *et al.*, 1990). This partly reflects a division of labour within families, where, almost regardless of married women's participation in the labour force, they continue to carry the main responsibility for housework and child care. It also reflects the fact that, even where women are in paid employment they are likely to be financially dependent to some degree on their husbands.

This idea has been pushed a stage further by those who have argued that, because of the primacy attached to marriage and the family, women are reluctant to encroach on what is seen as family time, territory or money to develop or maintain their own friendships. (A rather different cultural attitude exists in the case of men, who are typically seen as 'needing' or 'having earned' personal time and/or pocket money.) Oliker

(1989) rather provocatively suggests that 'Gender stratification allows women to exchange generously only those values they control or possess. Most married women own few material resources they can dispose of at will' (Oliker, 1989: 66). Even their work and their time are not really their own, so that even minding a friend's children can be seen as a drain on family resources. In this situation, all they have to offer is themselves: their intimacy, their understanding and the illusion that they will always be there if needed – an illusion that they are very careful indeed not to shatter by asking too much of their friends (or allowing too much to be asked of themselves). In this way, they try 'to strike friendship terms without exploitation' (1989: 68). Hence one might suggest that it is their very lack of material resources which moulds the shape of their very close friendships.

There is little evidence to suggest that friendships could substitute for marital relationships, other than in a situation where economic security was not provided by the marital relationship (e.g. amongst Stack's, 1974, poor black American woman living on welfare cheques). In this situation, the possibility of economic survival, through dependence on relationships with kin and friends, was greater than through dependence on unemployed men whose very presence within the home endangered the women's receipt of welfare cheques. Hence, in this situation, marital relationships were unstable, although indeed relationships with kin and friends were also conditional on their continued ability and willingness to be reliable sources of help.

It has been eloquently argued (albeit in small unrepresentative studies by Gullestad, 1984, and Oliker, 1989) that married women's friendships in fact effectively promote marital stability. They do this, they argue, not only by actually meeting intimacy needs which are not met by the marriage, but also by diffusing 'anger or other volatile emotions' (1989: 127), and managing these emotions so as to sustain married women's commitment to their marriage. Oliker explicitly argues that the net effect of this improvised individual 'marriage work' by friends was overwhelmingly in the direction of 'solving' marital conflicts. In fact, half of the women in her study said that their friendships with other women had made their marriage work more smoothly, and none said that they had affected it negatively. Thus Oliker (1989) describes how friends generated empathy for a women's husband and 'framed' the marital situation in such a way as to ennoble him. They used humour to defuse situations; they underlined the women's own awareness of their (frequent) financial dependence on their husband; and they reinforced their sensitivity to their children's needs, and what Oliker calls their 'communal responsibility' (1989: 142).

Occasionally, women in Oliker's (1989) study did support each other in subtle resistances (e.g. in negotiating 'favours' from their husbands or forming what she calls a 'counter culture'). Nevertheless, this was rare. Indeed, Gullestad (1984) argues that the attempt to maintain moral codes (e.g. by 'spreading rumours' about those who did not conform to these standards) reinforced marital solidarity at the expense of solidarity between the friends themselves. This was despite the fact that these women had strong expectations of loyalty from their female friends and tried to hide compromising information about their own best friends from the men (although they did not give their friends moral support to break the rules of marital fidelity). Gullestad (1984) suggests that when these women were together they struggled, through their talk, to work out ways of handling their lives, and especially ways of dealing with their husbands and the tensions potentially implicit in the conflicting cultural expectations of marital stability and sexual bliss. Hence, paradoxically, even these very close friendships, which were often perceived by husbands as undermining the marital relationship, contributed to its stability: the typical shape of these relationships (i.e. dyadic and intimate) arguably being influenced by the structural and cultural constraints on the women's situation.

WHAT OTHER FACTORS AFFECT MARRIED WOMEN'S FRIENDSHIPS?

Much attention has been paid to the influence of class position on various aspects of women's friendships, including their existence and the joint/segregated nature of the networks in which they are embedded. This section will provide an overview of this work. Attention will also be paid in this section to work which has highlighted the importance of other explanatory variables (namely, life stage, geographical mobility and women's participation in the labour force).

Firstly, then, various studies have drawn attention to the importance of life stage in influencing the existence of friendships between women. Most are agreed that such friendships tend to be at a low ebb in the period after marriage or cohabitation (Aries and Johnson, 1983). There are different views about the extent to which the early child-rearing period either creates a condition which facilitates them, or indeed poses such barriers that it is difficult to maintain them. Certainly, it has been noted that the amount of time spent with friends decreases during the period when family responsibilities are heaviest (i.e. during the thirties, forties and early fifties, Larson and Bradney, 1988) and amongst those with young children, (Fischer, 1982b). However, Bradford Brown (1981), drawing on Weiss and Lowenthal's (1975) and Shulman's (1975) work suggested that by the time women were in their forties and fifties, although their networks had become smaller, interaction with friends was more frequent, and the content of their friendships more specialized.

There was a tendency for the working-class respondents in Willmott's study (1987) to be less likely than their middle-class counterparts to identify friends as people in whom they would confide. O'Connor (1991a) found that although class position (assessed on the Goldthorpe and Hope Schema, 1974) was not associated with the existence of a confidant within her rather marginal middle-class sample, those who had experienced financial insecurity during their married life were unlikely to have such a confidant. She argued that this reflected the fact that such experiences reduced the wife's ability to invest in friendships. A relationship with a spouse offered these women the best chance of economic survival; hence, they limited their friendship investments.

Class differentiated trends as regards intimate confiding have emerged in a number of studies. However, to some extent the whole issue has been confounded by the tendency of working-class respondents to see their relatives as their 'real' friends (Allan, 1979) – something which is further explored in Chapter 6. There is some evidence to suggest that, at the middle- and upper-class levels, friendships between women tend to reflect and reinforce both the class position of the couple and their identity as a couple. At lower-middle- and upper-working-class levels it has been shown that there is a tendency to restrict friendships to specific locations such as work or clubs (so that inevitably they impact less on their class position and their identity as a couple). This trend has been interpreted in various ways: for example, in terms of the greater social and/or geographical mobility of middle-class couples; and/or their higher levels of social skills. Allan (1979), however, argued that such class-differentiated trends indicated the existence of what he called the 'rules of relevance' in these relationships:

When the middle class respondents wanted to develop one of these relationships further and get to know a person better, what they tended to do was to change the implicit rules of relevance from those imposed by a given situation to ones which, in effect, emphasised the individuality of the interactants and their relationship, their liking for one another and their mutual compatibility. They did this by broadening and widening the situation and activities in which interaction occurred, thereby overcoming the limits tacitly imposed on the relationship by the initial situation.

(Allan, 1979: 51)

Bott's study (1957), as well as studies by Komarovsky (1967), Turner (1967) and Goldthorpe *et al.* (1969), suggested that husbands' and wives' networks were most likely to be segregated amongst working-class respondents. (The focus in this work is typically on sociable companionship rather than on the sort of intimacy referred to in the previous section.) Similarly, Willmott (1987) looked at the issue of whether friends were seen alone – something which indicates, at a very basic level, the extent to which the relationship was/was not shared by the spouse. He found that, as in Bott's study, class variation existed with working-class women, being more likely than middle-class women to see their friends on their own. As one might perhaps expect, this trend was particularly strong when the women were living nearby. Such women typically saw each other during the day – a strategy which provided them with privacy and to some extent side-stepped possible conflicts of loyalties between such relationships and their families.

Hess (1981) argued that, although there was general agreement that working-class husbands and wives retained premarital, sex-segregated friendships and/or developed sex-segregated ones after marriage, the situation was much less clear cut amongst the middle class. However, Aries and Johnson (1983) noted that: 'Even in middle and upper classes where couples tend to form friendships with other couples, husbands are more likely to share confidences with husbands and wives with wives' (1983: 1184). Studies which have focused on joint friendships and/or which have used regular social interaction as a measure of friendship have tended to underline the importance of the husband in initiating such friendships – especially amongst the middle class. Thus, for example, Edgell (1980) found that in half of the middle-class couples he studied, the husband was the major source of those close friends who became joint friends of the couple (a trend which La Gaipa, 1981, suggested might be beneficial to the marital relationship). This pattern had been noted a considerable time before by Babchuck and Bates (1963) in their study of young married middle-class couples in the Mid-West United States. Thus they found that husbands initiated more joint friendships than the wives; and the husband's friends from before marriage were more likely than the wives to remain mutual friends after marriage. However, Hess (1981) noted that 'their tables show that fully half of the couples were not in full agreement over friend choice' (1981: 108). She also commented that they tended to ignore the fact that husbands and wives might have important individual friendships. In fact, she notes that, in her own earlier work on middle-aged managerial migrants, there was almost no overlap between the husbands' and wives' best friends.

Indeed, Willmott's study (1987) also found that although the working-class couples in their study were likely to have mainly different friends, where the respondent was a woman, the first member of the couple mentioned was also a woman. Thus, one might conclude that a more differentiated approach might well produce a rather different picture. McRae's (1986) study of cross-class families, where both partners were in paid employment, provides a very interesting insight into the influence of a husband and wife on friendships (unfortunately, these were simply defined as 'the three friends seen socially on a regular basis'). It shows that wives in these cross-class families were the main initiators of joint friendships: a pattern which is unusual but which must be seen in the context of the fact that the wives had the higher class position within the couples. She argues that:

> previous research which indicates male dominance in friendship choices actually indicates status dominance. It is not that husbands are more likely than wives to dominate *friendship choices*, but that husbands are more likely than wives to dominate *occupationally*. Reverse their positions in the occupational hierarchy, and their positions of dominance in initiating joint friendships reverses as well.
>
> (McRae 1986: 175–6)

McRae's small study clearly suggests that class is more important than factors related to gender in influencing the joint friendships of the couple. Through their mainly work-related friendships, these women enabled their husbands to become effectively upwardly socially mobile by sharing some of their own middle-class friendships. When one looked at those friends who were not shared with the spouse (i.e. those people seen socially on a regular basis away from the spouse), it is clear that middle-class wives socialized almost exclusively in middle-class worlds (and their husbands socialized predominantly in working-class ones). Hence, implicit in McRae's work is the recognition of the relationship between joint friendship and the class position of the occupationally dominant partner (separate friendships reflecting each partner's own occupational position). McRae's study thus implicitly suggests that the absence of clear class-differentiated trends in small-scale studies of middle- and/or working-class samples arises from the fact that such samples include cross-class couples whose joint friendship patterns reflect the class position of the superior partner. This possibility has not been widely recognized because studies for the most part continue to classify couples simply on the basis of the male's occupation.

The importance of exploring the process through which friendships contribute directly and indirectly to marital patterns and class structuration is quite clear. The neglect of these topics obviously reflects the continued failure to see friendships as other than a residual institution which has some importance in meeting individual needs.

Numerous sociological studies (Bott, 1957; Young and Willmott, 1962; Willmott and Young, 1967; Pahl and Pahl, 1971; Allan, 1979; Gouldner and Symons Strong, 1987; O'Connor, 1987, 1991a) have noted the effect of geographical mobility on friendships. Indeed, it is possible that the importance of class position has also been modified or even obscured by geographical mobility. At any rate, O'Connor (1987, 1991a) found that in her lower-middle-class sample, class position was not associated with the existence of a confidant, while geographical stability was so associated. In that study, those who were born in the local area were particularly likely to have a confidant. These women were likely to be effectively surrounded by people whom they had known at work and at school (i.e. potentially ready-made friendships) and by relatives who could act as links to further potential friends. O'Connor (1991a) suggested that this could be interpreted as indicating the importance of what Bowlby (1979) described as a 'secure base' in providing both the emotional security and social opportunity to develop a confidant relationship.

Gouldner and Symons Strong (1987) drew attention to the fact that other changes in women's lives could also affect friendships: 'Work, family and health changes of many sorts, new interests and activities, and new stages in the family life cycle may precipitate the process of finding new friends by breaking up the older personal order' (Gouldner and Symons Strong, 1987: 154). This idea is provocative partly because it challenges the idea that friendships are permanent, psychological realities, uninfluenced by social factors – a view which in any case sits uneasily with the stress on similarity in friendship relationships.

Various studies (such as O'Connor, 1987; Willmott 1987) have shown that the overwhelming majority of married women meet their friends in a domestic situation. This is perhaps not surprising since, as outlined earlier, there are relatively few public arenas for female interaction (and even if such venues were available it is by no means clear that married women would have the time and/or the financial resources to use them). Furthermore, as previously mentioned, ideas about respectability, sexuality and appropriate behaviour for wives and mothers militate against their use of pubs and/or sporting facilities. Willmott noted that, at least in his outer-London sample, women, when they did meet outside the home, still mainly met 'outside the children's school, at the shops or at a local group such as a keep fit class or a mothers and toddlers' group' (1987: 26). Wimbush (1986) similarly identified the street, local shops, schools, health centres and community centres as potential meeting places.

Such venues are not particularly conducive to the formation of what Morris (1985) called 'collective friendships', that is, friendships based on a group activity. Morris' (1985) work is provocative in so far as she highlights the idea that group-based single-sex relationships are an important source of group pressure. The absence of group-based friendships amongst married women weakens their group identity and limits the development of those strong normative pressures which, potentially at least, challenge aspects of the patriarchal culture. (The importance of such structures in reflecting and/or maintaining male attitudes is indicated by Morris' findings (1985: 337) that, of the unemployed steelworkers she studied who were involved in such collective interaction, twice as many identified one area of domestic activity that they would not consider being involved in, as compared with those who were not involved in such interaction.) Hence one might conclude that an effective challenge to gender-role stereotyping requires the presence of female group-based friendships: a pattern which is not typical of married women's friendships.

Regardless of the actual nature of the work done, women who are in paid employment are, by definition, outside the world of what Bernard (1981) has called 'Blut' and 'Bod' (i.e. blood and place). The time and resources they have available for friendship are typically rather different from those who are full-time housewives. A more detailed consideration of work-related friendships will be provided in Chapter 6. However, as Wellman (1985) noted, pressures deriving from attempts to combine work with family roles can often inhibit the development of friendships between women, for example, married women may shop during lunch hour and omit coffee breaks so as to finish earlier in the day – thereby reducing the possibility of initiating or developing work-related friendships. Hence, although paid employment increases married women's opportunities to meet potential friends, it restricts the time and energy they have to develop them.

It is also true that many married women are often employed in activities which are considerably below their ascribed class position. Hence, it is by no means inevitable that their co-workers in these settings will be similar to them in terms of class position: a factor which may further inhibit the development of these relationships.

The increasing participation of married women in the labour force also has obvious implications as regards the potential availability of female friends for interaction during the day within the neighbourhood, and for the existence of a local female world. These implications are potentially very acute in view of the well documented tendency for married women to have difficulty in gaining access to resources which might enable them to maintain non-local friendships (such as interrupted time, personal spending money, child care and transport). Levy (1981) suggested that full-time housewives were least willing or able to understand a friend's desire to make status transitions (e.g. to return to college and/or to paid employment). They were most likely to resent such behaviour – depriving them, as it did, of potential daytime friendships. Inevitably perhaps, then, sooner or later in the face of changed identities, life styles and domestic timetables, many friends just drifted apart.

The trends emerging from the work reviewed in this section are complex and by no means clear-cut. To some extent this reflects differences in the nature of the samples and in either the definition of friendship used in these studies or the aspect of friendship on which attention was focused. It is clear, however, that married women's friendships are likely to be affected by life stage and geographical mobility and that the influence of class is particularly complex. McRae's (1986) study is, however, provocative as regards the importance of the class position of the occupationally dominant partner at least in influencing joint sociable friendships.

It is also clear that in so far as friends are similar on what are seen as socially significant characteristics (such as marital status or, indeed, paid employment) changes in these characteristics inevitably pose problems for the maintenance of the friendship. Finally, the paucity of 'acceptable' public interaction venues, combined with ideological constraints and lack of resources, arguably discourages group-based friendships between married women – and so further weakens their group identity and inhibits the development of strong normative pressure which potentially at least, challenge aspects of the patriarchal culture. It will be argued in Chapter 7 that this pattern is beginning to change even amongst married women – but this change is not as yet evident in the research being undertaken.

THE EFFECTS OF FRIENDSHIP

Most of the studies which have been concerned with this issue have looked at it at an individual level, that is, in terms of the association between particular types of provisions of friendship and various psychological indicators – such as psychological well-being, enjoyment, etc. However, a small number of studies have moved beyond this and have looked at its effect on other members of the family, on the marital relationship itself or (more generally) on the part played by such friendships in creating and/or maintaining class-related cultures.

Typically, the presence of a relationship is depicted as positively associated with psychiatric health. As outlined earlier, there are difficulties in interpreting this relationship (e.g. do supportive relationships simply reflect positive psychiatric health?). Brown and Harris' (1978a) work is the classic example of a study documenting the importance of confidant relationships. However, their model combined those who had only an intimate relationship with their husband with those who had both an intimate relationship with him and with a close friend (see O'Connor, 1991a). Because of this methodological decision, Brown and Harris' (1978a) work was popularly interpreted as indicating the importance of a high level of confiding in the marital relationship. This conclusion, however, was clearly modified in their subsequent longitudinal study, when it was shown that neither confiding in the husband nor in a very close relationship was associated with the subsequent onset of depression amongst married women. However, crisis support 'from a husband and from a very close tie were associated with an equally low risk' (Brown *et al.* 1986: 825). None the less, in a subsequent overview of the entire body of work (Brown, 1987) the importance of the marital relationship was highlighted, while the contribution of very close ties were again ignored.

O'Connor (1991a) argued that for support to be a realistic possibility in a very close confidant relationship, the person should be seen at least every two to three weeks. In her own study she found that those who had such a confidant were less likely to have an affective disorder than those who did not. (However, as will be shown in Chapter 7, the most vulnerable, in psychiatric terms, were not those who said they had no close friend at all, but those whose only close friend was seen infrequently.) At any rate, in that study the existence of intimacy in both relationships was positively associated with psychiatric health. Those who had an intimate relationship with the husband only were in fact just as likely to have poor psychiatric health as those who had only an intimate relationship with a close friend. Similarly, Goodenow and Gaier (1990) found that in their study 'when married women were analysed separately, those who did have one or more close reciprocal friendships were significantly less depressed, were more satisfied with their lives, and had higher self esteem than those who did not have such a friendship' (Goodenow and Gaier, 1990: 18–19). Interestingly, they noted that these married women were less likely than their single counterparts to see these relationships as important, although their protective effect (in terms of psychiatric health) persisted, regardless of the quality of the marital relationship. These studies are, however, comparatively unusual in actually looking at the extent to which close friendships and marriage are alternative or complementary contributors to their psychiatric well-being.

A small number of studies have argued that being with friends, unlike being with family members, is associated with an intense positive feeling – one which comes from shared enjoyment with equals. Thus, for example, Larson and Bradney (1988) noted that although after marriage and starting a family the amount of time their respondents spent with friends declined dramatically, these latter relationships remained a reliable source of positive experiences. When they were with their friends they were able to transcend their usual preoccupations and to experience what Larson and Bradney described as an 'all absorbing enjoyment' (1988: 124). They conclude that, contrary to romantic ideology, most of the time their respondents spent with their spouses after marriage was routinized and dominated by everyday concerns and that 'it was still friends that generate the best times with others' (1988: 122).

Argyle (1987, 1990) also noted that friendship was an independent source of happiness over and above marriage and family life, and that 'for some married women, friends are more important than husbands' (1987: 19) in the sense of providing advice, sympathy, intimacy or simply sharing a way of looking at the world. His work, however, stressed that friends were particularly important as sources of joy, making new friends and seeing old ones being identified by his respondents as the main sources of such experiences.

Even less attention has been paid to the more indirect effects of women's friendships. However, Wellman (1985) looked at the way in which friendships were used by Toronto women in job finding. There has even been some evidence to suggest that, where the mother had a dependable friend, there was a positive effect on her children's adjustment – in the sense of their own assessment of their happiness, their social skills and their general adjustment in school (Homel *et al.*, 1987). Such work has, however, been limited – thereby prompting one to conclude that there is little ideological pressure within a patriarchal culture to explore the extent to which such positive effects arise from women's friendships (academic interest in the negative effects of married women's participation in the labour force providing a salutary contrast).

The social consequences of friendships were further elaborated on by Cohen (1978) and Cheal (1986). Thus, Cheal argued that middle-class women, through the use of home entertaining, played an important role in the creation of a class-appropriate life style – an idea which has been given little attention in class terms, although it can be traced back to Veblen's (1970) notion of conspicuous consumption. Indeed, it is not clear to what extent similar patterns may exist amongst the owner–occupier and more affluent sections of the working class. Typically (e.g. Goldthorpe *et al.*'s study, 1969), working-class respondents have been shown to be unlikely to entertain at home. In this way, as Allan (1989) noted, they can more easily conceal their life style, conserve their financial resources, limit the demands for resources made on them and maintain a sex-segregated division of roles inside and outside the home. Allan (1989) argued that, for middle-class respondents, bringing friends into the home not only offered the opportunity to flaunt a class-appropriate life style, but also affirmed their identity as a couple: 'In this respect, two aspects of middle class life styles are particularly relevant: the character of the home and the construction of marriage' (Allan, 1989: 138). Cohen (1978) went a stage further in so far as she suggested that the suburban middle-class women she studied, sharing the common problem of rearing children with little support from their husbands, developed and sustained what she called 'particular cultural forms, which had the effect of clearly marking the boundaries between themselves and outsiders' (Cohen, 1978: 137). In this way they were able to create and sustain a middle-class environment which fostered their children's middle-class identity and educational aspirations. Such identity and aspirations thus both facilitated and limited their friendships with each other: 'through the estate culture, they minimized their own internal differences, but accentuated the differences between themselves and women from other social classes outside the estate' (Cohen, 1978: 142). Cohen's work is similar to Oliker's (1989) and Gullestad's (1984) in drawing attention to the processes operating within friendships in creating 'moral discourses'

> about what is right and wrong. Their talk includes rightness and wrongness in child rearing practices, in division of labour between spouses, in relationships with parents and parents-in-law and other relatives, issues surrounding work, issues raised in films on the TV or picture magazines etc. . . . Their relationships with men are the focus of an intensive interest.
>
> (Gullestad, 1984: 220).

Such work provides a fascinating insight into the way in which micro-level behaviour (i.e. talk) can have a significance other than in terms of psychological well-being. Unlike Cohen's work, however, Gullestad (1984) and Oliker (1989) were concerned with the way in which friendships created moral universes which were ultimately supportive of a marital-role ideology. Hence, these friendships, despite strengthening women's individuality, subordinated the claims of that individuality to their marriage and their family responsibilities. They thus re-echo Whitehead's (1976) scepticism about the extent to which married women's largely home-based, female personal networks are a potential basis for the generation of competing ideologies. However, they go beyond her work by showing the processes through which 'Paradoxically, the very support networks offered by women to other women, although frequently positive and benign are often fraught with contradictions in that they can function to reinforce patriarchal power and limit the possibility of challenges to it' (Green *et al.*, 1990: 119). They thus provide an insight into the nature of friendship which is lacking from more methodologically sophisticated studies; and they highlight the partiality of a concern with the effects of friendship on psychological well-being – a perspective which has been by far the most dominant one in the area.

ISSUES ARISING FROM THIS WORK

In this chapter, an attempt has been made to draw together material on the existence, content and quality of married women's friendships. The trends which emerge are complex – partly reflecting diversity in the definitions of friendship and partly variation in the samples used. It is clear that although most attention has been paid to intimate relationships between women, in reality, married women's friendships vary considerably. They can be – and indeed often are – simply companionable: rooted in easy sociability and casual interaction. In a highly individualized society, where women's roles frequently still have a strong normative tone, such friendships can provide important identity validation. They can be nurturant, providing them with practical help and/or with important identity-enhancing experiences. Equally, these friendships may be little more than mental constructs – albeit ones that are highly valued because they embody an important perception of self and/or act as a security figure whose very presence is felt to be in some way reassuring.

Typically, this work has been concerned either with simply documenting their existence or with exploring the extent to which they are characterized by a limited number of relational provisions. It is ironical, then, that relatively little of this work has specifically addressed the issue of the extent to which marriage and friendship are competing or alternative sources of intimacy. Indeed, the theoretical positions taken up on this issue arguably simply reflect the writers' assumptions about the nature and importance of marriage. There has been some evidence to suggest that such friendships – although often providing very important emotional and/or practical support and sometimes, indeed, even being perceived by the husbands themselves as a threat – were unaffected by the level of intimacy in the marital relationship (O'Connor, 1991a). Rather, it appeared that the existence of these relationships, which were predominantly not shared with their husbands, reflected the respondents' own embeddedness in the local area and/or the level of material resources they had to develop or maintain such relationships. Thus, there was no evidence to suggest that the husbands' perception of these relationships as a threat was justified; although this situation reflected as much the cultural valuation and economic underpinning of the marital relationship as its content or quality.

A number of factors were identified as influencing these friendships: the most popular of these being class position. Work in this tradition has by and large remained at a fairly micro level, for example, Allan's work (1979) on the identification of the rather different 'rules of relevance' amongst middle- and working-class respondents which led them to have different conceptions of friendships and different attitudes to generalizing such relationships beyond the initial interaction context. However, implicit in work such as McRae's (1984) is the germ of a more class-related structural approach to friendship, the idea that friendship plays an important part in maintaining a class structure, and that class position may be even more important than gender in influencing the selection and maintenance of friendship relationships.

At a structural level, feminism has also made a contribution, highlighting the conditions which inhibit and/or facilitate the development of married women's friendships, e.g. the cultural denigration of women, which with their lack of power and status makes them socially and structurally unattractive as friends; women's frequent lack of easy access to time and resources to create and maintain relationships; the lack of cultural validation of women's obligations towards each other; the disruption of such relationships because of geographical mobility – often consequent on a partner's job-related mobility; and the paucity of non-home-based interaction venues where women can meet and have an opportunity to initiate or maintain friendships. These features are not peculiar to the situation of married women, and hence relatively little specific attention has been paid to them in this chapter. Nevertheless, they are a very real aspect of their situation. As Allan (1985) has noted, the processes involved in generating friendships in this situation, without much institutional support and back-up, has received little attention.

Equally little attention has been paid to examining the impact of women's increasing participation in the labour force on friendships between women. Such participation in many ways divides women, rooted as it often is in very different perceptions and assumptions about women and their roles. The tensions and difficulties of maintaining friendships through changes in employment status have only begun to be explored. The whole issue of friendship between work-mates will be examined further in Chapter 6.

There is an increasing volume of evidence to suggest that married women's friendships make an important contribution to their psychological well-being – in the sense that their absence is associated with psychiatric ill health and/or that their presence is the source of positive life-enhancing feelings. The recognition of this contribution has important implications as regards the cultural valuation of such relationships – both in their own right and as compared with marriage. It also has implications as regards the cultural legitimation of the expenditure of resources (time, money, etc.) in creating and/or maintaining such relationships.

To a considerable extent, a very limited range of questions have been asked about married women's friendships. Little attention has been paid to the processes involved in maintaining relationships. Conflict and dissolution have typically not been explored. Neither has the issue of physical contact between friends been discussed; nor has much attention been paid to marital jealousy. Overfacile assumptions have been made that the main importance of friendships between women lies in their provision of intimacy. It is almost as if such friendships have been seen purely in terms of the extent to which they can meet psychosocial needs which, given current patterns of gender-differentiated behaviour and the current division of labour, cannot be met by the marital relationship. Indeed, even studies such as Acker *et al.*'s (1981) which look at the friendships of feminists have implicitly perpetuated this focus on women's friendships as 'oiling the wheels of marriage'.

It is suggested here that a more useful perspective is one which identifies the conditions which facilitate or inhibit the development and maintenance of various kinds of friendships between married women. This might include the ideological primacy of the couple in Western society, social class factors, women's access to resources (time, money and public interaction venues) and social-psychological factors such as their level of social skill, their need for validation and/or security, desire for intimacy, etc. Such work might also usefully highlight the processes through which friendships create moral discourses, and the association between these and the class context and marital ideological framework within which they occur. This type of work, which is essentially processual and qualitative, has, however, typically been neglected in favour of more methodologically sophisticated studies which frequently have provided very little insight indeed into either the importance of friendship in married women's lives, or indeed the conditions associated with the emergence of particular types of friendship.

— 4 —

Friendships: A refuge for single women?

INTRODUCTION

This chapter is concerned with single women: a focus which at first glance is an obvious one in view of the previous chapter. However, the concept of singleness is deceptively simple: sometimes it is used to refer to the never married; at other times it is used as a residual category so that it also includes the divorced/separated and the widowed. The criterion of maintaining a separate household can also sometimes be confounded with unmarried legal status – the position of cohabiting adults or single parents living with their own parents highlighting this issue. In fact, it is arguable that the apparent clarity of the concept of singleness reflects a cultural stereotype whereby it is equated with 'spinsterhood'; the latter being a vivid and negative cultural image which is typically juxtaposed with an equally stereotypical image of romantic love.

Buunk and Van Driel (1989) defined single women as 'unmarried individuals who do not cohabit with an intimate partner, although they may share a residence with a friend, children or relatives, and may have a more or less stable intimate relationship with someone living elsewhere' (1989: 22). Such a definition poses problems as regards separated people who have not yet divorced (and so are not unmarried). Hence, in this chapter, single women are defined as women who are unmarried and/or not maintaining a household with an intimate partner. Hence, this concept includes the never-married, the divorced and the separated. It excludes those involved in lesbian relationships or in cohabiting heteroosexual relationships. In addition, however, the chapter includes some reference to marriages which are 'at risk' and where 'singleness' is clearly one possibility being considered (e.g. violent marriages, or marriages where one or other partner is in touch with marriage counsellors).

This chapter, then, deals with single women of various ages, in various domestic situations and life stages. What they have in common is the fact that they are not cohabiting with a male. Elderly women and widows (who are statistically likely to be elderly) are for the most part excluded from this chapter. Thus the focus is on women who are, at least on the basis of age, potentially available as heterosexual partners. This heterogeneous universe of women is arguably constrained by gender-role ideologies about romantic heterosexual love which depict friendships between women as very much second best, as well as by those traditional stereotypes of femininity and respectability which constrain their social participation. Hence, although these women are arguably considerably freer than their married counterparts to create and/or maintain female friendships, in their situation there is little cultural validation of any attempt to do so. Indeed, for separated, divorced or battered women, the limitations of friendships with other women may become an all-too-real experience when these relationships are put under pressure by status transitions and/or by a need for help which is seen as in some way inappropriate. By including this rather heterogeneous group of women in this chapter, it is hoped to underline the common factors which inhibit the creation and/or maintenance of their friendships.

The definition of 'woman' (and hence the age at which one moves to a discussion of the friendship of single 'women' as opposed to single 'girls') is potentially equally ambiguous. Legal, social and cultural definitions of adulthood all vary. Indeed, it is not uncommon for middle-aged women to refer to each other as 'girls'. In this chapter, onset of puberty is taken as a simple criterion of adulthood. This allows the chapter to include a discussion of adolescent female friendships: an important area and one which potentially illustrates the popular perception of women's friendships, and which is the focus of much of the work on friendship.

However, much of the material on non-elderly single women in fact deals with American college students – a population which has obviously limited generalizability. This work, although empirically limited, has raised important issues concerned with the processes involved in initiating and terminating relationships.

Since the early 1970s there has been a steady trickle of work concerned with the role played by friends in the wake of life events such as divorce, separation and marital violence. This work looks in a more traditional way at the provisions of friendship and the effects of its absence. It does allow one to raise the issue of the extent to which, in the words of the cliché, 'A friend in need is a friend indeed', that is, the extent to which receiving support in stressful situations is the real testing ground of friendship. Such a perception contrasts with the trends emerging in other chapters, where it is clear that friendships are, to a considerable extent, adjusted at times of status transitions. Hence, this chapter will continue the discussion of the 'real' nature of friendship. Finally, it will look at the effects of friendship, in the sense of its association with global indicators of single women's personal well-being: an extremely complex issue and one which can only be touched on here.

Before looking at these issues, it seems useful to indicate very briefly the wider cultural and structural context within which singleness exists in Western society.

STRUCTURAL AND CULTURAL CONTEXT

In Western society we have become accustomed to think of singleness as a relatively rare phenomenon – and one which is only explicable in psychological terms (e.g. in terms of attachment avoidance). The popular conception of singleness is thus implicitly based on the concept of 'lifelong' singles. Hence, since most women in Western society today do marry, we see it as a minority phenomenon. In fact, as Buunk and Van Driel (1989) noted, it is far more common than this popular notion would imply (with 35 per cent of all American women over the age of eighteen years in 1985 being either unmarried and/or not cohabiting with a sexual partner).

For most of these, however, the stage is a temporary one, either before marriage, between divorce and remarriage or after widowhood. Some single women will be maintaining families, either because of divorce, separation or widowhood. Hill (1986) estimated that in the United States, fewer than one in five of these female heads of families were single, never-married women, the overwhelming majority being divorced or separated, with just over one in ten being widows. White women were very much less likely than black women to be in such female-headed households (and men were even less likely than white women to be lone parents).

In the United States the proportion of the total adult population which experienced divorce increased more than threefold in the 1970s and 1980s. Nevertheless, three out of every four divorced women do remarry, half within three years (Buunk and Van Driel, 1989). This is not, perhaps, particularly surprising in view of Hill's (1986) comments that female-headed households were predominantly below the poverty line in the United States – particularly if they were rearing children, when child-care costs were added to low pay and vulnerability to unemployment: 'With such inhospitable conditions facing the divorced with children, the attractiveness of a second marriage is understandable' (Hill, 1986: 24). Such remarriages are particularly vulnerable to a second divorce and a return to single status. Hence, quite clearly, this part of the universe of single women is continually changing. Only 16 per cent of widows remarry (Berardo, 1982) and their marriages are less vulnerable to divorce than the re-married divorcees. Indeed, Buunk and Van Driel (1989) noted that, for very different reasons, the elderly widow and the well-educated young professional career woman are equally likely in Western society to find themselves in the involuntary single position.

In the late nineteenth century, the typical west European pattern involved a high incidence of permanent celibacy. This pattern persisted in Ireland long after it had been abandoned in other west European countries. In fact, Clancy (1991) noted that in Ireland, of those born at the beginning of the twentieth century, 25 per cent of the women (and 30 per cent of the men) did not marry. Allen (1989) noted that more than a quarter of the women aged 40–44 in Ireland in 1911 were unmarried, partly because of economic reasons (related to the combination of agriculture, and a particular type of extended family structure) and partly because of cultural attitudes encouraging strong 'family keeper' roles and negative attitudes to sexuality. This pattern is one which has now changed (Clancy, 1991). However, even in Britain: 'despite the fact that never married women (25 and over) have comprised between 20 or more per cent and (currently) 8 to 9 per cent of the female population in Britain, we know little about their lives' (Leonard and Speakman, 1986: 40).

Stein's (1981, 1983) and Shostak's (1987) typologies of single people highlight the heterogeneity within the universe of single people. Stein (1981, 1983) suggested that the two crucial axes were the temporary/ stable nature of people's single status and its voluntary/involuntary character. Within the group who are unlikely to marry and/or who have become committed to singlehood, Shostak (1987) differentiated between the 'resolved' (those who have chosen to be single) and the 'regretful' (those who would wish to marry but seem unlikely to do so). Amongst the temporarily single he similarly differentiated between those who were voluntarily as opposed to involuntarily in that position: labelling them as the 'ambivalents' and the 'wishfuls' respectively.

Regardless of these subtleties, however, there is a certain stigma attached to being single in Western society. Thus, despite an attempt in the nineteenth century to rehabilitate cultural attitudes to singleness through the cult of 'single blessedness' (i.e. a movement amongst educated spinsters 'to bring dignity to their place in society' – see Adams, 1976; Allen, 1989) a quarter of US respondents still see an unmarried woman as immoral or mentally disturbed (Buunk and Van Driel, 1989). Similarly, Allen concluded on the basis of her study of single women that

> singlehood is still devalued and considered a personal failure. Stereotypes of single women are couched in pathological terms, such as lack of sexual attractiveness, or the inability to form an intimate relationship with another person . . . and research has focused on the psychological deficits in single women's personality as compared to the relative health of married women.
>
> (Allen, 1989: 24)

Interestingly this perception is not a universal one even in Western society – with much more tolerant attitudes being documented in the Netherlands (Buunk and Van Driel, 1989). Stein (1983) has very sensibly noted that the major tasks which have to be faced by single adults are the same as those which have to be faced by all adults: finding work; maintaining their emotional and physical well-being; adjusting to ageing; building friendships; achieving intimacy and meeting their sexual needs. However, to the extent to which their social position is stigmatized, one would expect them to have greater difficulties meeting these needs. Thus, for example, one would expect few opportunities to be provided for single women to meet and interact together – a particularly important issue for the development of friendships.

There has been some recognition of the importance of ideology and its potential implications as regards unattached women's friendships. Bland *et al.* (1978), McRobbie and McCabe (1981) and Hudson (1984) have explored the elements in the ideology of femininity (i.e. having a boyfriend, spending time with him, pleasing him and giving him priority in their lives). Beechey (1986) has drawn attention to the issue of 'glamour' as an element in young women's ideas about femininity. These definitions of femininity play a part in implicitly devaluing friendships between women and endorsing the ideology of romantic love and domesticity. Green *et al.* (1990) suggest that once women begin seriously considering marriage, they begin to conform to traditional stereotypes of femininity and respectability: for example, not going out to discos or pubs with friends; cutting down, if not eliminating, their involvement with their own circle of friends; and generally restricting their friendships and activities to those which are seen as respectable for soon-to-be-married women. Rubin (1985) has wryly commented that friendships, which were encouraged during childhood and indeed were seen as an indicator of adjustment, begin in adolescence to be seen as potential threats to core institutions: 'But from adolescence on, these very friendships will often be seen as outlaw relationships – as a threat first to the authority of the family, then to the stability of the marriage' (Rubin, 1985: 110). Over the past fifteen years women's evaluation of themselves and other women has arguably increased; friendships between women are seen in a less 'pathetic' light, although they still lack the institutional supports typical of other close relationships (Leonard and Speakman, 1986; Wiseman, 1990). Some studies have noted (e.g. Griffiths, 1988) that British adolescent girls now keep Friday night as 'lasses night', when groups of them hit the town together (keeping Saturday night for their boyfriends). There was also some evidence in Green *et al.*'s study (1990) that lone parents availed of their 'freedom' during school hours to go to town or just have a laugh with friends – an alternative which was less available to their married counterparts.

A variety of studies (see Gove 1972; Jong-Gierveld, 1980; Bernard 1982) have shown that unmarried women are generally in better mental and physical health, less lonely, less vulnerable to suicide, etc. than unmarried men. There is also some evidence to suggest that, in general, the never married have better physical and mental health than the divorced, separated and widowed (Gove, 1974; Buunk and Van Driel, 1989; Whelan *et al.*, 1991). Hence one might suggest that the transition to singlehood, including dealing with loss, creating appropriate networks, etc., poses greater difficulties than remaining single. In fact there has been a strong tendency (see Buunk and Van Driel, 1989) to ignore the fact that for women lifelong singleness may constitute a viable life style and one which is associated with positive mental health (Bernard, 1982).

It has been suggested that the availability of close female friendships may be at least part of the reason for the relatively advantaged position of single women. However, Goodenow and Gaier (1990) found that in their study those who had a close friend were not consistently different in terms of mental health from those who did not. The sheer fact of being in employment also, however, has an important effect on the psychological health of single women (Whelan *et al.*, 1991). Further research is thus necessary to disentangle the importance of friendships in contributing to the mental health of the single.

It is also necessary to explore such theoretically interesting topics as the extent to which friendships between single women can transcend differences in age and education; the nature and type of friendships between women in their early twenties who are sharing flats and/or who holiday together; or indeed between celibate women in religious communities. Some attention has been paid to adolescent friendships between females, and it is to this that we now turn.

THE CONTEXT OF ADOLESCENT FEMALE FRIENDSHIPS

There are two diametrically opposed views of adolescent female friendships: one drawn from psychoanalysis, and the other from feminism. In the former tradition, theorists such as Erikson (1950) have seen intimacy as the property of heterosexual relationships. Reis and Shaver (1988), in summarizing and drawing out the perspectives of a variety of writers in this tradition (including Erikson), suggest that these writers see same-sex friendships as important in providing understanding, validation and clarification of identity. Nevertheless, the clear implication of their work is that such relationships are a preparation for, or a prelude to, heterosexual relationships.

Coming from a very different perspective, writers such as Smith-Rosenberg (1975) and Rich (1980) have seen these attitudes as part of the 'institution of compulsory heterosexuality': 'It is possible to speculate that in the twentieth century a number of cultural taboos evolved to cut short the homosocial ties of girlhood and to impel the emerging women of thirteen or fourteen towards heterosexual relationships' (Smith-Rosenberg, 1975: 27). This context, they argue, makes it extremely difficult for friendships between women to blossom despite the fact that female companionship has been shown to be highly beneficial (e.g. Wheeler *et al.*, 1983, found that amongst college seniors, loneliness amongst both women and men was negatively related to the amount of time spent with women). Nevertheless, like writers in the psychoanalytic tradition, they conclude that for women – especially young women – boyfriends: 'Represent social success and status, a secure symbol of acceptable femininity, someone with whom to share experiences and tentatively explore love and sexuality, someone to take them out and give them a good time' (Sharpe, 1976: 214). Milardo (1987) and Allan (1989), on the basis of their research reviews, argue that there is considerable evidence to suggest that adolescent and early-adult friendship patterns alter in the later stages of courtship. At this stage, they suggest, respondents report fewer friends, smaller networks and more couple-based interactions. The common popular and scientific perception is that 'Establishing a heterosexual relationship will probably affect the termination of women's same sex friendships more strongly than men's' (Rose, 1984: 267). It has been part of the conventional wisdom to see such patterns as indicating women's fickleness and/or the primacy of the conjugal role. Rose and Serafica (1986), however, implicitly suggest that this pattern may rather reflect differential power within the couple, and the impact of this on their patterns of friendship. Here in microcosm one sees the situational and cultural context which inhibits the maintenance of female friendships. The weakening of the female network is sometimes accompanied by the assimilation of the women into their boyfriends' social network; in other cases it is not. The process is seen as an inevitable one – in fact, a psychologically sound one. Very much less attention has been paid to it as a socially generated and culturally validated process which effectively weakens women's relationships with each other, and hence implicitly weakens a female power base.

Griffin (1985), on the basis of her qualitative study of friendships amongst English working-class adolescents, referred to this as the process of 'deffing out'. She noted that this process was more marked amongst young white girls than amongst Asian and Afro-Caribbean girls – partly because the latter were under less pressure to get a boyfriend and partly because their cultural backgrounds offered them stronger models of female friendship and support. She saw the fact that the sites of teenage girls' interaction were typically in their bedrooms, bathrooms and in the toilets and changing rooms at school as being significant: these were the only places where they could exert control. She also suggested that the process of breaking female friendship networks occurred partly because of individual boyfriend's insistence on this and partly because of the loss of structured public interaction areas and the difficulty of using others (such as clubs, discos, etc.) because of sexual harassment, shortage of money, parental control, etc. Hence her work very much underlines the social and cultural context which weakens these female friendships rather than seeing their abandonment as an indication of female fickleness, disloyalty or jealousy.

Green *et al.* (1990) put forward a similar line of argument, drawing attention both to the ideology of romantic love; the notion of reputation and the idea that the adolescent period is seen as preparation for the 'real world' of marriage and motherhood, where women's time and emotional energy will be concentrated within the home.

Hobson (1981) suggests that amongst adolescent females 'this pattern of acquiescence in their own subordination even at the time when they were potentially and theoretically most powerful' (1981: 138) can only be understood in the context of an ideology of femininity, and in particular, adolescents' recognition of the fact that their primary task is to find a man. This can be seen as very rational in so far as it has been clearly shown that in Britian

> a man's absolute mobility chances are greater than those of a comparable woman; he will benefit from better returns on his formal qualifications; and within every class location will find his market and work situations superior to those of occupationally similar females.
>
> (Marshall *et al.*, 1989: 83)

Purely in these terms, then, and apart from the ideology of romantic love or the arguably higher cultural valuation given to males over females, women's concern with their future class position should lead them to a pursuit of eligible males – if necessary, at the expense of female friendships.

Indirect support for this argument emerges from Candy *et al.*'s (1981) study, where, in her middle-class sample, female friends were chosen less and less by respondents ranging from adolescents to those in their twenties and thirties, for what she called status (i.e. prestige) reasons. Rose (1985) found that in her study women's friendships with each other were seen by them as providing less 'companionship' than their friend-ships with men. She suggests that this may be due to the fact that her measure of companionship in fact includes a status or prestige dimension (1985: 72). Certainly, in Griffin's (1985) and Hart's (1976) studies there is a strong feeling that female friends are not status enhancing, but rather that: 'women may acquire status by having males as companions and this may compensate for the lack of intimacy and acceptance in these relationships' (Rose, 1985: 72). In this context it seems important to look at the types of friendships that single women have.

WHAT KINDS OF FRIENDSHIPS DO SINGLE WOMEN HAVE? WHAT FACTORS AFFECT THEM?

It is very clear from the considerable body of work done (albeit mainly on American college undergraduates), that single women have various types of friends. As in the other chapters, however, it is more difficult to identify the content or quality of these relationships. It is also unclear to what extent the trends emerging from these studies can be generalized to single women in their twenties and thirties and/or those outside a college population. Furthermore a very substantial proportion of this research has been specifically concerned only with comparing and contrasting male and female friendships. Nevertheless, it does provide information on the content and quality of such friendships, and documents the peculiarly emotionally satisfying character of female friendships.

Thus Rose (1985) noted that, in her sample of white middle-class undergraduates and graduates, same-sex friendships were clearly preferred by both males and females, and were seen by both as providing more help and loyalty than cross-sex friendships. Furthermore, females saw their same-sex relationships as providing more acceptance and more intimacy than their cross-sex ones. These trends help make sense of Wheeler *et al.*'s (1983) finding that loneliness amongst women was negatively related to the amount of time they spent with other females.

Caldwell and Peplau (1982) in their study of unmarried college students found that the women identified, on average, just over three intimate and just over six good female friends (a pattern which was basically similar to that emerging amongst the males). However, in that study of roughly 100 undergraduates, women's interactions with their best friend were more personal and intimate than men's with theirs. This type of pattern has been broadly reproduced in a series of studies. For example, Williams (1985) found that in a study of over 500 under-graduate students of the University of Texas, females were more likely to confide in their close female friends, to be affectionate towards them, to discuss personal topics and issues with them, to spend more time talking than doing things with them, and generally to be more emotionally vulnerable to them than males were to their same-sex friends. Indeed, as previously mentioned, Wright (1982), on the basis of a review of a large number of studies, mainly but not exclusively dealing with college populations, typified women's friendships as 'face to face', with the partners 'mutually oriented to a personalized knowledge of and concern for one another' (Wright, 1982: 8). However, both in this early work and in later (1988) work he stresses that this generalization is too simplistic and that differences between women's and men's friendships diminished as the strength and duration of the friendships increased.

There has been some evidence to suggest that single adults were more likely than married ones to create and/or maintain friendship ties and/or to see their friends more often (see Rose and Serafica, 1986; Palisi and Ransford, 1987; Hays, 1988). There has also been a suggestion that the pattern varies by age. Thus Hess (1972) suggested that diffuse reciprocal relationships were only possible in adolescence when those participating had few other competing claims. At this time, Hays suggests a friend is:

> More or less a constant companion, a confidant with whom one can share very private information, a critic/advisor whose counsel is acceptable, a standard against which to measure oneself, an ego support whose affection and respect for one are known and reliable, an understanding ally, and a moral support in times of crisis.
>
> (Hays, 1988: 393)

Friendships, he argues, become more compartmentalized after this stage. Nevertheless, as Stein (1981) has noted, for many single people (particularly the voluntarily single) they remain an extremely important source of intimacy, sharing and continuity, and fill the gap left by the absence of a husband and children. Very little attention has been paid to this group of women; however, Goodenow and Gaier (1990) found that, amongst the single women in their study of American college alumnae, only just over two-fifths had at least one close friend, but in their terms this referred to a relationship which was reciprocal and with a high level of attachment, intimacy and equality.

Even less attention has been paid to the factors influencing the content and quality of friendships between single, never-married women in their twenties and thirties (other than those in American undergraduate and postgraduate college programmes). At these ages the availability of single women of similar age, social class, etc. is obviously limited. Hence, in this situation, where a structural shortage of 'similar' others exists, friends may be chosen from amongst those who are different in age, social class, marital status, etc. An examination of the strategies used on a short-term basis to 'create' equality in such relationships might well prove illuminating, the stability of these friendships enabling one to explore the importance of equality as a defining characteristic of friendship. However, with the exception of theoretical work by Blumstein and Kollock (1988), suggesting that these strategies might well include affirmation of the lower-status person's contribution to the relationship, devaluation of what the higher-status person has to offer and symbolic reduction of the latter's position, this topic has not been explored.

Typically too, the topic of age-related variation in women's friendships is dismissed rather summarily:

> The early twenties appear to be a period of high contact with friends . . . and of reliance on friends to discuss the issues of early adulthood . . . . By the mid twenties expectations for friends change: more emphasis is placed on communication and the individuality of the friend.
>
> (Rose and Serafica, 1986: 277)

Griffin's qualitative work on working-class British adolescents, while based on a small unrepresentative sample, makes three interesting and important points about adolescent friendships. Firstly, she highlights the strong element of identification implicit in female 'best' friends: 'These best friendships were typified by young women going everywhere together, walking along arm-in-arm, wearing exactly the same clothes, shoes, hairstyles, even jewellery' (Griffin, 1985: 61). Secondly, she notes that female friendships were not restricted to one person, but that they were embedded in a loose network of other friendships which was a source of resistance to the teacher's authority in school ('we girls together') and a challenge to male culture in the engineering industry ('more than three or four and they have one table at tea-break to themselves, they tend to become their own little community' (Griffin, 1985: 157)). Such perceptions have, however, generally been ignored, with the main attention being simply focused on girls' face-to-face 'best' friendships. This focus makes sense in terms of the discourse of femininity, where femininity is defined in terms of the skill to make lasting relationships and the ability to care very deeply for very few people (Hudson, 1984: 47). The disproportionate attention paid to such 'best' friends arguably reflects the dominance of this discourse and (as previously mentioned) reflects what Cancian (1986) has aptly called 'the feminization of love'.

Finally, Griffin (1985) noted that amongst her female respondents, many 'best' friendships were quite stable and had lasted for several years. This pattern is rather different from that suggested by popular and scientific discussions of the effect of courtship on adolescent friendships, and is something which might well be explored in more systematic studies of single women's friendships.

At any rate, it is clear that females are the preferred people to confide in (Cline Welch, 1989) and that the majority of single women have no problem identifying a best friend – who is almost always a woman (Rubin, 1985). Nevertheless the status of such friendships is low, especially amongst adult never-married and divorced females. It is possible that, as argued by Hart (1976), the cultural primacy attached to coupleness means that friendships between single women, whether individual or group-based, and regardless of their provisions, will never be seen as satisfactory. Thus, as the divorcees she studied graphically commented: 'there were no personal pay offs to identification with a group whose outward appearance was in the words of one respondent, that of "a bunch of social cripples" ' (Hart, 1976: 230). Hart acknowledges that the focus of her work on members of an association for divorcees arguably leads her to paint a grimmer picture of their relationships than might otherwise be the case. Nevertheless, this work, together with the qualitative work on adolescent friendships suggests that a neglected question is the perceived evaluation by single women themselves of the cultural value of their friendships.

TRAUMATIC SITUATIONS: THE TEST OF 'REAL' FRIENDSHIP?

Some of the most common types of difficulties faced by women in our society are those related to problems within the marital relationship – problems which may eventually lead to singleness. Typically, work in this area looks at the contributions made by friends in such situations (e.g. in violent situations and in separations prior to or after divorce). This is also one of the foci in this section. In addition, however, the impact of trauma on the content and/or sheer existence of friendships will also be explored.

There is a common-sense belief that 'true' or 'real' friends are characterized by the provision of help in such situations. Hart's (1976) and Brannen and Collard's (1982) studies vividly outline the way in which notions of marital privacy and what Cobb and Jones-Cobb called 'the marital taboo' (1984: 59) inhibited the contribution which could be made by any relationship in the face of marital difficulties. These studies showed that respondents were unwilling to discuss their marital problems as long as there was any possibility of resolving them. Hence, they often withdrew physically and emotionally from friends – a pattern which was sometimes resented by friends, and which made continuing the relationship later at the same level very difficult. In this situation, the contribution that friends might potentially make was limited: by fears of gossip; by a desire to present the marriage in the best possible light for as long as possible; by strong ideas about privacy and loyalty, etc.

> This attitude [i.e. fear of disloyalty] seems to reflect a widely held inhibition about talking about marital relationships which arises from their exclusivity and privacy. But it also reflects the unequal and deferential position of wives who are thereby bound by loyalty to their husbands.
>
> (Brannen and Collard, 1982: 127)

Nevertheless, there is some evidence to suggest (Hart, 1976; Brannen and Collard, 1982; Milardo, 1987; Allan, 1989) that friends can be supportive, especially those who are not shared with the husband, who are of long standing or those whose friendship developed during or after the separation. Typically, however, such friendships rarely provide more than active listening, reassurance, encouragement and moral support – albeit that these are very much appreciated and appear to make an important contribution to the respondents' emotional adjustment.

Brannen and Collard (1982) noted that respondents who had what they called 'differentiated friendship networks' (i.e. consisting of a relatively large number of members, with at least four friends in the network and which had 'a varying degree of connectedness', 1982: 98) were more likely to get the emotional support they wanted, partly because their networks were largely composed of friends and partly because in such networks they could choose who to confide in without the risk of having the whole network involved. Close-knit networks seemed particularly likely to provide practical or instrumental help but to be less adequate sources of emotional help.

In the long run, however, there is a tendency for some of the friendships of those who become divorced or separated to atrophy. Thus, for example, Rands (1988) found that roughly 40 per cent of the respondents' preseparation networks were dropped after that separation. Similarly, on the basis of a wide-ranging review of the literature, Milardo (1987) concluded that although ties with married predivorce friends were retained in the short term, in the long term, these frequently deteriorated – especially in the case of women.

Milardo (1987) suggested that women, especially those who had custody of children, were unlikely to develop new friendships. Rather, they intensified their relationships with kin – a trend which could be seen as helping them meet their responsibilities to their children, but one which was likely to be negatively associated with their own level of adjustment. Hetherington *et al.* (1977) and Acock and Hurlbert (1990) also noted that divorced women consistently reported fewer friends in comparison to their married counterparts. This pattern they see as part of a social process where 'Ties will be replaced by others which are more consonant with the new identity and which serve to bolster it more effectively' (Allan, 1989: 61). This led Rands (1988) and Allan (1989) to suggest that after divorce, a network is likely to resume the character it had before marriage (i.e. mainly consisting of single people). Wilcox (1981) noted that, in his study, many of the respondents' friends before the separation were spouses of their husbands (his business associates or friends). Such relationships nearly always 'cooled' after divorce. Hart (1976) and Allan (1989) also noted that joint friendships were particularly vulnerable to disruption – sometimes because the friendship was initiated by, or rooted in the spouse, sometimes because of lack of resources to maintain the relationship, lack of acceptance of a single person in couple venues, or because friends, being equally close to both partners, felt embarrassed and unable to deal with taking sides, and so withdrew. Hart's study (1976) also briefly opened up the issue of the vulnerability of upwardly socially mobile (and often also geographically mobile) divorcees: 'who had hitched their waggon to a spiralist marriage, and now found themselves, after it had broken down, with no current reason for being where they were' (Hart 1976: 178). Typically, in popular comment this provokes an examination of these women's ability to choose 'real' friends: and/or an examination of the extent to which these friendships were 'real' anyway, a discussion which partly reflects the assumption that 'real' friendships should provide any or all resources required in crises, that they should be strengthened by crises and in any case, should not end in such circumstances. Such expectations are, of course, highly idealized since it is widely recognized that the essence of friendship is not the unilateral provision of practical help (Allan, 1989).

This type of argument also obscures the fact that some relationships simply reflect and reinforce class position and couple-based identity. Furthermore, since similarity is widely accepted as an important element in friendship relationships, it is obviously desirable that divorced and separated people should surround themselves with those in similar marital positions. Doing this, however, may well involve the development of new close relationships and the attenuation of those which were previously very close.

Women who are in families where there is violence are in an even more difficult situation than those who are separated or divorced, because of the stigma attached to their situation and the fact that the damaging potential of gossip about it is even greater. Prior to the 1970s the popular opinion was that such families represented a tiny minority. However, a large nationally representative American study by Straus *et al.* (1980) concluded that more than a quarter of those interviewed had experienced some kind of physical violence in their marriages (and for roughly half of these it had been severe). Marsden (1978) estimated that in Britian, serious assault happened in one in every twenty marriages; while Andrews and Brown (1988) found that in their sample of working-class women, one in four had experienced physical violence at some time in their lives (with the exclusion of the separated and divorced, this fell to one in nine of those women who were currently married or cohabiting – a still far from negligible figure).

Relatively little is known about the role of friends in providing support in this situation. Gelles (1974) suggested that abused women lacked the social networks that would enable them to leave their abusive partner. On the basis of his review of the literature, Allan (1989) concluded that between a half and three-quarters of abused wives did approach friends for support at some stage during their violent marriage. Friends, he concluded, do act as a resource for some abused women.

Dobash and Dobash (1980) found that in their Scottish study of a sample of women who had experienced marital violence, just over half had never even mentioned the assault to friends. Just under one in five of those who contacted anyone contacted a friend as regards the first episode; but this fell to one in twenty when one looked at either the last episode, or the worst episode (1980: 249). These trends partly reflected the women's hope that the violence would stop; their adherence to the idea of the privacy of the marriage; their sense of shame and guilt (patterns which are typical in studies of violence); and their own and others' perception of the problem as something which probably could only be solved through divorce – a step which these women were not always or immediately ready to take.

In this situation, even if women had friends (and Pahl's, 1985, work suggested that this was not always the case), they usually simply provided a sympathetic ear, gave them advice, looked after the children, took them to doctors, solicitors, social workers, etc., and perhaps provided them with a loan or temporary accommodation. As Dobash and Dobash (1980) suggest, their help was inevitably limited both by beliefs about the inviolability of the marriage; the fact that both women were typically economically dependent; had a mutual responsibility for child care; and typically lacked access to 'spare' rooms or other long-term accommodation possibilities. Indeed, Strube and Barbour (1984) found that having nowhere else to go was clearly associated with remaining with a violent husband.

Work such as this clearly challenges facile asssumptions about the nature, existence and supportive provisions of friendships. It highlights the importance of looking at the social context constraining the provision of help – rather than simply concluding that such relationships were not 'really close' anyway. There is implicit cultural pressure to retain the concept of friends as people who would be willing and able to help out in a crisis. It is argued that this concept implies a distortion of the nature of friendship. It also (indeed, like the ideology of romantic love itself) sets up an impossible ideal against which friendships embedded in day-to-day life are likely to be found lacking.

In this situation, the 'best' friendships are almost inevitably likely to be those which are purely mental constructs: people who are seen rarely but who are believed to be willing and able to help out 'if they were really needed'. Their existence as security figures may well be seen as extremely important. Clearly, however, these relationships, by definition, provide little ongoing help or support; but equally, they demand little time or energy and pose very little real threat to the primacy of other responsibilities in these women's day-to-day lives. As such, they fit easily with both the ideology of romantic love and the cultural requirement that 'everyone should have friends'.

THE EFFECT OF FRIENDSHIP

Arguments concerning the effects of friendship implicitly presuppose that it is more than a mere mental construct. In the context of this chapter, there are typically three main types of approaches to this question: firstly, those that look at the effect of divorce or transition to college on the composition and quality of the respondents' social networks (a topic which we began to explore in the last section); secondly, those that look at the buffering effect of friendship in the face of these and other 'life events'; and thirdly those that look at the association between relationships and broad social-psychological variables (such as mental health, adjustment, loneliness, enjoyment, etc.). The area is a methodological minefield (e.g. do underlying personality factors create both deficits in friendship and poor mental health? does one focus on the supportive content of relationships or on the perceived existence of support? etc.). However, it seems important to raise a number of issues specifically related to such studies on single women.

As previously mentioned, it has been consistently shown that the separated and the divorced have poorer mental health than the never married or the still married. It is, however, difficult to interpret this relationship. Similarly, there is, within the general social-support literature, a well-recognized difficulty in disentangling the association between supportive relationships and feelings of satisfaction, loneliness, etc.

> Thus the question becomes: do inadequate relationships cause loneliness, or does loneliness cause inadequate relationships, or both? Similarly are such aversive psychological states as depression (which often accompanies loneliness) a consequence of feeling lonely, or do they result from exposure to situations and events that presumably could cause both loneliness and depression.
>
> (Jones *et al.*, 1985: 228)

The issue of the effect of friendship on adjustment to divorce was first raised by Weiss, on the basis of his work on parents without partners (1969). He concluded that although friendships were important, they could not compensate for the loss of the marriage. He thus put forward the 'fund of sociability' thesis, which in essence stated: 'The presence of some elements of social support did not make up for the absence of others' (Cobb and Jones-Cobb, 1984: 61). However, Cobb and Jones-Cobb on the basis of their review of the literature also concluded that the existence of friends was associated with stress reduction in all the studies they reviewed with only one exception – and that the 'time frame' of the latter study (i.e. four months or less after separation) could partly explain that result.

Gerstel *et al.* (1985) have been amongst those who have shown that (using Fischer *et al.*'s north Californian sample) the divorced were less likely than the married to have a confidant, more likely to have smaller networks, less likely to have homogeneous networks (i.e. consisting of only divorced and separated people) and were more likely to feel lonely and to see their networks as burdensome. However, in that study these characteristics were less important than material conditions (i.e. available income and number of children) in explaining women's heightened psychiatric vulnerability (both factors together explaining almost all of the relationship between marital status and mental health). Later work by Gerstel (1988), however, suggested that turning to kin, especially for money or to confide in them, was inversely associated with the likelihood of depression amongst these separated and divorced women (1988: 216). One might speculate that although women's responsibilities for their children made kin support attractive, the quality of these relationships was also important.

There has tended to be an assumption that a large network is a highly supportive network. However, as Milardo (1987) suggested, size could also be associated with a high degree of interference. Similarly, there has also been a tendency (noted by Leslie and Grady, 1985; Milardo, 1987) to assume that close-knit networks were more likely to be supportive than loose-knit ones. In fact, however, there is some evidence to suggest that such dense (often kin-filled networks), although conducive to the provision of material support, were not necessarily conducive to the provision of emotional support or to the woman's own positive adjustment to divorce (Colletta, 1979; Leslie and Grady, 1985; Milardo, 1987).

The issue of the importance of network density also appeared in Hirsch's (1979, 1981) and Wilcox's (1981) studies: studies which Morgan (1990: 201) referred to as 'often cited but still little understood'. Thus, Hirsch (1979, 1981) suggested that low-density networks were more adaptive in situations that resulted in a great deal of change. They provided access to a greater variety of role partners and, as one's needs and interests changed, they increased the probability of finding someone similar and/or changing the opinions and attitudes of individual dyadic role partners. Hirsch's own data drew on college students and on women returning to college. In his first study, which used college students, Hirsch (1979) found that denser networks provided greater quantities of support (possibly indicating the input of parents) although students were less satisfied with that support. In the latter case he found that the denser networks were associated with less satisfying support and poorer mental health.

This latter trend re-appeared in Wilcox's (1981) study of fifty recently divorced women (half of whom were identified as having successfully adjusted to their divorce and all of whom were still single at the time of interview). He found than those who were poorly adjusted had denser networks that those who had adjusted more positively. In a qualitative examination of his data, he suggested that this was related to the fact that the friendships of the less well adjusted were more likely to have been based in their husband's world prior to their divorce. Inevitably perhaps, then, these ties were lost on divorce, and equally inevitably, perhaps, they turned to kin in that situation (kin who were often critical of their decision and/or tried to exert unwanted control in that situation: see Milardo, 1987). A similar reaction was unlikely to occur amongst friends – partly, indeed, because such overtures, if unwelcome, were less likely to be tolerated from them. Milardo (1987) noted that what he called 'separate friendships' (1987: 88) were positively associated with adjustment to divorce. However, it was not clear to what extent this reflected the supportive properties of these relationships or the fact that women who had them were less involved in their marriages anyway, and so were better able to adjust to divorce.

Hays and Oxley's (1986) work showed even more clearly that the most adaptive social networks for first-term university students were those which were most permeable (i.e. in that they included other college students) rather than those where the student simply held on to old high-school or neighbourhood friends. Stokes (1983) did not find that density was important in his study of college students in their mid-twenties: a conclusion which he interpreted as indicating that low density is only particularly important in dealing with certain kinds of transitional crises. He also suggested that density might be less important *per se* than the existence of networks where there were relatively few relatives or clusters of friends tied to relatives. Indeed, he found that it was the existence of confidants which was particularly important in such situations: a finding which has been widely noted in other studies (see Milardo, 1987).

Shaver *et al.*'s work (1985) attempted to deal with methodological difficulties by differentiating between students who experienced what they called 'state' loneliness (i.e. in the wake of their move to college) as compared to 'trait' (i.e. more long term feelings of) loneliness. They found that 'state' loneliness changed in these college students' first year at college, paralleling changes in peer relationship satisfaction. 'Trait' loneliness, on the other hand, tended to be associated with a perceived lack of social skill (e.g. an inability to initiate relationships, to self-disclose, etc.). Such skills accounted for only 7 per cent of the variance in loneliness before coming to college, but for almost 40 per cent during the first term of college. They suggest then that 'trait' loneliness is a chronic condition for some students who lack social skills and who, anticipating failure, do not take the initiative. 'State' loneliness, on the other hand, arose due to disruptions and changes in the students' networks during their move to college.

In that study, as in the studies of divorce, the effects of friendship are clearly being assessed within the context of a more or less defined event. Hence one is concerned with friendship acting – either directly or indirectly – as a buffer. Other studies were less event-focused. Thus, for example, Cauce (1986) found an association between the perceived emotional support received by young black working-class adolescents and their levels of self-esteem and peer competence; between their networks' positive attitude towards school achievement and the adolescents' own school performance; and between their number of reciprocated best friendships and what he called their 'independence orientation' (i.e. the extent to which they do or do not feel under pressure to conform to the attitudes and values of their friends). Such studies, in so far as they deal with feelings of support, show similar, if not more acute methodological problems than those within the stress buffering tradition.

Larson and Bradney's (1988) work was unusual in so far as it required the participants to carry electronic 'bleepers' and to indicate what they were doing and feeling at random times when they were 'paged'. Their sample included, although it was not restricted to, high-school students. Their results clearly showed that being with friends was associated with positive feelings of excitement and happiness: 'On the average, their emotional states with their friends were extremely high, much higher than their typical states with their families. Clearly, for adolescents it is with friends that precious moments with others are most likely to occur' (Larson and Bradney, 1988: 112). They suggest that this reflects the fact that these relationships are typically non-hierarchical; they are between those who have similar goals and problems, interaction is rooted in 'fun' activities, is more likely to be assessed as 'joking' rather than 'serious' and is more likely to provide positive feedback. Work such as this supports other work (such as Bradburn, 1969; Argyle, 1990) which has suggested that friendships are associated with positive states: an 'assets benefiting' type of model but dealing with transient positive outcomes –

conceptualized as excitement, happiness or joy.

It is arguable, however, that every focus on what friends 'do' (a focus which is very much to the fore in the social support literature) leads to a distorted picture of the very nature of friendship. Indeed, in the next section it will be shown that even the sheer existence of a friendship is a much more ambiguous reality than those studies concerned with its psychological effects would suggest. In that section, we turn to a more explicit consideration of work done on the creation, maintenance and termination of friendships: work which is located in this chapter since it has been predominantly done on single women.

CREATING, MAINTAINING AND ENDING FRIENDSHIPS

As mentioned previously the 1980s have seen an attempt being made to identify the factors associated with the maintenance of such relationships and/or the processes operating at each stage. Much of this work has not dealt exclusively with single women, although the latter have often been disproportionately represented within those studies which have been concerned with process. Some of this work has dealt specifically with friendship, while other parts (e.g. Dindia and Baxter, 1987; Reis and Shaver, 1988; Leatham and Duck, 1990) have been concerned with the processes operating in other types of relationships. Much of this work is empirically limited – drawing largely on American college samples. Nevertheless, it does provide some insights into the processes operating within the friendships of single women and for this reason it will be discussed in this section.

Thus Hays (1985), on the basis of a twelve-week longitudinal study of same-sex friendships among college students, showed that, despite being frequently ignored in friendship studies, there were costs involved in both close and non-close relationships – costs such as emotional aggravation and time. Furthermore, these costs increased as the relationship developed: with roughly one-third of all the dyads mentioning them after nine weeks. He argued, however, that in the case of those relationships which became close, such costs were more than offset by benefits: close friendships reporting more benefits than those which were not close. (Companionship and confidancy were most often mentioned as the benefits of friendships – with the latter being particularly important in

close relationships.) Possibly because of the student dormitory environment generating them, these friendships tended to develop rather rapidly
between the third and sixth weeks: the friendship level established at that
time being quite highly correlated with their score five months later.
Subsequent work by Hays, (1989), using a diary approach, basically
confirmed these earlier findings, that is, close friends provided more
emotional and informal support than casual friends, although there was
no difference between them in terms of the level of fun, intellectual
stimulation and task assistance they provided.

Hays does not locate these insights within a wider social and cultural
perspective. Gender is only used by him as a categorical variable, although
even as such it proves to be rather interesting, with female students
reporting that they offered their friends more emotional and informatio-
nal support and experienced less interaction costs than their male
counterparts – a finding which is consistent with other work in the area.
Hays (1985), however, simply interprets this in terms of differences in
support styles.

Rose (1984, 1985), noting the extent of the change in young adults'
same-sex friendship networks when they went to college, simply concluded that they had not yet developed strategies to maintain geographically inaccessible relationships where there was no situational context for
interaction (such as the school or the neighbourhood). Later work by
Rose and Serafica (1986), on the basis of a study of ninety young adults
aged 20–25 years, noted that best friendships were actually maintained by
letters, phone calls and/or exchange of gifts. Rather interestingly,
however, in that sample those who had never had a best friend thought
that such friendships were self-maintaining (1986: 280, 286). Shaver *et
al.*'s (1985) study looked at the effects of the transition to college on
young peoples' friendships. Their study showed that in the period
between the summer prior to college and the winter of their first year
there, the average number of friendships fell from 6 to 4.8, and they also
declined in perceived quality. New close friends developed over the year
within the college setting, although only one-third of these retained that
label during the year. Shaver *et al.* note that regardless of distance, visits
to old friends were infrequent during the year and phone calls and letters
decreased in frequency as the year went on, leading them to conclude that
these pre-college friends were 'more or less forgotten, at least for a while'
(1985: 206). It seems plausible to suggest that such students were in the
process of 'adjusting' their friendship ties to conform to their own change
of identity and situation.

As previously mentioned, Duck and Sants (1983) argued that relationships were processes not states, and that hence researchers should investigate these processes rather than simply looking at the predictors and outcomes of interaction (i.e. in Duck's 1990b analogy, simply to identify the ingredients and the end product provides little insight into the process of cooking). In this context, Miell and Duck (1986) attempted to identify the strategies used by first-year university students in intensifying and restricting a friendship's development – both with a potential friend and a close friend. They argued that the partners' plans as regards the future of the relationship determined the content and style of the communication between them. Thus, for example, they suggested that those who wished a new relationship to develop asked questions; reciprocated disclosures and were responsive and observant (the opposite behaviours being shown by those who did not wish it to develop further). They suggested that these strategies were obscured at the beginning of a friendship by polite conversation, a limited range of conversational topics, a general level of discussion and infrequent contact. At a later stage, strategies were directed to creating a predictable pattern of interaction – as indicated by an attempt to plan interaction, to be in frequent contact, to deal with a wide range of conversational topics and to introduce intimate topics, sometimes in an ambiguous, general, joking or hypothetical way, so that the appropriateness of moving towards what they call a close-friend script could be assessed. In so far as one partner did not wish the relationship to develop further, such strategies would be resisted. However, these manoeuvres took place within an atmosphere of acute uncertainty: 'People have generally little confidence about the relationships' future form, are constantly storm tossed by the vicissitudes of daily life, and are full of mild "existential terror" about their friends and their friendships' (Duck and Miell, 1986: 134). For these undergraduates, the most important element in their interaction with each other was the public and apparently superficial chat through which these subtle negotiations took place (an idea which obviously belies the common popular and scientific notion that friendships develop through 'meaningful' conversations).

McCabe (1981a), on the basis of her qualitative work on female adolescents, also vividly illustrated the role that talk, their main leisure pursuit, played in such relationships:

Talking for girls and women is not relaxation, but managing contradictions, and its centrality to girls' activity is no surprise. They see talking as positive, sorting out problems with your friends, establishing their own space and time, but it is always over-determined by boys.

(McCabe, 1981a: 129)

A very similar sort of picture was presented by Gullestad (1984) and Oliker (1989) as regards the importance of 'talk' in the lives of small samples mainly of married women (see Chapter 3). Work such as this provides a fascinating insight into the processes operating in relationships and could well be more widely undertaken in order to provide an understanding of the processes operating in single women's friendships.

Even less empirical work has been done on the dissolution of their friendships. Wiseman (1986, 1990), like Rose (1984) and Helgeson *et al.* (1987), but in the contrast to the trends emerging in Wright (1982), suggests that the ending of a friendship rarely involves confrontation. Rather, the participants involved redefine the nature of the relationship and end or curtail their involvement accordingly. Obviously, further work is necessary to explore the reasons for this discrepancy in findings – although it clearly could simply reflect different methodologies, samples, etc. At any rate, Rose (1984), in explaining the dissolution of friendships, noted that physical separation was mentioned most often by female college students (i.e. roughly by two-fifths of them), followed by the presence of new friends and of behaviours that they disliked. Only just under one-fifth referred to the impact of dating or marrying, a trend which is interesting in view of the frequent assumption that romantic involvements are the main reason for the break-up of female friendships.

It seems clear that friends can play a very important part during the dissolution process of a relationship – particularly during what Duck (1982) called the 'social phase', where partners consult and involve the network as regards that relationship, and at the 'grave-dressing' phase, when the partners and their relevant networks construct publicly negotiable accounts of the course of the dead relationship and the cause of its demise. Work on accounts of friendships has barely begun to tackle these issues – arguably because this work is, like most of the work on creating, maintaining and terminating relationships, coming from a social psychological and psychological perspective and so is not rooted in a discussion of the social position of women and/or the sociology of gender.

ISSUES ARISING FROM THE WORK

Work on single women's friendships has disproportionately drawn on American college undergraduate samples, and hence the generalizability of these findings is questionable. Very little work has been done on the friendships of single women in their twenties, thirties and forties – especially those who have, for whatever reason, chosen to be single. The initiation and maintenance of such relationships is arguably quite different from other friendships, in view of the sheer paucity of such women in the population in Western society at any one point in time. This situation raises issues about the extent to which friendships amongst such women might be based on singleness rather than on similarity in age, occupation, education, etc. It raises the issue of the extent to which their friendship networks are likely to include married women, and the implications of this as regards managing such dissimilarity (topics which are taken up again in Chapter 7).

In fact, most of the work done on single females and their friendships has focused on what, in Stein's (1981, 1983) terms, can be described as 'involuntary singles'. It is arguable that female friendships would be least important to these groups since their main priority is finding a mate. Indeed, there is some evidence from Hart (1976) that a club structure which had set out to provide individual support and to act as a social centre for generating friendships had, by the time her study concluded, become a marriage market.

Work such as Hart's (1976) or indeed Griffin's (1985) raises issues about the cultural valuation of female friendship – a valuation arguably increased by the rise of the Women's Movement. The value and importance of such friendships has received unexpected support from work such as Wheeler *et al.*'s (1983), which has shown the psychological importance of interacting with females. Furthermore, even in Griffin's work there is some suggestion that friendships between young women are both stable and enjoyable, and that wider networks of female friendships exist – networks which are, potentially at least, a power base for these young women.

Work such as this illustrates the importance of locating a discussion of friendships between women within a social and cultural context. In fact, relatively little of the work in this chapter has done this. Indeed, there has been very little attempt even to spell out the factors which facilitate and constrain the development of friendships between women (e.g. their level of income, access to resources including transport, the availability of public spaces in which to interact, cultural attitudes which make it difficult for women to go out alone, the availability of a network through which contacts can be made and the increasing unavailability of single companions for women in their twenties and thirties).

Work from within the social-psychological tradition has provided important insights into the processes involved in initiating, maintaining and terminating friendships. As previously mentioned, the majority of such work has been done on American college-based populations, and so its conclusions need to be tested on other populations. Theoretical work such as Baxter's (1988), which has been concerned with the dialectical processes of relational development, and Duck and Pond's work (1989) on talk could usefully be tested on single women's female friendships. This has not yet been done, although Baxter and Dindia (1990) have applied these ideas to marriage.

The work in this chapter raises the issue of the importance of identity validation and hence of status similarity in friendships, and the inevitability of changes in friendships in the wake of events (such as divorce) which imply a change in status. This perception of friendship as a social construction which validates social identities sits uneasily with the popular view of friendship as an immutable loving relationship. This indicates that there is in friendship (as in marriage) a clear tension between the ideology of a long-term relationship and the recognition of the effects of status discontinuities on individuals' life styles:

> Certainly relationships can sometimes survive significant abrupt changes in one of the selves. But it is indeed a matter of survival, because newly adapted selves create new demands on the other to give role-support, demands that cannot always be met, even with the best of intentions.
>
> (Blumstein, 1990: 15)

Friendships are, of course, potentially particularly important in so far as they are freely chosen and so can be used to reflect and maintain burgeoning identities. They are also, however, the least structurally embedded relationships, and hence on this basis alone are the most vulnerable to termination (Milardo, 1986; Wiseman, 1986).

Studies of friendship in crisis situations (e.g. in divorce or in violent situations) implicitly raise the question of the extent to which the giving of help in such situations is the criterion of 'real' friendship. This in turn is related to the question of the relative usefulness of dense versus loose networks. It seems clear that with the possible exception of practical help, loose networks are most useful: a conclusion which implicitly highlights the variety of resources and role models typically needed by respondents at such transitions. Thus, even on this basis, it is questionable to what extent this willingness to provide help is an appropriate indicator of 'real' friendship.

Overall, it is true to say that work on single women has provided important insights into the nature and importance of friendship and the processes operating within it. It has (with a few notable exceptions) provided very much less insight into the experience of singleness and/or femaleness, and the nature and importance of friendship to the single female. Thus it is not clear to what extent life-stage variation exists, whether voluntary/involuntary singleness affects friendship patterns and/ or whether the statistically and normatively deviant status of being single and female has an impact on friendship patterns.

— 5 —

Elderly women and their friends

INTRODUCTION

In Western society, women typically live longer than men. Hence one might argue that even if friendships between women were not important at any other age, they were likely to become so in old age. Furthermore, often in old age other roles such as spouse or worker cease, so that friendships may well be one of the few available sources of social integration, status and companionship. This issue was concealed in the 1950s by a predominant focus on the family relationships of elderly people (Blau's work, 1973, being a notable exception). In the 1960s Cumming and Henry's (1961) notion of disengagement continued to obscure the issue by suggesting that old age was a period of social and emotional withdrawal. In the 1970s concern with the care of elderly people in the community again distracted attention from their friendship relationships – although studies of the support networks of elderly widows suggested that friends, particularly confidants, played an important part in their lives. However, it was only with the rise of the Women's Movement, and the increasing legitimacy of friendship as a topic for investigation, that serious attention has been given to the study of elderly women's friendships.

Over the past ten years considerable attention has been paid to this topic. In fact, with the exception of the study of friendships among student populations, more attention has been paid to friendships amongst this age group than to any other. In this chapter, as in these studies, the concept of 'elderly' is interpreted rather loosely to include those in late middle age (i.e. in their fifties and older). Furthermore, as mentioned in the previous chapter, for practical reasons, widows (who are for the most part likely to be in this general age group) are also discussed here. The age range included is thus quite broad, although for the majority the continued availability of a heterosexual relationship is arguably problematic.

Studies which have been concerned with the existence and quality of friendship relationships amongst the elderly have typically focused on their psycho-social provisions, often relating these to some measure of psychological or emotional well-being either in a general way or in specific situations (e.g. in the face of major life events such as retirement or widowhood; Blieszner, 1988). Such theoretical work as has been done has been concerned with exploring the relative validity of Litwak's (1985) task-specific model and Cantor's (1979) hierarchical compensatory model. According to Litwak's model, friends, because of their similarity in age and experience, are most suited to providing companionship and helping people learn new roles, as well as being potentially important sources of affective support. Cantor's (1979) model suggests that relationships with friends are essentially compensatory, 'that is they stand in for kin when kin are non-existent or unavailable and thus are an important adjunct to family in the support networks of the elderly' (Crohan and Antonucci, 1989: 137). Much of the work has, however, been atheoretical and has simply been concerned with exploring the provisions of friendship and/or identifying aspects of the elderly person's present and past material and social circumstances which have shaped their friendships (i.e. their class position, marital status or health: see e.g. Dickens and Perlman, 1981; Adams and Blieszner, 1989; Allan and Adams, 1989). Selected themes from these studies will be highlighted in this chapter. In addition, some attention will be paid to the interesting work which has been done on the social processes operating within groups of friends (Jerrome, 1984) and to variation in friendship styles (Matthews, 1983, 1986; Adams, 1987). It is necessary, however, first to indicate briefly the context within which friendship operates in the case of the elderly and to highlight the diversity implicit in the latter concept.

WHAT KINDS OF FRIENDSHIPS DO ELDERLY WOMEN HAVE?

There is an enormous complexity behind this apparently simple question. Firstly, it has been widely recognized that in studies of the elderly as well as younger respondents, various definitions of friendship have been used ranging from simple identification of close or best friends to definitions which have included both statements of closeness and either frequency of contact and/or geographical propinquity, to more complex measures of the provisions of such relationships – including their level of intimacy, their primary quality, etc. Furthermore, some studies have not differentiated between friendships and relationships with kin who are also identified as very close, thereby making comparisons difficult. In addition, there is some evidence to suggest that friendship patterns differ between the still-married, the widowed and separated and the never-married. Many studies, however, have included one or the other group only in their analysis. Finally, the concept of the elderly itself is very loose – and can effectively embrace a forty-year age span.

Within these studies there is a huge range of variation in the proportion of respondents identifying close friends – reflecting, no doubt, both variation in the nature of the samples and in the definition of friends. Adams (1985) found that the overwhelming majority of her respondents had at least one emotionally close friend. Similarly, the majority of the widows in Lopata's study (1979) said that they had close friends both in the year before their husband died and since their widowhood (a small proportion having actually developed friends for the first time since their widowhood). The overwhelming majority of Wenger's (1984) respondents said that they had 'real' friends nearby; while Lawton (1977) found that three-fifths of their old respondents claimed to have friends, and these normally lived nearby and usually were seen frequently. On the other hand, O'Connor (1991b) found that in a sample of very frail elderly Social Service Department clients living alone, less than one in five had a very close friendship.

Ambiguity in the definition of friendship has continued to bedevil the study of the friendships of elderly people – even over the past ten years. The importance of age similarity as a defining characteristic of friendship has been challenged by a number of studies such as Cantor's (1979), Weiss and Lowenthal's (1975) and Powers and Bultena's (1976). Thus, for example, in the latter study of seventy-year-olds, a quarter of the women's friendships were with people at least sixteen years younger. Hence, the very meaning which is attached to age similarity and/or its importance as a defining characteristic of friendship is questionable.

Frequency of contact has been widely used as a crude indicator of friendship intensity. Particularly amongst the elderly, it is likely to be associated with geographical proximity. Matthews notes that a number of studies, however, have even included such geographical accessibility in their definition of a close friend (e.g. by asking their respondents to identify those to whom they feel close 'within the community' (1983: 143)). This strategy seems particularly questionable in view of the fact that it has been widely recognized that long-standing, even if infrequently seen, friends can be extremely important figures in the respondents' emotional lives: indeed, often the elderly's most cherished relationships persist over miles and years (Dickens and Perlman, 1981; Jerrome, 1981; Shea *et al.*, 1988; Allan, 1989).

Matthews (1983) differentiated between friendships where the other person was valued as a unique and irreplaceable individual and a friendship which was valued for its relational provision (and so was eminently more replaceable). The same kind of distinction was implicit in Adams' (1985) comment that people considered themselves to be very close friends because their friendship was an enduring one or because they saw that person often. In 1989, however, Allan and Adams were still reiterating the observation that

One of the more important ambiguities within our cultural conception of friendship arises from the distinction between a friend as a more or less regular sociable contact on the one hand, and as someone with whom one has developed a high level of intimacy, trust and loyalty on the other.

(Allan and Adams, 1989: 47)

Elderly respondents are likely to experience the loss of personal primary ties as they age. Such ties are inevitably irreplaceable and this in itself may account for the perception of old age as a time of loss. Such ties, however, rooted as they are in self-definition rather than in current sociability or intimate confiding, are unlikely to be dissolved by infrequent contact, geographical inaccessibility, low level of resources, etc. The validation provided by the sheer existence of such friendships has tended to be ignored – with, as will be shown, intimacy being most typically used to explore the support provided by friendships. At any rate, in so far as frequency of contact is chosen as the main indicator of friendship, the importance of such long-standing friendships will be underestimated, since typically these relationships, although very close, are not likely to be in the local area, and hence are likely to be seen less often. The extensiveness of these ties is indicated by the finding that in Adams' (1985) study almost four-fifths of the respondents had an emotionally close non-local friend. Finally, to focus simply on a crude measure, such as frequency of contact, obscures the content of the relationship, and so makes it more difficult to differentiate between various types of friendships.

Lopata (1979) suggested that although the importance of friends as sources of emotional support increased enormously after widowhood, this aspect of the relationship was still very much less important than that of sociable companionship. Fischer (1982b) and Wenger (1984) saw companionship as a particular provision of friendship, while Jerrome expressed this even more graphically:

> A widespread feature of the friendships I have encountered has been the emphasis, in practice, on pleasure as opposed to help or the exchange of confidences . . . the main need seems to be for companionship in an enjoyable activity, 'someone to do things with'.
>
> (Jerrome, 1981: 192–3)

This was re-echoed by Rook (1989) on the basis of an extensive review of the literature: 'Friendships are particularly conducive to interactions characterised by spontaneity, playfulness, permissiveness and candour . . . and interactions of this sort tend to make the greatest contributions to feelings of happiness' (Rook, 1989: 166). Similarly, Sinclair *et al.* (1988) found that, amongst their elderly Social Service Department clients, friends and neighbours were mentioned most often as sources of social integration – half of the respondents in the study mentioned them in this context. O'Connor (1991b), using the same data base, focused specifically on same-sex relationships identified as very close. These relationships were overwhelmingly these respondents' main sources of social integration, while only roughly half of them were confidants.

Hence, quite clearly, although there are various types of friends, the provision of companionship in some form or another can be seen as a peculiarly defining characteristic of the relationship amongst the elderly. Nevertheless, in the area of the elderly, as in the case of the wider social-support literature, attention has tended to focus particularly on the existence of confidants. This concept is frequently loosely defined, with actual confiding behaviour being very often confounded with more general feelings of trust or acceptance as implied by a willingness to confide.

Given the variety of samples and questions used, etc., it is difficult to get any overall picture of the existence of confidants. Strain and Chappell, on the basis of their review of a wide range of studies, concluded that 'most studies indicate that elderly persons have at least one confidant' (1982: 481). Lowenthal and Haven's work (1968) suggested that the probability of having an intimate friendship was greatest for those aged 65–74 years, while those aged 75 years or more were least likely to have one. Booth (1972) found that roughly half the females in his middle-aged Nebraskan sample had a confidant – a trend which was broadly similar to that emerging in Powers and Bultena's (1976) rural Iowan sample of individuals over seventy years, with roughly three-fifths of the women in that study, as in Adams' (1985) older Chicago sample, having confidants.

However, Strain and Chappell (1982) found that although more than four-fifths of their stratified random sample of home-care users (the majority over 70 years) in Winnipeg had a confidant, only just over one-third identified a friend as a confidant. In Cantor's (1979) inner-city study, the trends emerging were not very different, in so far as roughly two-fifths of their respondents had an unrelated person to whom they felt very close, that is, someone they saw often, could share confidences and feelings with, someone they could depend on. Thus it is obvious that the existence of a confidant cannot always be equated with the existence of an intimate friendship.

In the 1970s and early 1980s particularly, the existence of intimate confiding has been seen as the defining characteristic of friendship. This perspective has tended to ignore the very different attitudes to confiding amongst age cohorts, and in particular the reluctance of many elderly people who had grown up in the 1920s and 1930s to discuss intimate topics, such as money or sex, with anyone, especially those who are not relatives – regardless of their closeness.

Lopata (1979), Wenger (1984) and Adams (1985) looked in a more comprehensive fashion at the type of help provided by friends. In all of these studies, the majority of these friendships did not help during either sickness or other emergencies, or routinely with shopping or housework, with gifts or loans of money or with advice on money matters. The most common type of practical help given was help with transportation and this, even in Adams' (1985: 68) study, was given by less than half of the friends. Physical distance did, by and large, make it less likely that help would be given. Nevertheless, it was obvious that these low proportions reflected a view of friendship which tended not to be rooted in or expressed by practical help:

Admittedly in the abstract, our cultural image of friendship does contain a strong element emphasising the responsibility that friends have to help each other out as need arises. . . . Most friendships are simply not like that and are not created with the expectation that they should be.

(Allan, 1986: 10)

Allan (1986) and Jerrome (1990) recognize that some friends do provide practical help and caring – but they suggest that they are, in fact, qualitatively different from other friendships. This difference is, they argue, typically recognized by the respondents themselves. They are often described in kinship terms or are referred to as 'real' or 'true' friends: thereby in a sense obscuring the popular categories of kin and friend (a topic that is returned to in Chapter 6).

The importance of friends as a source of identity and self-worth in old age is vital in Western society, where being old tends to be seen in negative and stereotypical terms. Chronological age, declining health and mobility and the social structure itself frequently make it impossible to work and difficult even to hold positions within formal organizations. Hence the task of self-validation falls entirely on the informal sphere of relationships. Theoretically, this property can be seen as a type of nurturance – and one which is considerably more characteristic of 'old' or 'true' friends than the giving of practical help: 'Old friends are valued for their role in preserving one's self-image and confirming one's sense of worth'. (Jerrome, 1981: 191). Wright (1978), O'Connor (1987), Crohan and Antonucci (1989), Shea *et al.* (1988) and Allan (1989) have all drawn attention to the importance of status validation or enhancement as an often neglected but crucial provision of friendship. For Wright (1984) this dimension simply refers to friends' favourable evaluation of one's personal qualities; while Candy *et al.* (1981) refer to the reflected glory derived from associating with high-status friends: both elements being included by O'Connor (1987) in the concept of the identity-enhancing character of friendships.

It is obvious, then, that the question 'Do the old have friends?' is a deceptively simple one. The answer to it presupposes a degree of consensus about the definition of friendship which exists neither amongst researchers nor amongst those interviewed. Variation in the trends emerging in these studies partly reflects these various definitions and partly variation in the nature of the samples used. It is possible to identify the various types of friends implicit in these studies: for example, the purely sociable companion; the long-standing but not interactionally active relationship; the very close intimate and/or identity-enhancing relationship; and the pseudo-kin friendship. In so far as studies have failed to differentiate adequately between these various types, it is perhaps not surprising that very different trends have emerged in these studies.

FACTORS INFLUENCING THE DEVELOPMENT AND MAINTENANCE OF ELDERLY WOMEN'S FRIENDSHIPS

Five main types of factors have been very widely used to explain variation in friendship patterns amongst the elderly: age, health, social class, marital status and geographical accessibility. Typically, the impact of these factors has been examined in a variety of cross-sectional studies drawing on samples of varying sizes and composition. The influence of these factors is frequently confounded, given the nature of these samples. In fact, it has been argued that 'Attempts to analyse friendship in terms of age, say, or class, or gender, or marital status or whatever, are too gross to be very useful' (Allan, 1989: 91). Within these very considerable constraints, an attempt will be made to highlight the main trends emerging from these studies, and so to identify the sorts of themes and issues which need to be tackled in the future.

Traditionally, age itself has been seen as a factor which is inevitably associated with the attenuation of social bonds: this idea lying at the heart of disengagement theory (Cumming and Henry, 1961). This idea came increasingly under pressure in the 1970s, with Weiss and Lowenthal (1975) suggesting that healthy individuals with adequate resources could increase or re-invest in friendship during this period. Bradford Brown (1981), however, was less optimistic about this, arguing that such factors increased friendship only on a temporary basis. Certainly, Ferraro *et al.* (1984) found that age was negatively associated with friendship levels (amongst both the married and the widowed). Similarly Wenger (1984) found that only two-fifths of those over ninety years in her study felt that they had real friends, as compared with twice that proportion in the sample overall.

However, it is obvious from various studies (such as Jerrome, 1981; Matthews, 1986; Shea *et al.*, 1988) that old age is not simply a period of losing friendships. In so far as friendship is a peer relationship, as respondents age there is an increasing likelihood that they will lose friends through death. Nevertheless, friendships may also be acquired in old age. Lopata (1979) herself noted that over two-fifths of her respondents identified new friends (i.e. friends made after their widowhood). Adams (1987) has done one of the very few longitudinal studies of friendship. In her study of a small community sample of non-married Chicago residents, she noted that the women averaged more friends in 1984 than they had in 1981; but on average they saw them less frequently and felt emotionally distant from a higher percentage of them, although they also lived closer to a higher percentage of them (1987: 224). Simplistic notions about social disengagement were further challenged by her finding that 'Status group membership affected the course of friendship network evolution' (1987: 226). Thus, she found that over the three-year period the three types of respondents she identified – the 'marginal', the members of 'high society' and the 'pillars of the community' – simply changed their friendship patterns. For example, the 'marginal' (who were identified as middle- and lower-class respondents, who had lower incomes than the other respondents, and belonged to fewer organizations in 1981) took advantage of the Senior Citizen Centres to expand their social horizons in 1984. Hence, Adams' study raises the possibility that old age may be a period of greater freedom from social constraints, and hence provide an opportunity to try out new patterns of sociability – albeit within the often formidable limits imposed by health, economic resources, etc.

A very similar conclusion was reached by Jerrome (1981) on the basis of her small study of people ranging in age from late fifties to mid-eighties. She found that in this sample of predominantly single, widowed or divorced women, the overwhelming majority had made new friends since retirement. Furthermore, a substantial minority (i.e. more than a quarter) had met the friend(s) whom they regarded as closest after their retirement.

Within the past ten years there has been a move away from a focus on age as the sole determinant of friendship levels amongst the elderly. Health, social-class position, marital status and residential-location patterns are now all seen as important factors in influencing such friendships. According to Fischer (1982b), the crucial factors seem to be the existence of relatively few restrictive commitments, on the one hand, and the availability of various resources, on the other, to enable one to create and maintain friendships.

The importance of health as a resource was outlined by Bradford

Brown: 'The infirmities that often accompany old age create obstacles to maintaining contact with close associates, thus diminishing both the number of friends . . . and the amount of contact with those who remain' (1981: 42). Ferraro *et al.* (1984) noted that, in their study of disadvantaged elderly, amongst married respondents health was the strongest predictor (although amongst the widows its importance was matched by that of education). Its importance was reiterated by Allan and Adams (1989: 57) on the basis of their updating of evidence in the area; while O'Connor (1991c) found that only a minority of the very elderly Social Service Department clients in that study who were, by and large, in very poor health, had close friendships.

Apart from the direct effect of health or mobility on face-to-face contacts with friends, health also has an effect on their participation in clubs and activities, venues which are potential sources of new relationships. However, it is worth noting that participation in such organizations is itself affected by national and class factors, such organizational participation being particularly high in the United States in contrast to Britain (Deem, 1982; Dixey and Talbot, 1982) and being class-related (Allan, 1989; Allan and Adams, 1989).

Because friendship is essentially seen as a relationship rooted in similarity and in a non-instrumental kind of exchange, numerous questions have been raised about the effect of changes in the status or resources of the participants, for example increasing disability, widowhood, changes in financial resources, place of residence etc. Retsinas and Garrity's (1985) and Adams' (1986) work suggested that the crucial factor was the salience of the dissonant characteristic. For example, in the former study in a nursing-home setting similarity in terms of level of handicap and degree of care was far more important in influencing friendship formation than similarity in socio-economic characteristics.

There are considerable difficulties in locating elderly women in a class position on the basis of their occupation. However, education, pension rights, housing conditions and current level of income have all been used as indicators of class position. What evidence there is clearly suggests that, with very few exceptions, those with low socio-economic status are less likely to have friends than those with high socio-economic status.

Thus, for example, Lopata (1979) found that in her relatively large sample of roughly 1,000 Californian widows the most important factors influencing the identification of friends were their own level of education, the total family income when their husband was alive and their total family income now.

> Women with more schooling marry men earning a better income in a
> higher type occupation and together they develop a middle class life style
> that involves non-kin friendships: the differences are rather dramatic. . . .
> Friendless women are most apt to have eighth grade education or less.
>
> (Lopata, 1979: 212)

Other studies (such as Ferraro *et al.*, 1984) also found that the existence
of friendships varied depending on their respondents' income and
education, and that the effect of education was particularly strong also
amongst the widowed in that study.

Allan (1989) has argued that little attention has been paid to the
effects of material well-being on friendship patterns. The availability of
private transport is obviously one indicator of such well-being and is
closely associated with class position. Allan and Adams (1989) drew
attention to the dramatic effect the presence of such transport can have on
face-to-face contact with friends – especially amongst the elderly in urban
areas, because of fear of using public transport after dark. Hence one
might conclude that although friendship is typically described as a
voluntary, egalitarian relationship, it is not equally available to all:
'Friendship, in generic terms, involves systems of exchange that are more
available to some people than to others, depending on their particular
social position' (Allan and Adams, 1989: 47).

The fourth major variable which is traditionally used in explaining
variation in friendship amongst the elderly is marital status. The
evidence in this area is conflicting. Dickens and Perlman (1981)
conclude that 'The bulk of the evidence . . . suggests that married
individuals score higher than widowed seniors on quantitative friendship
measures' (Dickens and Perlman, 1981: 118). Studies such as Lopata's
(1979) found that the average number of friends her respondents had as
widows was roughly half what they had prior to her husband's death
(1.25 versus 2.69): a trend which she suggested could be due to a variety
of factors including the effect of the loss itself, women's dependence on
friendships made at a younger age, on couple-companionate friendships
which were not available to them in widowhood, or the absence of
social roles to provide them with an opportunity to form new friendships. Wenger (1984) also found that, in her study of the elderly in eight
rural communities in North Wales, friends were most important to the
widowed. Similarly, Troll *et al.* (1979) found that widowed females
had a higher level of interaction with friends than the currently married
and the never-married.

Booth (1972), however, showed that widowhood limited involvement with friends – especially married friends. Blau's (1973) study suggested that the crucial factor was the age at which widowhood occurred (and hence the extent to which it was a structurally unusual event). Thus she argued that widowhood was only likely to affect a woman's friendships if it placed her in a deviant position relative to her age and class peers. It was not, she argued, the experience of widowhood *per se*, but its effect on the person's interests and experiences and the availability of others in a similar situation, which was the crucial factor. Ferraro *et al.* (1984) developed this further by suggesting, on the basis of a study of a sample of elderly low-income respondents in their mid-seventies, that a widow's intense involvement with friends appeared at a particular stage (i.e. typically between one and four years after the death of the spouse).

Bankoff's work (1981) on American widows in their fifties who were at either the crisis stage or transition phase in their widowhood provided an early challenge to facile assumptions about the positive effects of confiding relationships. Thus she found that intimacy in friendship relationships had a positive effect at the crisis stage but it had a negative effect at the transition phase (1981: 120). Furthermore, her subsequent analysis showed that, even at the crisis stage, it was not intimacy *per se* which was important, but specifically the intimacy provided by married friends. She speculated that this could indicate the importance of relationships which predated the loss in facilitating the expression of grief and the sharing of that grief. At any rate, she concluded that, at the crisis stage, it was these married friends who were the critical support providers.

A very different picture emerged, however, at the transition phase, where the contribution of these still-married friends was predominantly negative in effect: 'In fact, our findings suggest that the more the transition phase widows confide in their married friends, the worse off they are' (1981: 131). At this stage, their relationships with widowed and single friends become important. Furthermore, the best predictors of their well-being at this stage were these friends' companionship, guidance and emotional support. Bankoff suggests that these types of support are increasingly important as women try to adjust to the status of widow-hood, and that they can best be accepted from people who are in the same situation as themselves. This piece of work – which is extremely insightful – has generated far less interest than it deserves.

Very little indeed is known about the friendship patterns of the elderly never-married. Ward (1979) argued that the possibility of maintaining a satisfactory single life style involving friendships rests very heavily on the availability of financial and health resources – and that this situation becomes increasingly difficult to maintain with age. However, the complexity of the situation is indicated by his comment that 'A few British studies indicate that single older persons are more isolated than those who are married . . . but are not necessarily more lonely' (Ward, 1979: 861). Jerrome (1981) suggested that the ideology of marriage supports a couple's preoccupation with each other. A similar ideology does not exist for single women, who, she suggests 'have to work hard in creating moral justification for their existence and way of life' (1981: 183). For this group, friends thus may be particularly important. Indeed, Wenger (1984) found that, in her study, those who were never married were five times more likely than their counterparts to report that they had 'real' friends nearby. On the other hand, Rubinstein (1987) found that in his study of residents within the community, the never-married women were less likely than the others to have very close friends. Half of them did so, as compared with 80 per cent of the married women and 65 per cent of widowed women. However, Rubinstein (1987), and indeed also Ward (1979) noted that single women were more likely than married women to have higher levels of education, and hence it is possible that education rather than marital status is the crucial variable in influencing their patterns of friendship. At any rate, Strain and Chappell (1982) found that the single, separated and divorced were equally likely to identify friends as confidants, while the still-married were least likely to do so, the widowed being in between (1982: 493).

Adams (1986) noted that segregated housing had a particularly positive effect on the situation of the never-married. They were unlikely to have emotionally close local friends other than in an age-segregated housing context, where the setting rendered differences in marital status irrelevant. She does note, however, that the age-segregated housing from which her sample was drawn did organize communal activities, the people in it had all moved in at the same time and they were all white, middle-class women who had previously been involved in one way or another with service agencies in the local community. It is thus unclear to what extent a similar pattern might exist in another setting.

It is obvious that there is a good deal of ambiguity surrounding the friendships of the elderly never-married, particularly when compared with other marital-status groups. This reflects the paucity of studies done in this area as well as the diversity of measures of friendship and samples used.

The fifth major variable which has been used to explain the level of friendship amongst the elderly is the proportion of old people in the local area. This is closely related to the fact that elderly people typically draw their friends from the local area. Thus Lopata (1979) noted that the local area was the primary source of both old and new friends amongst her widows. Cantor (1979) found that amongst her elderly inner-city respondents, 70 per cent of those identified as friends lived either in the building or within walking distance. To some extent, this reflects the paucity of other venues. Retirement obviously has an effect on their opportunity to make work-related friendships and to maintain those which, in Allan's terms (1989), are 'context-specific'. For those who have not been in paid work, increasing age may bring with it declining mobility and/or increasing responsibility for 'tending' (i.e. looking after a husband, aged parent or disabled sister or brother) – and this may leave them with few resources for servicing non-local friendships (Allan, 1986; Allan and Adams, 1989).

The importance of the proportion of old people locally was initially highlighted by Rostow (1967). On the basis of his study of 1,200 people living in three types of communities in Cleveland, he concluded that the more age-segregated the neighbourhood these old people were living in, the more integrated they were within it. The argument concerning age-segregated as opposed to age-integrated housing (and indeed the concept of sheltered housing itself) is partly related to this. Adams (1986) suggested, on the basis of her study, that

> In summary, age-segregated housing seems to foster the development of emotionally close, local friendships, because its residents have things in common, are aware of the similarities in their situations, are motivated to make new friends and have the opportunity for frequent interaction with potential friends.
>
> (Adams, 1986: 73–4)

Interestingly, Adams (1986) makes no reference to feelings of self-denigration arising from being surrounded by 'a crowd of old women'. The absence of such feelings may reflect the class position of the women and/or the arguably less negative stereotypes of elderly women prevalent in the United States than in Britain. At any rate, these feelings of the unattractiveness of elderly females as friends were very much in evidence in Jerrome's (1981) study of clubs for the elderly: 'A striking feature of these women was their ignorance about other women's lives, and their dislike of women. In their conversation they aired the usual negative stereotypes – women moan and bicker, women can't make up their minds' (Jerrome, 1981: 187). As one might expect then, friendships did not develop within the club setting (those that existed predated it). Hence it seems possible to conclude that accessibility of age peers – even those similar in occupational status and/or with similar interests – is not in itself necessarily conducive to the emergence of friendships. Furthermore, the development of friendships amongst stigmatized groups is itself difficult.

Despite the complexity emerging in these studies, it seems possible to conclude, firstly, that the level of resources (e.g. health, education, financial resources) are important in influencing friendship patterns amongst the elderly; secondly, within these constraints, that old age is by no means inevitably a time of friendship loss; and thirdly, geographical accessibility is important in facilitating the initiation and maintenance of friendship ties, although it is not in itself sufficient, and its influence can be moderated if not obliterated by other factors. Finally, although intuitively one would expect friendship to be most important to the single elderly as opposed to the married, it is obvious that the situation is a good deal more complex than that with different patterns emerging within the single group (between the never-married, the widowed and the separated) and within the various aspects of friendship (e.g. as regards frequency of contact as compared with confiding).

Amidst the complexity of these various trends it is easy to forget the reality of friendship in the lives of the elderly. Hence in the next section a number of vignettes will be presented illustrating various types of friendship and locating them within the context of the lives of these elderly women. These vignettes are drawn from a study of London elderly Social Service Department clients (Sinclair *et al.*, 1988; O'Connor, 1991b). Obviously pseudonyms are used to preserve anonymity.

VIGNETTES

Helen Brown is a 79-year-old non-housebound widow with two sons who are both living in New Zealand. In terms of her deceased husband's usual occupation, Helen is quite clearly middle class (i.e. her husband having been a manager of a very large chain-store where he did the ordering for about 1,000 shops). Her own usual occupation was also within the middle-class range.

Apart from a touch of arthritis, Helen's health is still quite good and she suffers from no major illnesses, impairments or disabling conditions. The day-to-day 'bread and butter' of affection and intimacy in her life is provided by Vera, her 71-year-old card-playing friend of thirty years' standing. Helen describes her as 'a lovely person, a lively, happy, healthy person'. She says of her: 'She's all I've got.' Vera lives just ten minutes away from Helen. Helen says that she would feel 'terribly lost' if she moved: 'My life would be terribly lonely, it would be a blank.' It is important to Helen to know that she is there: 'if I wanted anything I'd only have to give her a ring and she'd help me and if she was in any trouble she'd ring me.' 'She takes my advice same as I take hers.' Helen cannot imagine her not being there: 'I'd be lost.'

She says that Vera is the only person that she would really miss out of her life: 'We are proper pals. We can trust each other. She knows that she can come around any time she likes.' They met – along with two others – at a club thirty-odd years ago: 'four of us palled up – only two left – we've always been good pals.' Their relationship is such that they spend a very considerable amount of time together and yet they are never bored: 'I look forward to her coming.' They are together at the luncheon club on Tuesday and Friday afternoons, at bingo on Tuesday evening, at a local whist drive on Wednesday evening ('we've done that for thirty years'), and in their own homes on Monday, Friday and Saturday afternoon.

The relationship is not, however, simply a sociable one as Helen can and does confide in Vera: 'About the sons, her children, my children.' 'We can tell each other anything. We can trust each other. If I want anything she'll give it, if she wanted something, I'd give it to her.' 'There's nothing that I'd do or be ashamed of that I can't talk to Vera about.' Money, to Helen, is a particularly intimate topic ('the only thing I mind my own business about is money and what I have about money'). Yet this she can and does talk to Vera about: 'She's the only true friend I can tell anything to – any secret that I've got – if she thinks I'm unwise she'll tell me so.' Helen feels that even if they were living further away they would not drift apart: 'we'd still be friends.'

The relationship with Vera is identity enhancing in the sense that Vera sees her as 'the sort I am'. However, it also contributes to Helen's sense of her own self-worth indirectly because Helen sees Vera as someone who has done well in life: 'Her daughter married a professor. Her boy is a welfare officer at the school and out of his own pocket he buys the children shoes.' She says of Vera: 'as a woman to a woman I admire her. She's all the things I would like to have been and I haven't got the guts.'

The only difficulty in the relationship is that Vera is married and her husband is still alive, and so Sundays and holidays are spent with him and at these times Helen is very lonely. This relationship, no doubt reflecting Helen Brown's health and mobility, was quite similar to the very close friendships identified in a study of younger women (O'Connor, 1987). Neither provided the other with ongoing practical help, help with shopping or with 'trouble' with the Social Service Department. It illustrates the type of long-standing very close, sociable, intimate, identity-enhancing, albeit not practically helpful, relationship which added immeasurably to the quality of these women's lives.

Margaret John's friendship with her very close friend Dolly was of much more recent origin but it had many similarities with the previous one. Margaret is an 85-year-old, single, never-married woman who identified Dolly, a 78-year-old single woman who lived five minutes away from her, as 'very close'. Margaret's father had owned his own retailing business and so in these terms Margaret can be regarded as being middle class.

Margaret's sight is poor but apart from this her health is good, and she has no major impairments or disabilities. Their friendship is of only two years' duration and developed from their involvement in the Jehovah Witnesses: 'The word of God says bad associations cause useless habits. All my friends are true Christians and whenever I meet them, we talk on good wholesome matters and we help one another.'

They both enjoy each others' company and were initially drawn together by the fact that they were both single and both deeply involved in the Jehovah Witnesses. They both lost the sibs with whom they were living within the previous year and this brought them closer together: 'We weren't so close until then.' The relationship is still at an early stage, and they do not yet confide intimately in each other. 'She is getting to know me. I think I'm getting to know her better.'

Dolly went to her brothers' recently and stayed the night 'I quite missed her really because I didn't see her for two days.' If she wasn't there, Margaret feels that she 'would sadly miss her'. The importance of the relationship in terms of the feelings of security it provides is illustrated by the fact that 'I think we can both live on our own mostly because we can say "see you tomorrow".' Margaret is unusual in that she articulates her need specifically for a woman friend: 'I must have a woman friend, so I associate with Dolly. If she was to go, I'd get someone else from the congregation. I like a woman friend.'

Even amongst the housebound, the friendships of these elderly Social

Service Department clients typically did not provide routine practical help. It seems plausible to suggest that this reflects the fact that even where very close friendships were local and one of the partners was clearly in need of practical help, the equality implicit in the friendship militated against the provision of such help. Ironically, such appeared to be the taboos in this area that cross-sex friendships were more likely to provide practical help to the housebound than same-sex friendships (O'Connor, 1991b). Julie Barrett's friendship with Maggie, a local neighbour, was an example of the latter relationship. Julie is a 78-year-old widow, completely housebound for ten years. She was assessed as working class: her former husband was a painter and decorator and she herself had worked as a dinner lady.

Julie is prone to falling and unable to get up when she does fall. She is in continuous pain with arthritis, has had a prolapse and suffers intermittent but very severe pain passing water. She has one child alive – a son. Her friend Maggie is a widow in her seventies who lives less than five minutes away. Maggie drops in on her two or three times a week. They have been friends for nearly forty years. Julie describes her as 'the most marvellous friend and a very good person'. It is very important to her to have her there: 'I know if I'm distressed I've only got to get on the phone and she is here.' She says that she would feel lost if Maggie was not there. She does recognize that, 'if anything went wrong, she'd go to Wales to her daughters. I would miss her.' However, she feels that even if Maggie moved, the relationship would not end and that she would keep in touch by phone. She recognizes that it would be a great loss to her, but 'you can't live other people's lives. She's free to do what she wants, same as I'm free to do what I want.'

Julie sees Maggie as the person who is most concerned about her on a day-to-day basis: 'She worries if she does not see me. I know a little while ago she came over here and she didn't get an answer. She went next door and asked if I was right.' Yet despite the felt closeness of the relationship, and Julie's housebound status, Maggie does not provide any help with housekeeping or food preparation. She does help out when necessary with some shopping (although the bulk of this is done by the Social Services). Her visits are largely sociable: 'I can always talk to her.' 'She tells me bits about her family and I tell her about Brian [son] and his wife and she knows them and Dawn [granddaughter].' 'I can talk to her: she knows all what goes on here.' However, as is typical of many of the elderly, Julie goes on to say 'We don't discuss private affairs: I don't know what she gets [i.e. money] and she don't know what I get. We don't discuss private affairs. I don't think that is right – only to family.' Yet she describes her as 'easy to talk to: I can say – what do you think?' 'I can always talk to her.'

It is obvious that despite the felt importance of this relationship, it in fact contributes very little in terms of help with housekeeping, shopping, etc. This was typical of friendships between women amongst these housebound elderly Social Service Department clients.

In all the examples mentioned so far the respondents were fortunate enough to have very close friends living nearby. Harriet Boulton was one of a minority of respondents who did not conform to this pattern. She is a housebound widow whose former husband had been a qualified submarine engineer. Before her retirement from paid employment, Harriet was a manageress in a 'Lady's Outfitters' in the West End. She is now unsteady on her feet and has had several recent episodes of 'her legs giving way', that is, falling and being unable to get up. She has had intermittent attacks of bronchitis and arthritis, very poor eyesight and various other minor health difficulties. She has no children alive. She identified Grace, a 78-year-old widow now living in the south of England, as her very close friend.

Grace and Harriet had worked together in the West End and had known each other for over forty years. Harriet described the relationship as 'like sisters', 'I'm very fond of Grace.' She felt that Grace knew her and understood her: 'She's known me for years. We like each other. We suit each other with our ways.' She admires her, seeing her as a strong, competent person. However, their mutual declining mobility has made face-to-face contact difficult and in fact the last time they saw each other was three years before, when Harriet stayed with Grace for three weeks.

Harriet sees Grace as concerned about her. She had rung twice in the previous week saying: 'I'm terribly worried about you being ill and no-one with you.' Harriet does not feel dependent on Grace: 'I've had to manage without her.' She does derive a very limited feeling of security from the existence of the relationship: 'I like to know that she's around somewhere, that I can write to her.' 'I'd feel her loss a lot: I wouldn't like anything to happen to her.' Yet it is clear that distance has considerably weakened the relationship and limited its possibilities for support. Harriet says that she was 'very disappointed when she moved to Dorset – very cross with her. I didn't want her to go away.' Grace still presses her to go down to stay with her; indeed, she wanted them to share a house: 'she wanted to get a double bungalow – you see how much she loves me – she wanted me to go down.' Harriet decided against this, and their relationship is clearly now a very tangential part of her life. In fact, in an unguarded moment she says of Grace: 'We *were* very attached – we *were* more like sisters.'

These vignettes illustrate the reality of friendship in the lives of a sample of women who are least likely to have such friends, that is frail, elderly Social Service Department clients: a reality which is all too easily underestimated and ignored since such relationships do not typically provide practical help, and so do not potentially reduce the involvement of the statutory caring agencies in providing this minimal support. It is obvious that these relationships are an important part of their lives, although they vary considerably in content and quality. They can be crudely regarded as illustrating 'special', sociable and latent friendships respectively, although it is obvious that these labels capture very little of their character.

Up to now the main focus has been on dyadic relationships. A small amount of work has been done on groups of friends and it is to this that we now turn.

FRIENDSHIP GROUPS: THE CREATION OF A WORLD?

Jerrome (1981, 1990) has been one of the few to explore the ways in which friendships create normative standards and effectively weave a world of meaning and value for their participants. This world is, of course, particularly important for the elderly in view of both their marginal status within society and their closeness to sickness and death. Jerrome argues that 'An analysis of the content of conversation between friends reveals an important social process; the negotiation of norms of sickness behaviour' (1990: 53). On the basis of anthropological research on informal groupings of working-class women and of formal organizations (including nine old people's clubs and a church group), Jerrome (1990) concluded that through their interaction friends 'made sense' of their own and others' symptoms and developed and applied standards of appropriate behaviour in dealing with these. Behaviour which was either too independent or too self-indulgent in sickness was sanctioned: the overall picture of the normative standards emerging in the groups of club attenders being very evocative of Gluckman's (1963) discussion of gossip and its function in social interaction. Morgan (1986) also suggested that interaction between widows enabled them to develop what he called 'shared knowledge structures' by which they could assess the normality of their own grieving trajectory. This kind of approach is unusual, despite the fact that amongst the elderly there are public interaction venues (such as luncheon clubs, day-care centres, etc.), and these are typically regarded as one of the structural preconditions for the emergence of a group life.

Hochschild (1973: 35), although not specifically concerned with friendship groups, did note that the fairly homogeneous Merrill Court community, consisting of largely working-class, white widows in their late sixties, was 'what one might call tight'. Best friends were typically living on the same floor and most neighbours were also friends. Much of the conversation between residents was concerned with the development and maintenance of standards of appropriate behaviour. Within the community there was an 'honour' or prestige system which at least partially immunized these women against the stigma attached to being old and female. Through their conversations they also tried to deal cognitively and emotionally with the unpredictable arrival of death. They reflected and reinforced each others' views of the world but depended little on each other in more practical ways: 'the widows of Merrill Court took care of themselves, fixed their own meals, paid their own rent, shopped for their own food, and made their own beds; and they did these things for others. Their sisterhood rests on adult autonomy' (Hochschild, 1973: 69). Jerrome, in her study of the Tremendous Ten (1984) – a group of middle-class elderly women – looked specifically at friendship and illustrated the ways in which it enhanced their lives: that is, providing affection and intimacy, companionship, practical and emotional support in times of stress, stimulation, achievement and self-esteem. Jerrome, however, also drew attention to the structural implications of such friendships, arguing that both through the selection of friends and through the activities of the group itself, 'status differences are expressed and reinforced' (1984: 712). These women, she argued, are, through these friendships, involved in what Papanek (1979) called 'the politics of status maintenance', an informal – and neglected – dimension of social class.

Jerrome's description of this group is unusual and important in so far as, although she notes that there are several important and long-standing dyadic and triadic relationships between group members, her main concern is not with the level of intimacy in these relationships. Rather, she highlights the norms operating within the group, adherence to which creates and reinforces social solidarity (e.g. norms about the appropriate scale of entertaininng, material values, dress, conversational content, etc.).

> However, it should not be thought that the women's friendships compete with their commitments to husbands and families. The exclusiveness and solidarity of the group is in no sense threatening. On the contrary it promotes existing gender roles by providing moral support and advice for their performance. Conventional values are confirmed and a conservative ideology of marriage is upheld.
>
> (Jerrome, 1984: 710)

Jerrome's work is provocative in illustrating the kinds of relationships that can emerge between middle-class, geographically proximate elderly women who, although endorsing gender roles, do not see themselves as inferior to men or dependent on them. Rather, they use their considerable social skills to create a world which provides them with a variety of experiences, including fun and social integration, which supports, complements and, if necessary, compensates for the absence of these experiences in other arenas, while implicitly highlighting the importance of class factors. Unfortunately, however, it is an all too rare piece of work.

THE EFFECTS OF FRIENDSHIP ON PSYCHOLOGICAL WELL-BEING

For the most part, psychological well-being has been equated with the absence of psychiatric disorder, with morale, happiness and/or excitement. As previously mentioned, the whole area of the association between social relationships and these phenomena is a methodological minefield. Nevertheless, Dickens and Perlman's (1981), Crohan and Antonucci's (1989) and Rook's (1989) reviews of the literature reach broadly similar conclusions: 'Fairly consistent evidence has indicated, for example, that contact with friends enhances older adults' morale to a greater extent than does contact with adult children and other family members' (Rook, 1989: 188). Crohan and Antonucci's conclusion is perhaps more specific: 'Thus, friends appear to be most significant to older adults as a source of enjoyment, and as such, tend to have their greatest impact on the older adults' sense of immediate well-being' (Crohan and Antonucci, 1989: 134). There are occasional dissonant notes: for example Crohan and

Antonucci (1989) refer to Essex and Nam's (1987) finding that the relationships that are most important vary according to the respondents' social status; while Strain and Chappell (1982) note that although an association exists in their study, it explains only 2 per cent of the variance.

Furthermore, various studies have identified considerable complexities within this overall pattern. Thus, for example, Adams (1986) found that the existence of friends who were not very close and who were not living in the local area was associated with lower levels of positive affect (although it did not affect the level of negative affect). Ward (1979) found that the importance of friendships in contributing to an overall level of happiness amongst the aged varied depending on their marital status: contact with friends being a better predictor for the never-married than the married, widowed or divorced.

Bankoff's (1981) study of widows (outlined in the previous section) seriously challenged the assumption that the existence of a confidant was unambiguously related to psychological well-being in widowhood. Nevertheless, there is a very considerable body of literature which both preceded and succeeded that study, which simply looked at the association between confiding in a friend and various measures of morale (e.g. Lowenthal and Haven, 1968; Parkes, 1972; Arling, 1976; Strain and Chappell, 1982). In fact, in 1989 Crohan and Antonucci, on the basis of a review of the literature on old age, concluded that 'The presence of a confidant in one's support network is related to good mental health and high morale, and appears to act as a buffer to loosen anxiety and tension when stressful life events occur' (1989: 138). Allan (1989), on the basis of a review of sociological research on friendship in old age, concluded:

> What appears to matter is not so much having one or two friends with whom one's innermost thoughts can be readily shared, but rather being involved in different social activities that provide opportunities to socialize with others on a more or less regular basis and develop a range of less intimate friendships.
>
> (1989: 94)

Involvement in such sociable activities, as indeed also the existence of long-standing, albeit no longer interactionally active friendships, can play an important part in validating social competence and personal identity. Both can, however, be less than protective in particular situations. Thus, for example, a decline in mobility may lead to the disruption of sociable relationships. On the other hand, although 'special' individual friends may contribute to psychological well-being at any one point in time, the loss of such relationships may jeopardize it; and the latter possibility may account for the fact that those who saw friends as substitutable were more likely than those who did not do so to have a positive sense of well-being (Adams, 1986).

At any rate, the apparent inconsistency between Allan's (1989) and Crohan and Antonucci's (1989) conclusions as regards the relative importance of confiding and identity validation may simply reflect the different life situations of these elderly women. This interpretation is certainly plausible in view of both Wenger's (1984) and La Gaipa's conclusion that, after seventy-five years of age: 'Genuineness and authenticity become increasingly important whereas self disclosure becomes less important. These changes mirror changes in physical health and increased dependency' (La Gaipa, 1990: 134). Rook (1984) suggested that ties with others made an important contribution to well-being only when they involved what she called 'positive affect and sociability', and not when they simply provided support. Hence she argued for the importance of looking at the specific qualities and supportive content of ties. However, her study also suggested that negative social interactions had more powerful effects on respondents' emotional well-being than positive ones. She noted that, until relatively recently, little or no attention was paid to such negative phenomena even amongst the elderly. This is surprising since research in this area has been particularly sensitive to the complex reality of friendship relationships. Matthews' (1986) small qualitative study did suggest that friendships amongst the elderly were rarely terminated through conflict, but simply 'faded away' – to be revived if and when circumstances permitted it.

Rook (1984, 1989) suggested that conflict in the friendships of older adults arose from a number of sources – some of them being characteristic of any friendship (e.g. the others' negative reaction to intimate confiding; failure to perceive or honour obligations in the relationship; failure to see what is expected of them; invasion of privacy; lack of social skills; and/or low self-esteem). In addition, she suggested that strain and conflict could also arise if older adults, whose kin were unable or unwilling to provide them with material or practical help, turned to friends for this. Hence, quite clearly, her work suggests that amongst the elderly, friendships are by no means always unproblematic. However, Antonucci (1985) suggested that, compared with younger age groups, the elderly by and large reported higher levels of friendship satisfaction, were less likely to wish they had more friends and reported fewer negative feelings about them.

Furthermore, Roberto (1989) noted that older people were not dissatisfied when they were in friendships which were, in Roberto's terms 'underbenefited' (1989: 162). One might speculate that this reflected the fact that in this situation they felt themselves to be in a position of relational power, in so far as the other person was more dependent on the relationship than they were (O'Connor, 1991c). Roberto also noted that although 'overbenefited' elderly adults saw their relationships as less than satisfying, they still did not terminate them – arguably because they needed, for example, the practical help provided by the relationship and knew that they could not reciprocate. The implications of issues such as these for the level of conflict in these relationships and/or for the elderly person's psychiatric health have barely begun to be discussed in the area of friendship.

In fact, most of the work which has looked at the effect of friendship on psychological well-being has been rather static and has simply looked at the correlations between various relational provisions and psychological well-being – either in a general context or in crisis situations. It has typically not been concerned with the cultural and social position of dependency that the elderly usually find themselves in – although this will arguably have obvious implications as regards both their relationships and their psychiatric health.

ISSUES ARISING FROM THIS WORK

In this chapter attention has focused on the elderly – typically, in Western society, a group deprived of institutional support and frequently stigmatized. For them, friendship offers a potentially important source of validation and integration, largely unimpeded in its development by competing claims and obligations.

The three most popular foci of work on friendships amongst the elderly have been the following: the effects of such friendship on their morale, well-being, happiness, etc.; the provisions of such relationships; and the factors (such as age, class, health, marital status, residential location) associated with the existence of such relationships.

In a sense, this work has remained implicitly in a functionalist tradition and one which accepts the broad parameters of the social structure. Thus very little analytical attention has been paid to the fact that the social and cultural position of the elderly – especially the poor elderly – makes it difficult for them to have the resources necessary to create and/or sustain friendships. Similarly, the consequences of friendship for the societal structure have been little explored; nor, indeed, has any attempt been made to understand reactions to it (in the shape of the 'Gray Panthers' in the United States).

Ageism and sexism pose problems as regards the development and maintenance of positive relationships between women. Ironically, however, amongst the elderly alone does there appear to be a willingness to create the situational conditions (e.g. residential centres and retirement communities) which provide opportunities for interaction and potential locations for individual support, group cohesion and political awareness.

With the exception of Jerrome's (1981, 1984) work, very little attention has been paid to the processes operating in friendships. Thus, in 1988, Shea *et al.* noted: 'Researchers have ignored, however, the processes by which such relationships develop, the dynamics of the ongoing interactions upon which they are built and the depth of the caring involved' (1988: 84). Similarly, the issues of conflict and of termination of these friendships other than through death has been little explored. The ambiguities in the definitions of friend emerge again as an issue in this area, and obscure attempts to explore variation in types of friendships across the various age, class and marital-status groupings. However, on the basis of work done in this area, it does seem possible to identify various types, including the purely sociable companion, the long-standing but not interactionally active relationship, the very close intimate and/or identity-enhancing relationship and the kin-like friendship characterized by practical helpfulness and reliability.

In view of the non-institutionalized character of the lives of the elderly, it is not, perhaps, surprising that amongst them an attempt has been made to look at the processes operating within friendship cliques and to explore the ways in which norms and roles are created in such groups. Unfortunately, the insights derived from this activity have not been linked with the very clear tendency for respondents with higher education, income, social-class position, etc. to be more likely to have friends. Equally, no study has attempted to look at the extent to which membership of a friendship clique can, in and of itself, offset the stigma attached to being an elderly person in Western society.

Inevitably, because of life-expectancy patterns, the majority of elderly women are not currently married. Hence possible conflicts of loyalties between friendships and the marital relationship are unlikely for these respondents. However, it is easy to see how such conflicts could be generated in a situation of declining health on the part of both the spouse and the friend. The strategies used in dealing with this situation might well provide a useful insight into the limits and possibilities of friendship relationships. Furthermore, additional work might explore the extent to which, under various conditions, friendship cliques continue effectively to validate and support familial structures – both directly and indirectly.

The area of friendships amongst the elderly is a unique arena for the examination of these relationships, since they are, for many respondents, one of the most salient aspects of their lives. They are not in conflict with an institutional order, and indeed, the institutionalization of friendships in old age could well be an important step in dealing with the socially and culturally isolated position of the elderly. However, there is also considerable need to continue to examine both the small-group processes and the class ramifications of their friendships.

— 6 —

Is there something special about the friendship tie?

INTRODUCTION

There are considerable difficulties in defining the nature of the friendship tie. The classic position, initially outlined by Litwak and Szelenyi (1969) and subsequently restated by Litwak (1985), was that primary groups had become functionally differentiated – with kin, neighbours and friends each serving very different functions: that is, kin meeting needs requiring long-term commitment; neighbours performing tasks requiring geographical accessibility; and friends providing a peer group with whom one could enjoy oneself, and which could facilitate socialization, etc.: 'we typically have a good time with friends but turn to relatives in a crisis' (Fischer, 1982b: 132). In fact, however, the situation is a good deal more complex than this, and La Gaipa's conclusion that 'There is no consensus as yet amongst social scientists regarding the relationship between kinship and friendship' (La Gaipa, 1981: 84) needs little modification ten years later. The difficulties in defining friendship become more acute to the extent to which one highlights, as McCall (1988) has done, the institutionalized aspects of friendship or juxtaposes these with increasingly less institutionalized kinship ties. The question then arises of the extent to which kin and friendship ties now have discrete properties (indeed, La Gaipa, 1981, raises the question of whether they ever existed).

The situation is further complicated by the recognition that the meaning of friendship varies in different social classes (Allan, 1979, 1989). Allan's discussion highlights the suggestion that relationships

145

within specific contexts (such as work or recreational areas) lack the generalizability which is implicit in Western middle-class notions of friendship. Nevertheless, they can, in working-class terms, be thought of as a kind of 'buddy', 'mate' or 'pal' (and hence as one kind of friendship relationship).

At the opposite end of the continuum, it is necessary to raise the question of the limits of the definition of lesbianism. The essence of Rich's (1980) argument is that fundamental attachments exist between women and that these are diluted by the institution of heterosexuality. In this context, friendship relationships between women are, at the very least, part of the lesbian continuum – and need to be understood within a similar context to that used to examine lesbianism itself. Rich (1980) herself expanded the concept of lesbianism to include 'Not simply the fact that a woman had or consciously desired genital sexual experience with another woman . . . [but also] many more forms of primary intensity between and among women' (1980: 648). Indeed, in her eyes, lesbianism represented the essence of friendship between women.

In this chapter, the main focus will be on exploring the nature, content and quality of close-kin, work-based and lesbian relationships – within the context of elucidating the nature and meaning of friendship, and the significance of friendship at both the individual and structural level.

FRIENDSHIP: IS IT AN ASPECT OF SOCIAL STRUCTURE OR SIMPLY AN INTERPERSONAL RELATIONSHIP?

This argument implicitly lies at the heart of much of the discussion of the similarities and differences between close kin and friendship relationships. McCall (1988) argues that friendship is one type of social organization and, as such, has a social reality over and above the individuals in it. In this context, he identifies what he calls four 'organizational' features of friendship: the existence of an objectified social form; of a sense of collectivity; some form of role differentiation; and the existence of a shared culture. In the context of a discussion of kin and friendship relationships, the first of these features is particularly important (and this will be explored in detail). However, in the context of a more general discussion of friendship as a type of social organization, it is important to note that evidence in support of the other dimensions was presented in the earlier chapters. Thus, for example, a sense of collectivity was vividly demonstrated by the group of elderly women Jerrome (1984) referred to as the 'Tremendous Ten' (in Chapter 5). Thus they saw themselves as a group, identified with each other and had a sense of collective *esprit de corps*: all of these being seen by McCall as indicators of a sense of collectivity. Indeed, the description of this group also illustrated what McCall refers to as role differentiation, that is, different roles being played by the women within the group context (e.g. the group jester, the deviant, the zany character).

There are a number of elements in what McCall (1988) refers to as the creation of a shared culture. Thus, he draws attention to the ways in which interaction within friendships creates socio-cultural worlds through the process of interaction (especially through talk). Through this process normative expectations are clarified, priorities affirmed, relationship cultures develop, supported by relational symbols, rituals and ceremonies. Oliker's (1989) and Gullestad's (1984) work in Chapter 3, and Griffin's (1985) in Chapter 4, dealt with the ways in which friendships create and maintain views about the world. In Chapter 4 it was also noted that work on relational symbols, rituals and ceremonies was less developed, although Baxter's (1987) work on heterosexual dyads showed the possible future direction of such work.

These various features are ones which are often overlooked when attention is focused on friendship as an interpersonal relationship characterized by 'voluntary interdependence' (Hays, 1988). However, it is the existence of friendship as an 'objectified social form', an 'institutionalized mode of social organization' (1988: 469) which brings into sharp relief the similarities between friendship and relationships between close kin (such as sisters) and which is the main focus in this section.

McCall argues that in any society there are images of friendship and accepted ways of behaving towards friends, although these may well only be evoked when the relationship is under pressure from inside or outside. Indeed, Suttles (1970) had earlier suggested that

> When persons say they are friends, usually they can point to cultural images, rules of conduct, and customary modes of behaviour to confirm their claims. This is likely to be most apparent when one or both parties find their relationship questioned by outsiders. At these times there will be an appeal to standards, rules or 'facts' by which persons can validate whether or not they are indeed friends.
>
> (Suttles, 1970: 98)

As outlined in Chapter 1, the work of feminist historians (such as Smith-

Rosenberg, 1975; Faderman, 1981) made an important contribution in providing images of women's friendships. Despite such insights, up to very recently sociologists and anthropologists have not been interested in exploring these topics although the desirability of doing so was implicit in Hess' (1972) notion that fusion could exist between kin and friendship systems, and in Brain's (1977) recognition that, in non-industrialized societies, friendship could be a formal bond between two persons occupying specific niches in the social structure whose duties to each other involved reciprocal love supported by legal and supernatural sanctions. The latter relationship arguably came very close to what we define as a kinship relationship and so, potentially at least, opened up the issue of the similarities and differences in kin and friendship relationships as cultural forms. Indeed, Stack (1974) very clearly suggested that non-kin relationships could become institutionalized as 'fictive kin' relationships amongst the very poor, provided that friends were reliable partners in the exchange of material aid and the care of children.

There has been an increasing recognition that in any deep friendship short-term reciprocity is not the norm:

> The 'giving' of instrumental aid should be spontaneous but failure to reciprocate will eventually lead to the disruption of the relationship: short-term 'balancing of accounts' is discouraged because of economic overtones, but long term imbalance generally leads to the termination of the relationship.
>
> (La Gaipa, 1981: 80)

Friendship, Hirsch (1979) suggested, involves some degree of altruism. Inevitably, then, it implicitly incorporates the elements of non-reciprocal caring, thereby provoking the conclusion that the 'the separateness of altruism and reciprocity in principle begins to collapse in practice' (quoted in Bulmer, 1987: 165). This has obvious implications as regards facile distinctions between kinship and friendship relationships.

Argyle and Henderson (1985a) argued that friendship is 'rule-governed' and that there is general consensus on the rules appropriate to that relationship. They distinguished between various types of rules, including 'maintenance rules' (e.g. regulating relationships with third parties) and 'intimacy-reward rules', and noted that 'High quality friendships applied more of the intimacy-reward rules, such as discussing intimate topics, confiding and emotional support, than did low quality friendships. However most maintenance rules were similarly applied' (Argyle and

Henderson, 1985a: 78). They noted that amongst their respondents there was agreement that breaches of confidence, non-reciprocated affection or self-disclosure, invasion of privacy or critical or competitive remarks might all constitute reasons for withdrawing from or ending friendships.

There was some cultural variation in the rules endorsed within the samples studied by Argyle and Henderson (e.g. those dealing with ritual exchange and expressing affection); nevertheless, the general tenor of their work is that there is what sociologists would call a normative component to friendship relationships: 'Behaviour that most people, such as most members of a group, neighbourhood or sub-culture, think or believe should be performed or should not be performed' (Argyle and Henderson, 1985a: 63). The same theme, albeit in a much more qualitative form, emerges from Gouldner and Symons Strong's work (1987). They draw attention to the ambiguity of friendship as a cultural form, since friends in their study (unlike lovers) are loath either to tell each other of their love or to enquire about the other person's love for them. However, it is very clear from their work that there are rules as regards appropriate behaviour: 'The women expected their friends to "behave properly" when, for example they were called on for sympathy or help in an emergency' (Gouldner and Symons Strong, 1987: 143). Friendship, they argue, is a kind of contract for talking and listening, remembering and planning, and as such is taken seriously by good friends. Amongst their respondents there was what they called 'a norm of graciousness' in the conduct of the friendships, so that if a friendship was being terminated, this was done gradually so as to give the other person time to adjust to the breaking-off of the relationship. Typically, the issue of breaking off a friendship arose when one of the friends felt that she had been neglected, her confidence betrayed and/or that the other had been overintrusive. Similar themes emerge in Wiseman's (1986, 1990) work. She argues explicitly that the process of friendship dissolution is activated by the violation of unwritten contracts of friendship:

> The unwritten contracts of friendship are focused on expectations of aid and/or solicitous behaviour growing out of assumed bonds of investment, commitment and reward dependability which fulfil a friend's need. These assumptions of a quasi-contractual arrangement seem to exist despite the fact that there may have been no actual meeting of the minds as to the content of these responsibilities (and thus no real contract).
>
> (1986: 203–4)

A perceived unwillingness to help, or even an attempt to reduce the time and effort committed to the relationship, could be understood as a breach of the friendship contract; as could a change in basic values or ways of life, a betrayal of trust, failure to forgive or understand or simply 'using' a friend.

In Davis and Todd's (1985) work, violations of friendship (such as repeating confidential things or lack of trust) were recorded in roughly one-third of the close or best friendships; such violations being defined as 'Any behaviour which a respondent saw as indicating a failure to live up to his or her idea of what a friend should do' (Davis and Todd, 1985: 33). In these situations, as indeed between Wiseman's (1986, 1990) and Gouldner and Symons Strong's (1987) respondents, full reconciliation was difficult. Up to the point, however, when the friendship was broken off, there was an expectation that tension would be dealt with largely by ignoring the issue or joking. Indeed, the latter note that, at least in their study, 'Between most friends, there was a kind of conspiracy of good cheer' (Gouldner and Symons Strong, 1987: 145).

Such work clearly suggests that, in McCall's terms, the behaviour of friends is governed by 'rules of conduct and customary modes of behaviour' (1988: 469). It thus implicitly raises the question of the extent to which such relationships can usefully be seen as simply 'purely voluntary' interpersonal relationships. McCall's work is relatively unusual in so far as it transcends the purely interpersonal and attempts to locate friendship – even dyadic friendship – within a structural context. He sees his work as falling clearly within a Simmelian tradition: 'The cornerstone of the sociology of the dyad is the realization that *a dyadic relationship is a species of social organization* . . . the basic Simmelian point [is] that *a relationship is a social unit over and above the two individuals*' (McCall, 1988: 468). Interestingly, however, although he links his work to other dyadic work (on courtship, marriage and divorce), he makes no reference to close kin relationships (such as mother–daughter or sister–sister relationships). This may well reflect the fact that, up to relatively recently, the main concern continued to be with a functional analysis of the kinship system rather than a structural examination of any of its dyadic components (see Goetting, 1986; O'Connor, 1990). However, McCall's framework for the analysis of friendship clearly highlights potential similarities between kin and friendship relationships. We now turn to a more detailed examination of the similarities and differences in the content of these ties.

KINSHIP AND FRIENDSHIP: DIFFERENT
SOCIO-CULTURAL REALITIES?

There are two central issues here: firstly, the extent to which kin and friendship relationships can be differentiated simply on the basis of their obligatory/voluntary character; and secondly, the extent to which they are sufficiently similar in terms of content to be in some sense substitutable for each other. Finch's work (Finch, 1989; Finch and Mason, 1990) has made a very important contribution to the attempt to understand the quality of kin relationships. Prior to this it had been widely argued that relationships with relatives were universally dictated by obligation, mutual need and affection (see e.g. Litwak and Szelenyi, 1969). Firth *et al.* (1969), in fact, were among the first to document the increasingly voluntary nature of such relationships and to draw attention to the element of choice existing even in relationships within the family of origin. This point was made again by Hoyt and Babchuk (1983) and recently reiterated:

> Relationships with relatives may be more voluntary now and people may choose to be socially close to some relatives while ignoring others. Mutual interests, common statuses and similar values (the same bases for selecting friends) may now influence voluntary choice of socially close relatives.
>
> (Palisi and Ransford, 1987: 258)

Finch's work (1989) tackles these issues directly. She reviews the evidence as regards the extent to which kin relationships are/are not 'special'. Thus she identifies and largely rejects a series of theoretical positions which advert to material conditions and self-interest as the basis for all relationships including kin ones. She deals in much the same way with a series of explanations rooted in nature and biology, in what she calls 'the economics of family altruism' and in the idea that relationships within the family are 'special' because they have developed over time. Finally, she puts forward more sociological explanations. These see the 'distinctive character of kinship in the social organization of particular societies, rather than as something which is inherent in human nature' (1989: 229): in particular, looking for the roots of kinship in Parsons' (1964) concept of the particularistic (as opposed to universalistic) nature of relationships and Fortes' (1970) notion of prescriptive altruism. Drawing particularly on the latter two theorists, she argues that in British society, kinship has a 'distinctive moral character which divides the social world into people to whom we have obligations and the rest, and gives each of us a social place' (1989: 232).

Finch (1989) and Finch and Mason (1990) go on to note that the ways in which kin are to be treated 'differently' is ill defined; who is to be included as kin is ambiguous; and although general obligations towards kin are recognized, there is considerable room for negotiation as regards a particular individual's behaviour towards a kin member in a specific situation, within the context of what Finch calls 'public morality'. Furthermore, although she argues that the distinctive feature of kin relationships is one of morality,

> this can only be understood with reference to the sense which it enables people to make of their own position in the social world, rather than as a fixed set of prescriptive rules which people follow. . . . When it stops giving meaning and shape to the social world, the power of the moral imperative is reduced considerably, as it is when it conflicts with material self interest.
>
> (Finch, 1989: 236)

The attractiveness of Finch's examination of kin relationships is that it actually locates these relationships within a structural context (drawing on law, social policy, economics and demography), while at the same time seeing the individual very much as an active participant in the modification and construction of that world within their own social setting. She concludes that 'A distinctive morality does mark the boundaries between kin and other relationships, but it is a morality rooted in real ties between one person and another and the social meaning which these give to individuals' lives' (Finch, 1989: 236). This raises the question of the extent to which such a morality could (as indeed implied by Fortes', 1970, concept of the 'axiom of amity') exist in a friendship relationship. Finch's (1989) own work clearly demonstrates the conditional, negotiated and often ill-defined nature of kinship ties. It implicitly raises the possibility that the reality of friendship, like the reality of kinship, is a negotiated one, occurring within broadly agreed expectations for that particular type of relationship. These expectations might deal with issues related to commitment, intimacy, reciprocity or simply the locus of interaction. Specific decisions by friends as to the amount of time they spend together, the level of confidences they exchange or the amount they spend on a night out or on a gift might then be negotiated within these parameters. Work of this type has not actually been done on friendship. Nevertheless, it does seem plausible to suggest that the actual process could be very similar to the negotiations within the Mansfield kin network described so vividly by Finch and Mason (1990).

Hence it seems plausible to argue that there are certain similarities between kin and friendship relationships which can be obscured by overfacile generalizations about the obligatory nature of kin relationships as opposed to the voluntary nature of friendship relationships.

When one juxtaposes the actual content of kin and friendship relationships, similar sorts of issues emerge. Thus, as previously mentioned, intimacy has been widely noted as a characteristic of friendship – especially close friendship (Hays, 1988) – and this concept has frequently been simply operationalized in terms of confiding behaviour. It is increasingly recognized that intimate relationships are only one type of friendship. Sociability rather than intimacy is the key element in many friendships (see Fischer, 1982b; O'Connor, 1987; Hays, 1988). Furthermore, as will be shown later in this chapter, there is an increasing body of work showing that close sister–sister relationships are likely to be characterized by high levels of intimacy, primary quality and highly positive interaction (Allan, 1979; Aughingen, 1990; O'Connor, 1990).

Just as intimacy has been widely assumed to be the defining characteristic of friendship, so willingness to care has been seen as the defining characteristic of kin relationships. This equation has been facilitated by the tendency, prior to the 1980s, to obscure the difference between emotional caring and practical tending. This type of juxtaposition of kin and friendship relationships is being challenged at very many levels. Thus, there is widespread evidence to suggest that the obligation to care indefinitely for immediate kin – even a parent or a child – is being modified in Western society. Indeed, two-fifths of Finch and Mason's (1990: 154) own British sample agreed with the bold statement that 'Children have no obligation to look after their parents when they are old'; while the majority said that they would prefer care not to be given by the family in a variety of specific situations which were presented to them involving elderly parents.

On purely theoretical grounds it seems arguable that obligations to care for kin will be modified if what Noddings (1984) calls 'the ethical roots of care' lie in the way in which the infant is cared for by its mother; and if this changes with increases in women's participation in the labour force and fathers do not replace women as primary care givers of young children. Noddings argues that the early tending relationship provides a model for all others and is the source of purely 'altruistic' and 'other-regarding' behaviour. The continuance of such feelings of obligation etc., then, arguably rests on the continued provision of these sorts of experiences by a parent or some kin member. This, even today, cannot be taken for granted. (For example, in Denmark, 84 per cent of women with children under three years old are in paid employment; and half of the children under two years are cared for in state-provided nurseries and crèches; Jorgensen, 1991.)

At the other end of the life span, women, mostly daughters, are still typically the main care givers in Western society, although there is an increasing recognition of this as an aspect of the state's exploitation of women: 'In a very real sense the social basis of community care rests upon the backs of women, particularly kin, who perform the labour of care' (Bulmer, 1987: 25). It is arguable that such a pattern cannot be maintained in the face of both an increasing fluidity in family ties (consequent on high levels of marital breakdown and residential mobility) and women's rising expectations as regards their right to autonomy and self-determination. These various social and cultural changes are raising questions about the obligatory nature, and caring content, of kin relationships.

It is true that most studies, to date, have shown that friends play a very small part in the provision of practical help for the elderly – partly because of the respondents' attitudinal constraints as regards asking for that help, partly because of their own age and infirmities and partly because, in most types of friendship relationship, a lack of reciprocity is seen as incompatible with friendship (Wenger, 1984; Sinclair *et al.*, 1988).

Allan (1989) did identify what he called 'true' friends, and noted that such relationships sometimes provided long-term practical help without any regard to issues of reciprocity: 'their enduring commitment often being symbolized in kinship terms – "she's like a sister to me. I can always turn to her" ' (Allan, 1989: 113). He suggested that such relationships were relatively unusual, and that they typically were either with people who had been known for a long time or with people who had provided high levels of support in times of crisis. Matthews (1986) noted that, in her study, age-discrepant friendships tended to be portrayed in kinship terms – such relationships obviously possessing greater possibilities in terms of practical help, purely in terms of the relative youthfulness of that friend. Wellman (1990) also drew attention to the existence of such relationships in his study, and suggested that it was those who did not have active kinship ties who tended to develop these fictive kin ones. Indeed, a variation of the latter theme was also put forward by Jerrome (1990) to explain the existence of such relationships within her own study of elderly friendships. Thus she noted that often a friendship developed after the death of a friend: 'These new, often quasi kinship relationships based on inheritance, are established on apparently non-reciprocal terms' (Jerrome, 1990: 61). As previously mentioned, a much more ephemeral, albeit broadly similar, type of quasi-kin relationship was observed by Stack (1974) amongst the poor black American women she studied. They were subsisting largely on Social Welfare benefits in a series of unstable cohabiting relationships with unemployed men. In this situation, these latter relationships were not their main source of economic security. In fact, the existence of a male endangered their receipt of Social Welfare. Their most stable and important social ties were with their own close ascriptive kin and/or with fictive kin – the latter being simply identified as kin on the basis of their reliability as partners in the exchange of material goods, child care, etc.

Work such as this highlights the oversimplified nature of the distinction we typically make between kin and non-kin ties. This distinction is likely to come under further pressure in the face of the high levels of marital breakdown in the United States and Britain (i.e. is your ex-husband's mother kin to your children?) Such terminological issues apart, there is also an increasing recognition of the need to locate both ties in a wider structural and cultural context. Indeed, Rapp (1982) has made an interesting start to this by suggesting that working-class families use fictive kin to mobilize resources, while middle-class families 'convert' kin into friends to protect themselves from such economic pooling.

Mother–daughter relationships are, however, typically presumed to have a peculiarly close quality. It is to a more detailed examination of these ties that we now turn.

KIN TIES: IS A MOTHER A WOMAN'S BEST FRIEND? OR IS IT HER SISTER?

Sociological studies have traditionally emphasized the importance of the adult mother–daughter relationship (Young and Willmott, 1962; Rosser and Harris, 1965; Komarovsky, 1967; Adams, 1968). In these studies it has been portrayed as extremely caring – characterized by high frequency of contact, high levels of practical help and a generally high level of involvement in each others' lives. Indeed, O'Connor (1990) argued that there was a tendency amongst social scientists to see the mother–daughter relationship as the epitome of closeness, a view which, she argued, reflected both the equation of female tending in a relationship with emotional closeness and an idealization of the mother–child relationship.

Writers in a feminist tradition – both theoretical and popular (e.g. Chodorow, 1978; Friday, 1979; Eichenbaum and Orbach, 1984) – have made much of the importance of this relationship, highlighting its intensity, fusion and ambivalence. It has come to typify not only the closest kin tie but to be seen as a prototype of all close female–female friendships. Rossi has suggested that the

> pivotal role women have played in extended kinship ties and the special quality of a woman's culture that characterises the informal networks of female kin or friends whom women so easily transform into quasi-kin, are extrapolations of the unique bond between mother and daughter.
>
> (1980: 29–30)

However, on closer reading, it is apparent that Komarovsky (1967) and Young and Willmott (1962) recognized a lack of openness or intimacy in the mother–daughter relationships amongst their working-class respondents; while Firth *et al.* (1969), Allan (1979) and Walker and Thompson (1983) highlighted the lack of real depth or openness in relationships between mothers and daughters amongst their middle-class samples. Finch (1989) noted that although, theoretically, it was obvious that there was a distinction between the normative component of mother–daughter relationships and their actual content and emotional warmth, in practice, the distinctions between these elements had frequently been obscured.

It seems possible to suggest that the idea that 'your mum is your best friend' (Gavron, 1966) is most likely to be prevalent in situations where reliable practical help is essential for survival and where there are few equally reliable non-kin exchange partners. Certainly, in Allan's study (1979) it was the working-class women who saw their mother as a friend, who were willing to confide in her and accepted her high level of involvement in their lives as entirely desirable and appropriate. However, O'Connor (1990) found that, in her study of lower-middle-class married women, less than one-third of those who had a mother alive identified her as very close. The overwhelming majority of these saw her at least every two to three weeks, and more than half of them saw her more often than weekly. Interaction with her was, however, typically not highly positive: it was simply that popping round to see her was very much a routine event which indicated concern and fulfilled obligations. Thus, for half even of those who were very close to their mother, interaction 'was, to be honest, a little bit boring' (1990: 302). Her study also found (as indeed did Firth *et al.*'s, 1969; Brannen and Collard's, 1982; Cornwell's, 1984; and Willmott's, 1987) that mother–daughter relationships, even where they were identified as very close, were very unlikely to be characterized by a high level of intimate confiding – a finding that sits uneasily with the idealization of the mother–daughter relationship as epitomizing closeness. Hence she argues that, in its lack of intimacy, the routine obligatory nature of interaction, its strong component of concern rather than consensus and the focus on long-term rather than short-term reciprocity, the mother–daughter relationship is very different from a friendship relationship.

However, sister–sister relationships appear rather less dissimilar from friendship relationships and, in fact, the sister idiom is often used to indicate fictive kinship within friendship relationships. Furthermore sister–sister relationships are typically less institutionalized than parent–child relationships in Western society. Indeed, as early as 1969, Firth *et al.* noted that they represented the choice element of the kinship system.

In Britain, in the early studies by Young and Willmott (1962), little attention was paid to relationships between sibs, although even they noted that there was often a special tie between siblings who were nearest in age in large families. The overall trend of their study, however, was that sibs were linked to each other only through their relationship with 'Mum'. However, Allan (1977b, 1979) paid more direct attention to this relationship. He noted that, amongst his British working-class respondents;

> Without exception, these siblings were recognized by the respondents as being the most important people in their social network, and were frequently described as their 'best friends' despite the general inappropriateness of this label for kin relationships.
>
> (Allan, 1977b: 181)

Interaction with such sibs was much more likely to be enjoyable, and the range of social activities engaged in with them was much wider than in other sibling relationships (where the main concern was on simply keeping in contact). These 'best friend' sibling relationships were particularly striking since the working-class respondents identified their main non-kin sociable companions as 'mates' or 'not really friends'. Allan (1979) noted that, in his study, similar relationships with sisters did not appear to exist amongst the middle-class respondents, although there was some evidence that they still saw their relationships with them as 'like friendships' – albeit not special or very close ones.

Other studies have also provided insights into sister-sister relationships. Thus, in her small American study, Oliker (1989) noted that although being a sister did not guarantee identification as a friend, roughly one-fifth of her sample did identify a sister as their 'best friend' (as compared with one-twentieth of those who identified a mother in this way). These best friendships were in many ways similar to those with unrelated best friends, although she noted that they had longer histories and were often perceived as 'eternal' (1989: 79). Wellman (1990) found that, amongst his Toronto respondents, relationships between siblings had many similarities to friendships (e.g. in terms of sociability and emotional support), although siblings were more likely than friends to provide practical help. These elements of sociability and support in close sister–sister relationships also appeared in Hochschild's (1973) and Jerrome's (1981) studies of elderly respondents: the essence of these relationships being described by the former as 'reducing aloneness . . . [providing] laughter more than comfort, conviviality more than the act of being needed' (Hochschild, 1973: 65). Gouldner and Symons Strong (1987) also found that amongst their middle-class respondents there were sisters who were best friends – particularly amongst the older women. Argyle and Henderson (1985b), reviewing the evidence as regards contact between siblings, suggested that it fluctuated over the life cycle: being highest in adolescence, falling off in adulthood and rising again in old age. However, they concluded that even during the 'lowest' period (i.e. adulthood) relationships between sisters were important in particular circumstances.

O'Connor's work (1987, 1990) provides a more detailed illustration of the quality and content of sister–sister relationships. She found that in her study, highly positive interaction was much more likely to characterize very close sister–sister than mother–daughter relationships; and these relationships were much less likely than equally close relationships with mothers to be characterized by high levels of practical help or ongoing dependency. Relationships between very close sisters in her study had an intimacy and solidarity which is often thought of as characteristic of friendship. Thus, in her study, more than two-thirds of the sisters who were very close had a high level of intimate confiding (as compared with less than one in five of the mothers who were identified as very close). Similarly, the overwhelming majority of the relationships with these sisters had a high level of primary quality (as compared with half of those mothers who were identified as very close).

O'Connor (1990) noted, however, that the sheer existence of sisters by no means guaranteed their identification as very close. There was some evidence to suggest that (in contrast to the mother–daughter relationship) the husband's low level of involvement in child care, together with the sheer presence of sisters, was important in provoking the identification of them as very close. There was also some evidence that those respondents who included sisters were most likely to be stable working-class respondents. Nevertheless, only two-fifths of those who had a sister saw them as very close – a trend which is almost identical to that emerging amongst Allan's working-class respondents (1979: 109).

A flavour of the content and quality of these relationships can be provided through an illustrative vignette drawn from that study. Ruth Masterson was born in north London and both her parents and her sister live in her immediate neighbourhood. Ruth Masterson is a 32-year-old part-time kitchen assistant, married to a self-employed coalman (subcontracting to the Coal Board). Her father was an employed tailor all his life. They are thus regarded as stable working class. Both she and her husband left school at fifteen years. They have both a car and a phone but are renting a council house. Ruth has three children, aged seven, twelve and thirteen.

Ruth sees her sister Jean four or five times a week. She calls her 'my Jeannie' and talks to her about everything, including money, sex, trouble between herself and her husband and worries about getting pregnant. Their interaction is highly positive. She has strong feelings of attachment to Jean and it is important to her to know that she is there.

Ruth Masterson's relationship with her husband is not intimate in terms of confiding. She appreciates the fact that he works hard and that he has never been out of work and is dependable about money. He provides a low level of help both with housework and child care. He has provided her with financial security during their marriage but that is as far as the relationship goes. He frequently stays out for the night. He is poor company. They share no interests. She suspects that he may be having an affair at present. Yet to a large extent she feels less negatively towards him than one might expect since 'all men are like that anyway'. In this context her relationship with her sister provides intimacy and support which is absent from the marital relationship.

This vignette illustrates the possibilities of close sister–sister relationships and suggests the context in which they acquire friendship properties. Such relationships have provoked relatively little scientific interest. Indeed, one might suggest that the failure to explore them systematically reflects the continuing concern with women's tending capacities, and with effectively minimizing the potentialities implicit in women's relationships with each other – especially those which are not seen as essential in meeting physical dependency needs. At any rate, it is clear that there are similarities between close friendships and sister–sister relationships. We now turn to an examination of context-specific relationships.

CONTEXT-SPECIFIC RELATIONSHIPS: ARE THEY FRIENDSHIPS?

There is considerable evidence to show that working-class respondents consistently have fewer friends than their middle-class counterparts (see Mogey, 1956; Young and Willmott, 1962; Willmott and Young, 1967; Allan, 1979, 1989). Cohen and Rajkowski (1982) and Allan (1989) argue that this trend simply reflects the fact that ties of sociability are differently defined and organized within different subcultures. Indeed, such subcultural variation is consistent with the broad tendency for men and women to have different types of patterns of sociability (i.e. women being more likely to have dyadic, close, intimate friendships and men being more likely to have group-based, mate-type relationships).

One possible venue for such context-specific relationships is the work setting. Dillard and Miller (1988) and Brand and Hirsch (1990) have noted that relatively little attention has been paid to personal relationships there. Argyle and Furnham (1982), as well as Duck and Miell (1986) and Hays (1988), have suggested that friendship interactions typically involve leisure and recreational activities. It is obvious that such activities need not necessarily take place in recreational contexts, although, if they do not do so, the extent and range of activities is inevitably much more limited. It is, however, increasingly recognized that 'schmoozing' time generally exists at work, that is, time when there is an opportunity for employees to develop and maintain friendship relationships (Mangam, 1981). Thus Green *et al.* (1990) noted that, amongst their Sheffield respondents,

For many of them paid work offers considerable scope for leisure-like experiences. These can range from chatting at meal or break times or while working, through celebrating birthdays and other special events, or weekly trips to the pub at lunchtimes or more organized parties or outings.

(Green *et al.*, 1990: 8)

Allan (1979, 1989) has been to the fore in raising the question of the extent to which the study of friendship should include a variety of context-specific relationships (e.g. between workmates). In his earlier work (1979) he argued that working-class women do select people for apparently personal reasons from those with whom they interact in specific contexts; their interaction with these people is typically enjoyable and they see them as special in some small way. However, unlike their middle-class counterparts, they do not attempt to generalize these relationships beyond the limits imposed by the setting in which they are located – possibly because they want some control over the demands that can be made of them and greater flexibility as regards their degree of commitment to them.

In his later work, Allan (1989) recognized that what he called 'mateships', as well as being context-specific, have other characteristics: they are potentially more fragile than friendships; they are not characterized by dyadic commitment; and because of their 'contextual specificity' participants are able to ignore structural differences to a greater extent than is possible in friendship relationships. Nevertheless, he concluded that 'For purposes of analysis, the notion of friendship needs to be extended so as to include workmates, acquaintances and others who may not always be specified as friends' (Allan, 1989: 10). It is clear from very many studies (e.g. Sharpe, 1984; Griffin, 1985; Wellman, 1985; Green *et al.*, 1990) that relationships at work are an important and very real aspect of many women's work situations. McNally (1979), Pollert (1981), Cavendish (1982) and Sharpe (1984) suggested that these relationships were often the most positive aspects of the routine alienating jobs done by the women in their studies. For women like these, working in tobacco factories and other routine jobs, there were, in Westwood's vivid phrases,

No 'laffs' to be had on your own; bunking off to the toilets, spending too much time in the coffee bar made no sense if it was an individual activity; there was no way to organize a prank without your mates or to have a laff at a pornie picture or a coarse joke. The material base for all of these was the friendship group.

(Westwood, 1984: 90–1)

Leslie and Grady (1985) found that in their study, the workplace was the second most common source of significant relationships (with kin being the primary source); while Oliker (1989) found that although only roughly a quarter of her respondents saw co-workers as close friends, the majority of those who did do so saw them as 'best' or 'closest' friends. She also suggested that this latter group wanted to develop their friendship more gradually than her other respondents, and so welcomed the work-related constraints on the friendship.

Other studies (e.g. Cavendish's, 1982) suggested that although only a minority of the respondents had 'special' friends at work, group-based friendships were important. Indeed, it is possible that, as Allan (1989) has suggested, the real significance of work relationships may only become apparent when they do not exist (e.g. when the person becomes housebound, is unemployed and/or has young children at home). Certainly, many of the unemployed women in Coyle's study (1984) mentioned that they missed these relationships.

The development of work-related friendships appeared likely to be affected both by the characteristics of the employees (i.e. their permanent/temporary status, number of years on the job, number of hours worked; McNally, 1979; Fischer, 1982b); as well as by the characteristics of the organization (i.e. the physical proximity of the employees, the extent of supervision, organizational climate, time schedules, job design, levels of job mobility; Farrell, 1986; Hays, 1988; Wellman, 1988). Status differences between employees obviously further affect friendship possibilities. Indeed, it has been noted that within organizations those in high-status positions may base their friendships more on hierarchical considerations, whereas lower-status workers and/or those who are not occupationally mobile may select their friends on the basis of geographical proximity (Fine, 1986).

It has also been noted that group solidarity is affected by the structural isolation of the workers and by their degree of autonomy. Joking, rumour and gossip at work, as well as interaction rituals and work-based outings and activities, are all seen as contributing to the development of such group-related feelings (Fine, 1986). Of course, to the extent that women do not participate in the latter, they become excluded from such work-based friendships. In fact, Lorber (1989) argues that, except in organizations where women are in the majority, they tend to be excluded from such colleague peer groups, not only on these grounds but also because they are seen either as potential sexual partners or as what she calls 'traditional moral entrepreneurs' who cannot be trusted to collude with 'moral deviations'. She argues that the implications of this exclusion are very serious for women in so far as in bureaucratic organizations the formal organization of work is strongly influenced by work-based peer groups; in professional organizations careers are shaped through patronage; while in blue-collar work the peer group determines the managerial rules which are to be obeyed. Thus implicit in Lorber's work is the idea that the ease with which women do their paid work and/or their career prospects are likely to be affected by their work-based friendships (and within predominantly male-dominated organizations, she is pessimistic about their inclusion in such peer groups).

Sharpe (1984), Wellman (1985), Thoits (1986) and Allan (1989) have all drawn attention to the particular difficulties that employed married women have in creating and/or sustaining friendships in work settings. Wellman (1985) argues that their 'double-load'

> limits their exposure to neighbours, and while it exposes them to co-workers, it restricts the time and energy available to develop these ties. Thus, the double load paradoxically gives these women structural possibilities for engaging with social circles beyond the confines of neighbourhood and kinship solidarities, but at the same time it makes such major demands on their time and energy that they do not feel able to seize these opportunities.
>
> (Wellman, 1985: 176)

This was confirmed by Goodenow and Gaier's (1990) study of college alumnae, which found that women in full-time paid employment were less likely to have a best friendship than women who either were in part-time paid employment or were full-time housewives.

However, Evetts' (1988) work on primary-school head teachers implicitly raises the question of the extent to which relationships with female colleagues within a female-controlled environment can provide support in combining work and motherhood. In this context, head teachers and colleagues gave encouragement and advice in dealing with both the routine care of children and their care when they were sick; and, through their conversations, validated each other's work and family performances and their view of what it was to be a good mother and a good teacher. Evetts notes that: 'Amongst females, such mutual support might be termed "sisterhood" if this concept could be separated from its feminist, consciousness-raising connotations' (Evetts, 1988: 527). The primary teaching situation is, as Evetts recognizes, unusual in that it is one where women can and do achieve promotion (just under half of the primary head teachers in England and Wales are women), and so they are in a structural position to mobilize resources and create an appropriate cultural climate which encourages – or at least allows – helpful relationships between women to develop.

In so far as one regards housework as work (Oakley, 1974), the neighbourhood may effectively be regarded as a 'work environment' within which both particular friendships and more 'mate-like' relationships may be created and maintained. By and large, however, the focus of studies of such relationships has remained rather narrow (i.e. continuing to be concerned simply with practical help or sharing confidences and/or with the degree to which a neighbour is/is not 'very close').

Cohen's work (1978) is a notable exception in so far as she looked at the way in which talk between neighbours in a south London housing estate created an 'estate style': one involving the women's dress, their behaviour, their values and their attitudes to various aspects of their children's lives (including the importance of third-level education, acceptable levels of television watching, the desirability of after-school activities, reading, etc.). Cohen makes the point that this culture gave the estate an identity separate from the neighbouring local-authority estate, and was a response to, and a way of maintaining, its middle-class position. She also stressed that it in no way undermined the husband–wife relationship or provided the women with a substitute group through which they might achieve status in their own right.

Willmott's (1987) work is more typical. Thus, for example, he noted that neighbours played a crucial role in providing day-to-day help and support. Oliker (1989) found that, in her small study, roughly a quarter of the respondents included a neighbour amongst their closest friends. O'Connor (1987) found a similar pattern. Thus, for example, Julia Rodgers' relationship with Pauline was firmly grounded in their shared experiences of housewifery and motherhood: 'We lived next door, had the kids little together. We used to pop in and out of each others' for coffee and a chat.' For some of these women this kind of relationship, although it lacked the range of shared experiences which typically characterizes childhood friendships, had a fictive kin quality. Debbie Halley said of her relationship with Iris, whom she had known for about eight years through being neighbours and having children at the same time: 'It is like having another sister really – I can't get rid of her. Iris knows all my family and I know hers.' Tessie Halpin described the history of her relationship with her very close friend and neighbour, Brenda, equally graphically: 'We've been mates for eight years. We had the children when we were both young together. We've gone through bad times together . . . we've done umpteen things together. We've always classed our children as our children together.'

It is possible that important insights into the nature of modern neighbourly relationships could be derived by focusing, for example, on the information transmitted by them as regards job opportunities or shopping 'bargains'. Alternatively, a study of children's birthday parties could be illuminating as regards the ways in which such relationships are used to create and maintain class boundaries and networks of indebtedness. Such topics tend to be ignored – possibly because academic research is largely not done by people who are involved in such networks.

Compartmentalized friendships can also exist outside the arenas of work and home, although there are very few descriptions of such relationships amongst females. Rosencrance's (1986) description of male race-track 'buddies' is typical of the sort of relationship characterized by interaction and shared enjoyment but little else – a pattern which has continued to be seen rather derogatorily as '. . . No more than a mutual flight from boredom – a pact against isolation, with an amendment against intimacy' (Douvan and Adelson, 1966: 178). Green *et al.* (1990) noted that women are slightly more likely than men to be active in clubs, societies, leisure classes and/or voluntary work (typically, in areas that were single-sex, 'safe' and socially acceptable). It is, theoretically, possible for friendships between women to occur between those involved in such contexts. Oliker's (1989) small study suggested that this rarely occurred, although other studies (such as Lopata's, 1971) were less pessimistic about this. Gouldner and Symons Strong (1987) noted that such relationships did exist – both amongst that sample of middle-class respondents and in their earlier study of women who were active in the League of Women Voters in the 1950s. They argued that these relationships were most likely to be characterized by mutual respect and admiration. Typically, these women seldom saw each other outside the organizational setting and did not usually confide in each other about the non-organizational aspects of their lives. Yet they enjoyed the relationship enormously. 'They felt loyal to them, a feeling that appeared to develop in the course of sharing a kind of organizational intimacy rather than a personal intimacy' (Gouldner and Symons Strong, 1987: 81). There is also some evidence to suggest that solidarity and even intimacy may develop in situations where women find themselves in the same predicament, trying to re-establish their self-confidence and control over their lives in Women's Refuges (Dobash and Dobash, 1980) and in various kinds of community-development and adult-education settings. Typically, however, such relationships have not been seen as friendships.

Oddly enough, however, there has been a good deal less reticence about the possibility that relationships between couple-based socializing partners could be described as friendships, although it has been recognized that such relationships are also often rather limited and specific. Thus McCarthy noted that although almost four-fifths of those relationships he studied had been in existence for at least five years, the couples 'appeared to refrain from discussing intimate topics and also avoided dealing with those broad socio-political and moral/ethical issues, agreement on which has been seen by many researchers as the vital bonding agent of friendship' (1986: 88). Occasionally it has been noted (e.g. Granovetter, 1973; Willmott, 1987) that context-specific relationships can be extremely useful in providing information about jobs, in opening up social and cultural horizons and as sources of new friendships, etc. Such issues have, however, tended to be neglected in favour of an examination of the identity and properties of close, very close or confidant relationships – especially in the area of friendships between women.

In a sense, friendships rooted in a common political position can be regarded as context-specific. However, in situations of state oppression, such relationships may embrace life-and-death issues. Shlapentokh (1974) has discussed such friendships within the Soviet Union, and has suggested that they are both an obstacle to the absolute dominance of the state and a basis for the creation of underground networks of information, education and resistance of various kinds. There is a strong feeling that the essence of these relationships is rooted in their common political position – or, more appropriately, their opposition to the state.

It is possible to see Raymond's (1986) view of friendship between women as falling within this tradition: 'Female friendship gives depth and spirit to a political vision of feminism and is itself a profoundly political act' (Raymond, 1986: 29). She argues that friendship between women has to transcend obstacles such as therapism ('a tyranny of feelings where women have come to believe that what really counts in their life is their "psychology" ' (1986: 155), an androgynous acceptance of the male world and its values and victimization, where women make a cult of failure and emphasize their shared pain rather than their successes.

Friendship, in her eyes, creates and maintains feminism. In so far as this vision is all-embracing, then such friendships are equally so. Indeed, it can be argued that this perception of friendship is the truly authentic one, reflecting as it does the primacy of political ideas. Such a perception is not, however, typical of Western society, which has tended to privatize the friendship relationship – seeing it in terms of personality traits rather than socio-political implications. In this way, it is suggested, important insights into the social significance of friendship ties have been missed.

LESBIANISM

At first glance it might seem strange to include lesbianism in a discussion of the limits and meaning of friendship. However, it seems important to do so on three grounds: firstly, because of the argument that it was the emergence of lesbianism as a distinct sexual identity, indicating a particular type of person, which played an important part historically in inhibiting friendships between women; secondly, because of the idea that lesbian relationships represent the prototype of 'true' female friendships – and (it is argued) the only ones that can bring about change in the distribution of power within society; and thirdly, because an examination of lesbian relationships raises the issue of the extent to which Western relationship culture (whether homo- or heterosexual) is essentially exclusive and possessive – and so in this sense is basically opposed to the friendship ethos.

Firstly, then, Foucault (1981), Faderman (1981) and Ruehl (1983) vividly argued that the construction of the identity 'lesbian' only began in Europe in the nineteenth century and was not really established in public consciousness until the early twentieth century.

In fact, Ruehl (1983) argued that there was no distinct public consciousness of lesbianism as a sexual identity and a social type until 1928, when Radcliffe Hall's novel *The Well of Loneliness* was published.

The emergence of this sexual category as a social construct is thus a historically and societally relative one. It suggests that sexual acts with, and preferences for, women reflect a fixed sexual identity, a particular life style and a type of person. Since the identity of lesbian is a stigmatized one, the fear of being labelled in this way acts as an important control on women's relationships with each other – and in particular on their physical demonstrations of affection. Faderman (1981) argues that, since

Freud, we have become unable to avoid the sexual overtones in most adult relationships. Hence, to our worldly eyes, romantic, physically demonstrative or even emotionally important relationships between women may easily come to have sexual overtones. Inevitably, then, she argues, there has been strong pressure on women to avoid them – for fear of being labelled lesbian.

It is only since the rise of the Women's Movement in the 1960s and 1970s that this has been challenged. This movement has arguably brought about some lessening of the suspicion of female–female friendships. However, the acceptance of them has been limited by the anxiety that

> Love between women coupled with their emerging freedom, might conceivably bring about the overthrow of heterosexuality – which has meant not only sex between men and women but patriarchal culture, male dominance and female subservience.
>
> (Faderman, 1981: 411)

The second issue relates to the fact that within radical feminist circles, lesbian relationships have long been seen as almost the prototype of 'true' female friendships:

> [the] word lesbian has expanded so much through political definition that it should no longer refer exclusively to a woman simply in sexual relation to another woman. . . . The word is now a generic term signifying activism and resistance and the envisioned goal of a woman committed state.
>
> (Johnson, 1974: 278)

In this tradition, lesbians are juxtaposed with 'male identified' women (i.e. those who identify with men, live through them and get status and identity from them). Indeed, in this sense, they can be seen as women whose primary focus of attention and commitment is other women and in this sense they are women-oriented, regardless of their sexual proclivities.

Using the concept of compulsory heterosexuality, Rich (1980) argued that a heterosexual preference was developed and then enforced in women by a variety of mechanisms including rape, physical violence, the ideology of romantic love and the invisibility or marginality of lesbian existence (1980: 647). All of these mechanisms, she suggested, reinforced male power and assured males a right of 'physical, economic and emotional access' (1980: 647). Rich saw lesbian women and what she called 'women on the lesbian continuum' as challenging this power by their women-centred relationships with each other.

The essence of friendships between women, then, in the eyes of Rich (1980) and Daly (1978) – as indeed also in the eyes of Raymond (1986) and other radical feminists – is that of positive self-validation:

> Beneath the facade of male-derived identity, the Radicalesbians argued, there lay 'an enormous reservoir of self hate'. If her entire validity as a person derived from the man to whom she was attached, then she was nothing, in and of herself.
>
> (Eisenstein, 1984: 52)

Daly (1978) suggested that it was the ability to 'self-centre' that generated and reinforced women's ability to 'spark, that is, how to bond with other women' (1978: 373). Both friendship and erotic love between women, Daly argued, strengthened the individual's sense of self: 'Women loving women do not seek to lose our identity, but to express it, discover it, create it. . . . The sparking of ideas and the flaming of physical passion emerge from the same source' (1978: 373). Much of the debate between radical and liberal feminists in the 1970s and 1980s has revolved around the issue of the authenticity of a commitment to feminism when fused with heterosexuality. It was argued by the radical feminists that lesbianism was the only possible alternative for a woman-oriented woman. This view was strongly challenged by other feminists, who contended that:

> We like individual men. . . . We like individual women. Our solidarity doesn't need to be based on love, but, equally, our love doesn't need to be based on solidarity. We have solidarity with a 'sex class' but we *love* individual people.
>
> (Dhavernas, 1987: 106)

In Hite's study (1987) half of the women who identified themselves as lesbian saw this as a political commitment. Indeed, in the Hite Report, the permeability between sexual relationships and friendships amongst gay women was striking, with almost two-thirds of gay women remaining long-term friends with their most serious ex-lovers. Further-more, although only roughly one in four of the women in the Hite Report had sexual relationships with other women, the overwhelming majority of them had their deepest emotional relationship with a woman, and felt that it was far easier to talk to other women than to most men (including their current sexual partner).

Other work has noted that lesbians are particularly likely to emphasize the emotional quality of love relationships: 'to value closeness and permanence in relationships that are based more on love and romance than on sex' (Przybyla and Byrne, 1981). In this respect, they can be seen as similar to heterosexual relationships and compatible with an ideology which encourages women to see their sexuality in terms of long-term, stable, exclusive, possessive relationships. Very little attention has been paid to the question of the general priority given to such exclusive sexual relationships (whether with women or men) in Western society. A type of non-exclusive relationship existed in the Lesbian Community described by Barnhart (1975), and was also in evidence in the kibbutz in the 1960s (Bettelheim, 1971; Baker and Hertz, 1981). In the former situation, although it was accepted that 'a lover was also your best friend', it was expected that this dyadic relationship would be less important than the partners' overall commitment to the Community; and if it was not, the individuals left the Community, either by choice or because of pressure from the Community members. In this situation, as in some other lesbian communities (Krieger, 1982), priority was given to the less intimate, less exclusive but normatively prescriptive ideal of 'comradely' or 'sisterly' relationships within the Community as a whole: 'the Community does offer a coin – that of support and friendship, which mean true stability. Pair relationships also offer support, warmth, intimacy and friendship; however, for the members of the Community these pair relationships are not seen as stable' (Barnhart, 1975: 114). Similar patterns existed in the kibbutz, where Baker and Hertz (1981) noted that the ideal relationship was one of comradeship, and that exclusive and special relationships, including friendship, were devalued. The cultural unpopularity of this strategy arguably highlights the highly individual, possessive nature of our relationship culture – whether heterosexual, homosexual or asexual. However, there has been very little attention paid to this phenomenon either at a descriptive level or in terms of exploring its implications at the level of personal development or social structure.

A consideration of lesbianism thus raises several issues: firstly, the extent to which it is the best or indeed the only way in which patriarchy can be effectively challenged; secondly, it indirectly highlights the importance Western society attaches to exclusivity in any sexual relationship; thirdly, it draws attention to the centrality of physical intimacy in defining a relationship (and indeed, the lack of interest in understanding the meaning of physical intimacy between female friends in our society); and finally, it raises the issue of the nature of this tie and its similarity to, and difference from, friendship as we define it today.

Relatively little work has been done on lesbianism from within the personal-relationships tradition, so that the similarities and differences between it and friendship remain virtually unexplored.

ISSUES ARISING FROM THIS WORK

This chapter has highlighted the similarities between what is conventionally regarded as friendship and related social forms. It has explicitly challenged the assumption that friendship is purely and simply a private interpersonal relationship by arguing that it has an 'objectified social form' in the sense that it is characterized by rules of conduct relating both to the maintenance of the relationship and to its termination.

The chapter has also implicitly challenged the idea that friendship has a unique quality by highlighting the similarities between the content, quality and form of long-standing committed close-friend and sister-sister relationships. Equally, it has argued that context-specific 'mate' relationships (whether rooted in work or in a shared ideological position) must be included within a friendship spectrum: a continuum which already easily assimilates context-specific couple-based friendships. Even lesbian relationships, which at first glance can appear very different from what is commonly thought of as friendship, have clear elements of similarity. Radical feminists have regarded these as epitomizing 'real' friendship; while Faderman (1981) and Ruehl (1983) have implicitly raised questions around the extent to which friendship can be differentiated from lesbianism simply in terms of physical contact. Indeed, the whole question of the extent to which the shape of female friendships has been affected by the construction of lesbian identity is a very real issue for them. Thus Faderman's work (1981) suggests that, in the nineteenth century, female friendships had very much higher levels of physical contact than would be considered 'normal' today: the acceptability of such overt demonstrations of affection reflecting the segregation at that time of men's and women's lives; the absence of any preoccupation with fears of lesbianism and (most of all) women's lack of economic independence. In Western society today the latter has begun to change (although, as was noted in Chapter 1, the majority of women are still at least partially economically dependent on men). The ideology of romantic love extols the emotional primacy of the marital relationship but this relationship does not, in fact, structure the day-to-day rhythm of most men's lives, which remain to a very considerable degree rooted in the occupational sphere. For them, the emotional primacy of marriage is typically simply translated into sexual fidelity. Thus, the essence of that relationship is seen as its sexual reality: a cultural position which is complemented by the definition of lesbianism and its stigmatization. In this context the emotional primacy implicit in female friendships has a cultural ambiguity. Should they be seen as a diluted form of lesbianism? Are they a potential threat to the construction of emotionally important relationships on the basis of their genital reality? Are they a threat to the institution of heterosexuality and patriarchal culture, as Faderman (1981) has argued?

What this chapter implicitly suggests is that friendship can best be thought of as simply a form of social integration, but one which tends to be peculiarly 'distorted' in Western culture by an ideology which both idealizes and limits it, and which is most comfortable with it either as a static idealized mental construct or as almost a pseudo-kin-type caring relationship. Both of these themes are taken up in the next chapter.

— 7 —

The future of women's friendships

INTRODUCTION

It is obvious from the material reviewed in this book that over the past fifteen years there has been a good deal of interest in friendships between women. This interest has stemmed from a variety of sources, including sociology, social psychology, the science of personal relationships and feminism. This interest in friendships – including women's friendships – is particularly opportune in Western society, which is faced with growing instability in marriage, reduction in family size, attenuation of 'obligatory' kinship ties and an increasing recognition of the distinction between what Parker (1981) has called 'caring' and 'tending'. It seems clear that relationships will become more 'voluntary' and transitory – akin in many ways to those we currently define as friendships. In this context the importance of understanding the shape, course, content and impact of this relationship can hardly be overestimated.

Within sociology, Allan (1989) has drawn together the available research on friendship and highlighted issues related to various aspects of the social context within which it occurs. Within social psychology, Duck (1982, 1990b) has been active in examining the processes operating in the initiation, maintenance and dissolution of relationships. A re-evaluation of the importance of friendship relationships is implicit in network theory, social support and psychiatric sociology. Feminist thought, in what Eisenstein (1984) called 'the third stage of feminist theory', has moved to a positive evaluation of differences between women's and men's 'worlds'. She has argued that this initially led to what she called a 'false universalism' and a 'mystical feminism' (1984: 134). More recently, this has been replaced by an awareness of the complexity of women's class position and life styles, although it is still true that even radical feminists have paid relatively little attention to the nature and significance of friendships between women.

It is clear from the work drawn together in the previous four chapters that a good deal is known about women's friendships. Thus, for example, it is clear that women have various kinds of friends; that these friendships are no longer exclusively dyadic; that friendship has some similarities with kin relationships; that friendships tend to be positively associated with various indicators of psychological well-being (such as the absence of psychiatric disorder, morale, joy, etc.); that social-class position, age, life stage and marital status are amongst the factors which need to be taken into account in understanding them; that friendships play an important part in creating and/or maintaining women's social worlds and the moral discourses within them; and that we are just beginning to appreciate the process involved in creating, maintaining and ending friendships:

> There are certain 'truths' about friendship which most people hold to be self evident; that friends live near each other, that they share common attitudes and interests, that their relationship is subordinate to partners and kin ties, and that they are likely to value their relationship considerably if they are adolescent, but only marginally if they are adults. In each case, however, these great truths are only partially valid.
>
> (Bradford Brown, 1981: 44)

It is increasingly clear that not only are these truths partially valid, they are also very partial indeed.

Since this book is itself a review of work done in the area of women's friendships, no attempt will be made to provide a more condensed summary of the evidence than already exists within the substantive chapters. Rather, this chapter will identify what are seen as the key issues which will need to be addressed by future work in the area. This will be set within the context of a speculative discussion of the future shape of women's friendships. It will be argued that there is a cultural ambivalence about these friendships (indeed, this extends to other areas of personal relationships, although the tendency to trivialize and/or derogate them is, as was argued in Chapter 1, particularly strong in the case of women's friendships). Since such tendencies can find their most culturally legitimate expression in the idealization of such relationships, this issue will first be tackled. Indeed, it is only by demythologizing women's lives (de Beauvoir, 1972) that we can come to an understanding of their real nature and complexity.

This chapter is a personal synthesis and a provocative agenda. It demonstrates, however, the richness of the world of women's friendships, and the range of work on them which still needs to be done.

THE IDEALIZATION PHENOMENON

It is not difficult to argue that for most people relationships are important in the sense that they give meaning and significance to their lives:

> Through personal relationships, we may find our most profound experiences of security and anxiety, power and impotence, unity and separateness. Friendships and love affairs may gratify basic needs, fulfil fundamental values, meet developmental tasks, further instrumental pursuits, appease environmental demands or merely fill up free time.
>
> (McAdams, 1988: 7)

However, the fact that these relationships are neither the sole sources of these experiences nor unambiguously positive experiences has tended to be ignored by those involved in the study of friendship. Firstly then, despite Townsend's classic study (1957), which showed that there was no necessary relationship between social contact and the experience of loneliness in old age, and Gubrium's (1976) study indicating the happiness of life-long isolates, the assumption that personal relationships are the sole sources of happiness has become embedded in the thinking of Western society. It has been shown (e.g. Chapters 3 and 4) that friendship is associated with psychiatric well-being, joy, etc. It is not, however, too difficult to imagine that for some people, other activities may provide similar experiences. Indeed, it is obvious that at other historical periods the meaning and significance of life has been differentially located in people, work, nature or some spiritual reality that can be described as God.

The argument here is a subtle one. Thus, implicit in the very conception of this book is the idea that friendship is a valid and important focus of scientific study, and that particular kinds of friendship are associated with positive experiences – including joy and positive mental health (see Wheeler *et al.*, 1983; Jerrome, 1984; Larson and Bradney, 1988; Argyle, 1990; O'Connor, 1991c). Friendships are not, however, sole or unique sources of such experiences. Indeed, O'Connor and Brown (1984) showed that those who had no very close relationship, although more likely to have an affective disorder than those who had a confidant, were very much less likely to have an affective disorder than those whose only very close relationship was with someone who was seen very infrequently (their ability to face up to the fact that they had no close friend arguably reflecting their positive mental health). Gouldner and Symons Strong's (1987) work pushes this idea a stage further in so far as they note that in their study the feeling that one should have friends helped to keep alive many friendships that were far from ideal.

Secondly, friendships, like romantic-love relationships, seem in danger of becoming dominated by what Brittan (1977: 75) has called 'a language of make believe'. This type of thinking simplifies the complex psychological reality of friendship: 'friendship should not be considered as an unmixed blessing, as it sometimes appears in the psychological literature, but rather as a complex and sometimes problematic relationship' (Solano, 1986: 241). Implicit in this is the perception of friendship as involving costs and disappointments as well as joys and satisfactions. Furthermore, although Solano does not make this explicit, it is obvious that, as a living relationship, friendships will require resources (time, effort, money, etc.) to create and maintain them.

In Western society there is a reluctance to demythologize personal relationships; to see them as the products of what Lynch (1989) called 'solidary labour', as opposed to 'crocks of gold at the end of the rainbow' (Duck, 1988). This type of thinking is inimical to any real understanding of the nature of women's lives in general and their friendships in particular.

THE FUTURE 'FACE' OF WOMEN'S
FRIENDSHIPS: SOME SPECULATIONS

It has been argued in this book that friendship is not simply a personal relationship, but that it must be located in the wider socio-cultural setting. This setting influences both the cultural valuation of friendship;

and its shape at a particular moment in time (within the parameters of, for example, a paradigm such as that outlined by Davis and Todd, 1985). This section will speculate about the kinds of friendship which seem likely to emerge in the future – within the context of an examination of both the cultural ambivalence towards this phenomenon and the rise of related institutions.

In Western society, we have become accustomed to thinking in terms of the public and private areas: the world of impersonal and personal relationships respectively. The two worlds are seen as separate, so that, to our eyes, the New Guinea arrangement whereby 'when a man acquires a trading partner, he falls in love with him as part of the deal' (Brain, 1977: 10) appears very strange indeed. Typically, the most important institutions are seen as those in the public area: institutions dealing with economic production, power or social order. These are typically also seen as the 'male' areas, whereas the private world is seen as the woman's sphere and a place where 'personalized caring' (Porter, 1983) is valued, and where human, non-exploitative values are endorsed. Friendships, as non-exploitative personal relationships based on 'compatibility and liking rather than usefulness' (Jerrome, 1990: 56), fall within the private area. This world, like that of Bedouin women so vividly described by Abu-Lughod (1985), is neither self-contained nor economically self-sufficient. Unlike the Bedouin, however, it has tended to be ignored and trivialized by a public world that is 'doubtful of bonds of love' since such bonds are 'not compatible with the mechanism of its science or the utilitarianism of its policy' (Marris, 1982: 186).

On the other hand, friendship offers the opportunity for individuals to construct their identities. The fluidity of its form means that, in Simmel's terms (1971), the dead weight of institutional reality is least likely to affect friendships. The process of creating, maintaining and terminating them is thus in an important sense the process of creating and modifying an individual identity within a socio-cultural reality. Friendship with its strong voluntary ethos, its equality and emotional primacy is culturally an attractive genre in Western society: 'Friendship raised love to a higher plane and dispensed with its possessiveness, rejected standards of fidelity "set impossibly high", made no claim to abiding permanence, and thus relieved those who failed at friendship of responsibility or guilt' (Lasch, 1977: 104). Indeed, Simmel (1971) referred to friendships as relationships *par excellence* of individuation. As such, friendships between women pose an implicit threat in so far as women are typically defined by their relationships with others (particularly a husband and children). The cultural and structural pressures propel them in the direction of what Hochschild (1973) called 'altruistic surrender' and Baker Miller (1986) referred to as a search for attachment.

In addition to the pressures arising from this wider cultural context, the shape of women's friendships seems likely to be affected by the rise of related institutions. Three types of such phenomena will be briefly referred to here. Firstly, there has been the phenomenal rise of talk shows both on radio and television. Through these, moral discourses are created and/or maintained. Indeed, it is possible to see these shows as a way of transcending the essentially private nature of most women's lives – especially those who are not in paid employment. Porter (1983) noted that for all women working full-time in the home (but especially working-class women) there was a need for: 'an institution comparable to the unions that could mediate and interpret the information they do get' (Porter, 1983: 170). Talk shows are, of course, very different indeed from unions. They do, however, provide a public arena for the discussion of private issues; they play an important part in legitimating grievances, interpreting information and justifying choices. In fact, it does not seem too fanciful to see them as a public forum for the kind of talk which we see as characteristic of friendship – even intimate friendship. The implications of this phenomenon for the form and content of friendships between women have not even begun to be recognized.

The second type of phenomenon is very different. It is the emergence and cultural legitimation of social networks which reflect and maintain class and gender-based vested interests. Historically, there is nothing new in this, although the egalitarian ethos of the 1960s and early 1970s militated against it. Now, however, it is re-emerging with a vengence in socially legitimate forms. Thus, through channels of friendship, various types of fund-raising and pressure-group networks are being formed. These can be seen as more personal and less geographically based than such traditional British institutions as working-men's clubs or upper-middle-class gentlemen's clubs. They perform the same activities, however, in terms of perpetuating privilege, maintaining social closure and reflecting and reinforcing a gender- and class-differentiated world.

The third type of phenomenon is the commodification of physical contact and emotional support through a variety of venues and activities, including massage clinics, encounter groups, charismatic sessions, etc. The emergence of these reflects the extent to which emotionality and physical contact are typically seen as appropriate only within a heterosexual adult relationship: one which may be unavailable, or for various reasons, unwilling, or unable, to provide these kinds of experiences. Friendship between women in the gender-segregated world of nineteenth-century Europe and America dealt with this situation in an easy unselfconscious way. However, as Gouldner and Symons Strong's respondents noted, it is difficult today for women to say they love each other, since these words 'resonated too much of the vocabulary of heterosexual love' (1987: 108). Physical demonstrations of affection are even more fraught in view of the sexualization of what nineteenth-century women would have regarded as quite innocent physical contact. The implications of the presence of Aids (and the consequent risks involved in genital sex) in terms of obscuring the distinction between homosexual and heterosexual contact and/or legitimating physical contact between friends have not begun to be discussed. However, the Roman Catholic Church's desexualization of the handshake and/or kiss of peace, and the introduction of them into religious ceremonies, can be seen as an attempt both to extend the concept of friend and to legitimate limited forms of physical contact within it.

These three institutions can in a sense be seen as related to, but obviously very different from, friendship as we currently know it. They represent attempts to move the private area of friendship into the public area. They are part of the context within which the form and content of friendship is being moulded, although their implications as regards this relationship have not even begun to be explored.

Within the parameters of what we regard as friendship, there are a wide variety of patterns (and these have been documented throughout the book). Six patterns which seem likely to represent the future face of friendship are highlighted here: intimate confidants; dyadic friendships which are little more than mental constructs; group-based sociable relationships; the institutionalization of aspects of caring using the idiom of friendship; fictive kin relationships and friendships which reflect and maintain class positions. Obviously, not all women are likely to have all these types of friendship. Indeed, it is suggested that those which they do have are an important indication of the parameters of the specific situations within which they are living (so that, for example, confidant relationships are most likely to be characteristic of those women who are in a disempowering situation which they are unable or unwilling to change).

It has been noted that research attention has tended to focus disproportionately on such intimate or confidant relationships. Such a focus arguably reflects the dominant (male) cultural inability to deal with intimacy and emotional vulnerability and the projection of such feelings onto women. (Baker Miller, 1986; Cancian, 1986). This preoccupation with intimate relationships also arguably reflects and reinforces the power relationships between men and women, since it has also been shown that women tend to confide about their weaknesses rather than their strengths, and that:

> Interpersonal power appears to be an issue for men when deciding to engage in self-disclosure, but not for women . . . women avoid disclosing in order to elude personal hurt or relational problems while men avoid disclosing in order to maintain control.
>
> (Cline Welch, 1989: 9)

It has been widely shown that the opportunity to talk out distressed feelings is extremely important in the wake of life events such as widowhood, unemployment, illness, etc. Such events are frequently uncontrollable and have implications for the person's life style and their view of themselves. It is, however, worth considering why intimate confiding should be part of the routine of ordinary life, and why it was, for a very substantial period of time, seen as the defining characteristic of friendship. In this context it is arguable that intimate confiding represents what Raymond (1986) has called a retreat into 'therapism' or 'victimization', that is, where the main concern is with justifying an unwillingness to act, despite a considerable level of unhappiness. It can, in a way, be seen as pathological. The fact that it has not been seen in this way no doubt reflects partly what Montgomery (1988) has called the 'social ideology of intimacy'. This ideology has tended to conceal the paradox that, as Argyle (1990) succinctly stated, women, despite their high levels of confiding, have high levels of mental illness and a high consumption of psychotropic drugs (Gove, 1972, 1974, 1978; Cooperstock, 1978; Miles, 1988; Gabe and Williams, 1986). However, in a society where there is little evidence of dramatic changes in the balance of power between men and women, it seems likely to persist as one type of friendship between women in the future.

Dyadic forms of friendship – particularly amongst women – have been seen as the culturally dominant mode. This sits very easily with a focus on intimate confiding. Simmel (1950) noted that the very structure of the dyad itself (i.e. simply consisting of two members and so inevitably vulnerable to any change in its composition) ensures that it is 'The real locus not only of authentic sociological tragedy, but also of sentimentalism' (Simmel, 1950: 123–4). This sentimentalism is arguably reflected in the tendency, both amongst personal-relationship theorists and among the general public themselves, to idealize these relationships. Gouldner and Symons Strong's (1987) respondents, in a way which was strongly reminiscent of romantic-love fantasies, said that they expected these wonderful new friends 'simply [to] appear in their lives'. In the absence of such perfect friends, they romanticized and 'upgraded' old and infrequently seen friends. These latter relationships were often typically simply mental constructs, in the sense that they required little time or effort to maintain, although equally they provided little tangible support. However, they often had an important emotional reality in the respondents' lives and were highly valued. Indeed (like religious beliefs), they may be felt to make an important contribution to their ability to cope.

In societies where marriage is an unstable institution, the subsuming of women's identity within marriage becomes a highly doubtful exercise (albeit one which is extolled by the ideology of romantic love). The existence of friends who reflect and reinforce those aspects of personal identity which are not related to the marriage obviously becomes important in this situation.

Friends arguably provide identity validation and a solution to what was early identified by Friedan (1963) as a peculiarly female problem in patriarchal society: 'the problem that has no name' (i.e. the absence of a sense of personal identity). In so far as these relationships are latent (O'Connor, 1987) their emotional priority is, in a sense, fraudulent, if one takes Marris' view that: 'The meaning of a relationship in the structure of my life depends on its degree of priority in a hierarchy of claims, on what I willingly give up for its sake' (1982: 199). However, it is this very latency which makes them uniquely suitable within a cultural setting which stresses the desirability and normality of friendship – while at the same time providing little cultural legitimation for the expenditure of time and effort (especially by women) on creating and maintaining such relationships. As such, they seem likely to become an increasingly common phenomenon in Western society.

A very different cultural form of friendship is that which finds expression in sociable relationships between groups of women. In the past five to ten years, groups of women have come to see each other as acceptable partners in fun. Thus they run or drink or eat or walk together – sometimes in dyads, but often as a group. This pattern has been documented by Jerrome (1981, 1984) amongst the elderly, but casual observation shows that it is far more common. Sometimes, the setting is highly structured (e.g. bingo), sometimes it is single-sex (e.g. fitness clubs) and sometimes it is mixed (e.g. bridge, pool, darts). The main stress is on companionship and shared enjoyment – a pattern which has long been characteristic of male friendships and which is seen by Argyle (1990) as reflecting the true nature of friendship. Although, at first glance, this may appear to be a trivial development, it is an important one, since pleasure has, up to now, not been a highly valued element in women's life styles or identity: 'The traditional female life course is normative, socialized and supported by the ideology of compulsory marriage and motherhood' (Allan, 1989: 117). The recognition of women's ability to enjoy themselves with other women obviously implicitly undermines a romantic-love ideology which stresses that true pleasure is only possible in the arms of a man. It challenges social controls over women's behaviour, especially their access to public areas; it undermines the equation of femininity with maternity, domesticity and the private area, and the culturally legitimated tendency for women to base their identities on such 'caring' relationships. The future development of such relationships will be interesting, and will provide a litmus test of the relative pressures of commerical interests and neo-patriarchal tendencies within Western culture.

The incorporation by women of a public dimension of any kind to their friendships can be seen as potentially constituting a risk in a society where such action can easily be seen as undermining the institutional basis of marriage. Simmel (1950) suggested that, at the time he wrote, the point of tension within friendship was that relating to intimacy. This point of tension does not seem to exist amongst women's friendships today. However, a different kind of discretion now appears to be a point of tension: namely, one relating to commitment and the realistic limits of it within a society where women have very limited access to power and resources.

This tension was recognized by Oliker (1989) in her respondents' unwillingness to support each other in considering divorce as an option in marital difficulties. It is also obvious in the limited nature of the help which is frequently provided by friends to women in violent marriages (see Chapter 4). Even amongst the feminists studied by Acker *et al.* (1981) who were restructuring their lives, and for whom female friends were 'sources of support, affection and resistance', it was noted that 'there were structural limitations to these friendships. Feminist insights alone could not remove the conditions in which they were grounded and there were real barriers to making feminist ideology reality' (Acker *et al.*,

1981: 105). Two types of development seem likely to occur in this situation. Firstly, an attempt is likely to be made by organizations to institutionalize the concept of friend within the private area. A harbinger of this appears in the concept of the 'secret pal' in Hochschild's work (1973: 48), that is, the person who is responsible within that community for ensuring that everyone's birthday is remembered. A similar idea lies behind the notion of the 'faith friend' which has emerged in many Roman Catholic parishes (i.e. someone who is not related to the child but who will befriend them and explain to them the personal significance of their own faith). In these developments, friendship is still located in the private area.

The second type of development represents an attempt to institutionalize certain aspects of caring for unrelated people, using the idiom of friendship, by collectivizing resources through community-development programmes. In Britain and the United States this has found expression in women's aid refuges, victim-support schemes, in Greenham Common, single-parent organizations, poverty action groups, etc., which provide a vehicle for the tangible expression of women's care for each other and their attempt to create a better world. They are an attempt, usually by women's organizations or community-development projects, to institutionalize friendship by moulding it into a role, with responsibilities and rights in the public arena. In Western society these organizations typically lack resources and/or influential contacts. Hence, although they may be successful in moving issues from the private to the public arena; in creating a political dimension to friendship, and in changing the identities of individual women, the extent to which they can directly transform power structures is arguably very limited indeed. Nevertheless, they (like sociable friendships) can play an important part in challenging the equation of femininity with marriage and domesticity. In addition, by creating structures and discourses which encourage women's participation in the public arena, they can play an important part in acting as a lever for wider cultural and structural change (the part played by such groups both in the election of Mary Robinson as President of Ireland and in highlighting gender as a reality in Irish society is an interesting example of this sort of process). The whole question of the effect of such developments on the shape and content of friendships between women has barely begun to be explored. Indeed, the continued concern with women's intimate friendships has tended to militate against the examination of these issues.

It is plausible, albeit controversial, to suggest that given current trends, that is, the allocation of emotional and practical caring to women, high levels of divorce (with one in two marriages in the United States, and one in three in the United Kingdom now breaking down), smaller family size, high levels of geographical mobility, increased levels of married women's participation in the labour force and a strong element of negotiation even in parent–child relationships, it is no longer realistic to see the family as the sole locus of tending (i.e. in the sense of providing practical care for its dependent members). In this context, given its cultural plasticity, personal friendships potentially constitute a viable caring alternative (Jerrome, 1990) and one which is peculiarly compatible with an ideological context which favours 'love' rather than 'obligation' as the basis for such care.

This view of friendship is acquiring currency, especially amongst those involved with the elderly. In this perspective the 'real' friend is someone who provides long-term care. However, although the willingness to provide assistance has been recognized by Wright (1978) in the concept of the utility function of friendship, nevertheless it is clear that the unilateral provision of assistance sits uneasily with the current Western concept of a friend (Allan, 1989). Indeed, the use of the kinship idiom to label such friendships both indicates a recognition of this dilemma and suggests a possible solution to it. The positive attitudes to this sort of 'distortion' of the friendship relationship contrast vividly with the popular antipathy to the use of friendship to reflect and/or reinforce class position (which is the topic taken up below).

An increasingly important type of friendship is likely to be one which provides validation of one's class position. Since friends tend to be similar in class, it can be difficult to detect this phenomenon. However, the instability of marriage in Western society and the increasing stress on assessing the wife's class position independent of her husband's seem likely to bring this issue to the fore. At present, it is most obvious in the situation where the wife's friends are drawn from her more upper-class husband's milieu; or indeed where the wife and husband have both been upwardly mobile, and have surrounded themselves with friends who reflect and reinforce their newly acquired class position. In egalitarian humanistic societies this pattern has popularly been deplored, although this may change with the prevalence of a new right-wing 'worldliness' which sees such patterns as 'inevitable' or 'natural'. At any rate, the existence of these friendships with what are popularly known as 'the right people' seems likely to be an increasingly common phenomenon.

This section has raised the issue of the cultural ambivalence surrounding friendship and has speculated about the forms of friendship which seem likely to arise within this context. Within a radical feminist perspective, where the 'personal is the political', friendships between women can be expected to transcend the private arena. Although this may happen to some extent, it is also possible that new institutions will emerge in which the traditional concept of friendship is transformed and which will in turn influence the shape of friendship as a personal relationship. Furthermore, the emergence of these various types of friendship and their differential degree of acceptance, as well as being interesting in their own right, tell us a great deal about the wider socio-cultural reality.

This section has identified some of the types of friendships which seem likely to become prevalent between women: including group-based sociable friendships, dyadic friendships which are purely mental constructs, nurturant relationships – whether on a collective or individual basis, those which in class terms can be seen as 'the right friends', as well as fictive kin and confidant friendships. It is clear that, as argued throughout the book, a continued preoccupation with the latter is no longer sufficient. Part of the peculiar attraction of friendship lies in its fluidity as a cultural form, and the insights that its shape provides into the cultural context within which it is located. Friendships between women are also, however, very much a social reality and must be seen in the context of a social structure which is class-based and which institutionalizes women's economic, political, legal and personal dependence on men. The implications of such a structure for the identification of key topics in the future are taken into account in the next section.

KEY ISSUES FOR THE FUTURE

It is becoming increasingly clear that a focus on friendship which sees its significance only in terms of its contribution to individual well-being is inadequate. Friendship is a social reality and, as such, it reflects and reinforces wider social realities. Within this general perspective, key issues, which seem likely to be important in contributing to our understanding of the changing face of friendship between women in Western society will be identified, Thus, this section will highlight firstly the way in which class and gender are likely to affect the shape of women's friendships; secondly, the extent to which women's friendships are liberating or constraining forces; thirdly, the role played by friendship in creating and/or maintaining moral discourses which uphold class, gender and marital ideologies; fourthly, the impact of the wider social network on the shape of friendship; and finally, the importance of an examination of the processes through which friendships are created and maintained.

Firstly then, in Western society, women's world is differentiated in many ways – by age, class, life stage and marital status. Hence friendships between women must be seen as affected by these factors. However, it has also been stressed that friendships must be seen as 'creating' social worlds through the 'moral discourses' (Gullestad, 1984) which their conversations create and maintain.

It was argued in Chapter 2 (and indeed it was shown in the later chapters) that although attempts have been made to look at the effects of marital status, life stage and class position on women's friendships, much of this work has simply treated these as categorical variables and has not explored the processes and pressures operating within these contexts to limit the development of friendships. Thus, amongst single women, ideological, structural and situational processes weaken same-sex friendships; for married women, situational factors such as economic dependency, caring responsibilities, lack of personal resources and limited public interaction venues continue to restrict their friendships. It is only, in fact, in old age that structural and situational factors can be seen as fostering the development of such relationships. Thus overall, friendships between women may be seen as operating within a structural and ideological context which upholds marriage and gender-differentiated definitions of femininity and child-care responsibilities (and provides support for individual identities only within that context). This type of perspective, which is rooted in a structural analysis of women's position, seems likely to become an increasingly important one.

The way in which class position has been used in understanding friendship relationships reveals the academic community's interest in particular kinds of questions. Thus although it has been widely recognized that friendships tend to be between those who are similar in class position, and although there has tended to be an acceptance of the notion that the number and/or form of friendship varies between middle- and working-class respondents, little attention has been paid to the process through which class-based patterns emerge.

For example, in the context of friendship between women, it is arguable that friendship ties – both individual and couple-based – may play an important part in consolidating a middle-class life style and supporting middle-class values and privileges. Allan (1989) has suggested that within the middle classes such friendships may be expressed in couple-based dinner parties – a form of sociability which neatly combines an affirmation of couple identity and acts, in Veblen's terms (1970), as a form of conspicuous consumption, and thus reflects and reinforces class position. Such activities seem likely to be particularly important amongst those who have been upwardly mobile and/or who are in what McRae (1986) has called 'cross-class couples'. Allan (1990) has argued very clearly that 'as well as being about identity, friendship is also revealing about status' (Allan, 1990: 8). It indicates, he argues, the nature of the social system operating, what the categories are within which people are accepted as social equals and how permeable the boundaries are. Thus friendship, like kinship and education, plays an important part in reproducing the class structure. This issue has barely begun to be explored either in its own right or within the context of the ongoing discussion on the nature of women's occupational status. It is certainly plausible that married women have a vested interest in creating and maintaining friendships which are compatible with their husband's occupational status if it is superior to their own. The implications of this in terms of understanding married women's friendships in an era of rising divorce rates have barely begun to be discussed. At a more micro level, it was argued (in Chapter 6) that friendships could be regarded as having a cultural form, albeit one which is, like kinship (Finch, 1989) contextualized and shaped through negotiation. The cultural ambiguity of the concept of 'friend', both within classes and between them, has done nothing to facilitate the development of work in this area (work which might look at the formation and maintenance of culturally specific friendship rules within various types of friendship).

Any attempt to understand women's friendships must also arguably be rooted in the recognition that gender is a social category and that 'It [the evidence] reveals that the two sexes are typically in a relation of subordination and domination, and that women are disadvantaged in most societies' (Cooper, 1989: 14). This disadvantage is multifaceted: being reflected in their under-representation in positions of legal, political or economic power; in their frequently 'borrowed' and ambiguous class positions (i.e. typically being at least partially financially dependent on their husband); and in their over-representation amongst the adult poor in

Western society (partly because of their lower wage levels and partly because of their responsibilities for children; McLanahan *et al.*, 1989).

Secondly, one of the most important questions which needs to be addressed is the extent to which women's friendships are liberating forces or alternatively 'entrench them [i.e. women] further in deference, powerlessness and in many cases, personal misery' (Whitehead, 1976: 198). These friendships are for the most part located in the private area. The level of resources (time, money, etc.) which can be allocated to them is limited, and power, influence or economic support are rarely acquired directly or indirectly through them. It is argued that, in so far as they remain exclusively within the private area, they are unlikely to initiate societal change. Indeed, as Ringelheim (1985) noted, such relations, in so far as they are produced by a situation of oppression, cannot be liberating (an observation which seems particularly relevant in the case of intimate or confidant relationships). They can, however, arguably offer some element of identity validation. Oliker has, indeed, rather optimistically argued that: 'when friends keep a vision of mutualistic companionate love alive (in ideals and by example), they undermine male domestic authority – even when they cannot radically erode men's power' (Oliker, 1989: 164).

As outlined in the previous section, sociable relationships between women, preferably at a group level, seem to have the potential, in the long run, for bringing about social and cultural change. Such relationships, of course, typically require resources, although it is interesting to note that many women effectively minimize their need for these by restricting activities to those which require little expenditure of monetary resources (such as visiting, talking or walking). Indeed, the question of the availability of the public house or sports centre as a locus for female interaction only becomes an issue as women's disposable income increases.

Furthermore, it is possible that as women's structural resources (e.g. money, power, etc.) increase, their friendships may acquire elements of what Boissevain (1969) called 'patronage' (the latter being used to refer to a situation where patrons used their own resources to assist or protect a client). Maher (1976) noted that such relationships existed amongst the women she studied in Morocco. As previously indicated, an attempt is being made through women's business, political and academic networks to create ties between women within each of these areas, although there has been little or no research in this area.

It is arguable that such relationships may give power to individual women and/or increase the life chances of others within the context of the society in which they live. There is little support, however, for the hope that they will bring about an immediate radical restructuring of opportunities for women. Evetts' (1988) study of primary teachers is, however, clearly suggestive as regards the way in which even very limited change (i.e. female head teacher) can play an important part in facilitating further developments such as the continuance of other married women's participation in the labour force. Her conclusion contrasts vividly with Ryan's (1979) pessimism (based on her work dealing with the emergence of the Moral Reform Society in the United States in the nineteenth century) concerning the usefulness of female friendships as sources of structural change. The question of whether friendships between women are liberating or constraining forces thus needs to be located in the context of a structural analysis of women's position in society (especially their financial dependence on men), of ideologies about women's roles and considerations related to the nature of friendship and its location within the public/private arena.

Thirdly, as previously mentioned, work in the area of friendship has focused more on the effects of structural realities on friendship than on the way in which friendship creates and/or maintains them. It is only beginning to look at the way in which friendship creates and/or maintains moral discourses which uphold marital and gender-role ideologies (Oliker, 1989; Gullestad, 1984). This latter perspective is perfectly compatible with Gluckman's views (1963) on the nature and importance of gossip, and with Berger and Kellner's (1964), McCall's (1988) and Finch's (1989) work on the ways in which conversation creates and maintains a social world. It is ironical that this very basic phenomenon should have been largely ignored:

> What tends to be missing in the study of person relationships is the notion that relationships cannot go forward – cannot even exist – without a process of reality construction, and that reality construction is accomplished not simply attributionally, but interactively.
>
> (Blumstein and Kollock, 1988: 2)

The actual discourses which are created in various friendship relationships need to be explored. Thus, it is worth noting that although attention is increasingly being paid to the nature and importance of talk in friendships (Duck, 1990a, b; Leatham and Duck, 1990) there has been little attempt to see this as part of the construction of a discourse which reflects women's position in society.

Thus, for example, one might speculate that some of the most crucial issues discussed in friendships between elderly women are likely to be related to dependency (e.g. whether or not an elderly woman should ask her daughter to help her with her shopping and so risk being seen as a burden). Amongst married women, issues related to sexual fidelity and maternal responsibility are likely to be particularly important (e.g. discourses related to whether a wife is 'leading a man on' or 'asking for trouble', or whether an employed mothers' children are suffering because of the number of paid hours of work she does). Amongst young single women one might speculate that much of the conversation is likely to revolve around the interpretation of signals from boyfriends or authority figures ('Is he really interested in me – or could he just have been bored or wanting to make his old girl friend jealous?', etc.). Many of these themes appear to draw directly or indirectly on a feminine discourse, although some are also likely to occur within a class-related discourse (e.g. whether a couple are 'getting ideas above their station' because they are trying to join an exclusive golf club or sailing club). To date, empirical work at this level is very rare indeed, although it would arguably help us to understand the way in which friendship creates and maintains a social world.

Fourthly, at a different level, one might suggest that there has been less cross-fertilization than one might perhaps expect between the social network tradition and that tradition dealing with relationships such as friendship (Morgan, 1990). Thus relatively little attention has been paid to the extent to which friendships in dense networks are particularly likely to develop 'shared understandings' or 'shared knowledge structures' (Morgan, 1986). Given their high levels of visibility, these networks facilitate the imposition of informal social controls over behaviours, standards and identity itself. Such networks are thus arguably a comparatively conservative force within the society, limiting, as they do, access to resources across networks (and hence also arguably across social classes). It is also possible that, in such networks, friendships may become empty and ritualistic in so far as the complete termination of the relationship is impossible. Different types of 'accounts' (Harvey *et al.*, 1990) might also occur in close-knit, as opposed to loose-knit, networks. To date, work has not been done on this area either, although it potentially offers a fascinating insight into the ways in which personal-relational integrity and network cohesiveness may be maintained or sacrificed, and the conditions associated with both situations. This work can be seen as a logical extension of work dealing with the development of shared accounts of the endings of dyadic romantic relationships: a topic which has begun to be explored (Duck, 1982; McCall, 1982).

Finally friendships, although they are products, are also social processes. It is clear that relatively little attention has been paid to these processes. Thus some work has been done on the process of dissolution (Duck, 1982; Wiseman, 1986, 1990), although this needs to be developed. Less has been done either on the management of conflict or, indeed, on the selection and retention of unhelpful, invalidating or purely destructive friendships. At the opposite extreme, little attention has been paid (with such notable exceptions as Jerrome, 1984) to the processes involved in the creation and maintenance of group friendships, a phenomenon which, as was noted in the last section, is seen as particularly important.

The idea that friendships are equal relationships has also, arguably, been accepted rather too easily. Little attention has been paid to the extent to which relational attributes such as class background may be 'traded' for relational 'work' in particular types of friendship. Furthermore, as Blumstein and Kollock (1988) have recognized, issues related to the nature and limits of the process of creating equality within friendships have not been dealt with (e.g. 'creating' similarity in friendships by ignoring differences in marital status, age or education). Indeed, the assumption that equality exists in these relationships has pre-empted any examination of relational power strategies, including friends differential willingness to 'go along with' arrangements as regards activities etc. Work such as this sets the issue of relational power within a context which is more sensitive and insightful than that which typically characterizes theories of equity and equality. Work on these sorts of issues has begun in the area of marriage (O'Connor, 1991c), but the definition of friendship as an equal relationship has inhibited even the posing of the question in that area.

Thus, in the future, it is argued that it will clearly not be sufficient simply to identify factors (such as class, marital status and life stage) which are associated with the existence of particular types of friendship. Rather, it will be necessary to look at the ways in which such structural realities shape friendships, and are shaped by them. In this context, one of the most important questions which arises is the extent to which friendships between women bring about change in the social structure – or, alternatively, simply perpetuate it. This seems likely to be one of the central questions of the 1990s, in the same way that the effect of friendship on women's individual well-being underpinned much of the work in the 1980s. Both questions are, of course, far too simplistic and need to be reformulated within the context of a clarification of types of friendship, the wider cultural context and the structural position of women at that point in time. This work will also need to be rooted in an understanding of friendships as social processes. This poses methodological challenges, since the nature of survey methodology is not conducive to this type of work. Yet it is increasingly clear that an understanding of friendship must deal with issues related to the resolution of conflict, management of inequality and the creation and maintenance of relationships. These are in many ways the most difficult aspects to investigate. However, the fluidity of the friendship relationship makes it imperative that an attempt be made to do so.

CONCLUSION

This chapter has moved beyond a review of the considerable body of work which has been done on friendship during the 1970s and 1980s, to a speculative discussion of the future shape of friendship and the sorts of issues which arguably need to preoccupy future work.

It is obvious from the range of questions raised in this chapter that a great deal is not known about friendships between women. However, it is equally clear from the preceding chapters that much has been learned about the topic over the past twenty years. As outlined in Chapter 2, we can begin to identify the elements which might be included in a theoretical understanding of friendship. We can see how the questions that have been asked about friendship in the past have come from a perspective which has implicitly endorsed the primary importance of male–female relationships and seen friendship as of marginal importance – except, perhaps, for the elderly. Those who have studied married women have been concerned with the existence of confidants (who would arguably enable married women to cope with the difficulties and deprivations of their situations). Amongst those studying single women, the work has been located within a context which has accepted the inevitability – indeed, normality – of the lack of importance attached to such relationships (as compared with heterosexual relationships). Only amongst the elderly has there been a clear recognition of the potential complexity and centrality of these relationships in women's lives: lives which are seen as relatively unaffected by the dominant institutions of heterosexuality and economic production.

Yet, despite its starting point, this work has clearly demonstrated the general importance of such relationships. It has shown how, through such friendships, identities and social realities are constructed. It has recognized the reality of such relationships and has begun to look at its implications in terms both of the work required in creating and maintaining them and of the levels of conflict, disappointment and overload that they can generate.

Work on friendship between women is important in understanding one aspect of women's lives – lives which, for better or worse, remain relentlessly rooted in their attachments to others. The scientific community has been slow to become involved in the study of such relationships. Like much popular opinion, it has found it more comfortable to drift between idealizing and trivializing them. (Indeed, a similar fate, has until very recently, befallen the mother–child relationship.)

Yet friendship can provide important insights into the society in which we live. It is the relationship *par excellence* of individuation. It is a personal relationship which assumes a variety of cultural forms within particular social contexts. To attempt to understand friendships between women without recognizing this is to impose an attractive, albeit spurious, simplicity on the topic; it is also to ignore the opportunity for multidisciplinary work. Friendship between women is an area which has been strikingly neglected by women's studies and yet it lies at the heart of what Cheal (1987: 155) has called 'a female world of love and ritual'.

Indeed, paradoxically, work on friendship between women can be said to lie at the heart of our understanding of key issues in women's lives. Issues related to power and love, equality and dependency are all enmeshed within friendship: issues which are arguably at the centre of any understanding of women in Western society. Friendship is a personal relationship, but its importance transcends the purely personal: this has only begun to be appreciated.

Bibliography

This bibliography contains all the works cited in the text and, in addition, important source works to be used for background reading.

Abu-Lughod, L. (1985) 'A community of secrets: The separate world of Bedouin women', *Signs: Journal of Women in Culture and Society*, 10, 4: 637–57.

Acker, J. (1980) 'Women and stratification: A review of recent literature', *Contemporary Sociology*, 9, 1: 25–34.

Acker, J. (1988) 'Class gender and the relations of distribution', *Signs: Journal of Women in Culture and Society*, 13: 473–97.

Acker, J., K. Barry and J. Esseveld, (1981) 'Feminism, female friends, and the reconstruction of intimacy', in H.Z. Lopata and D. Maines (eds) *Research in the Interweave of Social Roles: Friendship*: vol. 2, Greenwich, CT: JAI Press.

Acock, A.C. and J.S. Hurlbert (1990) 'Social network analysis: A structural perspective for family studies', *Journal of Social and Personal Relationships*, 7: 245–64.

Adams, B.N. (1968) *Kinship in an Urban Setting*, Chicago, IL: Markham.

Adams, M. (1976) *Single Blessedness*, New York: Basic Books.

Adams, R.G. (1985) 'People would talk: Normative barriers to cross-sex friendships for elderly women', *The Gerontologist*, 25: 605–11.

Adams, R.G. (1986) 'Emotional closeness and physical distance between friends: Implications for elderly women living in age-segregated and age-integrated settings', *International Journal of Aging and Human Development*, 22, 1: 55–76.

Adams, R.G. (1987) 'Patterns of network change: A longitudinal study of friendships of elderly women', *The Gerontologist*, 27, 2: 222–7.

Adams, R.G. and R. Blieszner (eds) (1989) *Older Adult Friendship*, Newbury Park, CA and London: Sage.

Adler Lomnitz, L. (1988) 'Informal exchange networks in formal systems: A theoretical model', *American Anthropologist*, 90: 42–55.

Ainsworth, M.D.S., M.C. Blehar, E. Waters, and S. Wall, (1978) *Patterns of Attachment: A psychological study of the strange situation*, Hillsdale, NJ: LEA.

Alcoff, L. (1988) 'Cultural feminism versus post-structuralism: The identity crisis in feminist theory', *Signs: Journal of Women in Culture and Society*, 13, 3: 405–36.

Allan, G. (1977a) 'Class variation in friendship patterns', *British Journal of Sociology*, 28: 389–93.

Allan, G. (1977b) 'Sibling solidarity', *Journal of Marriage and the Family*, February: 177–84.

Allan, G. (1979) *A Sociology of Friendship and Kinship*, London: George, Allen and Unwin.

Allan, G. (1985) *Family Life: Domestic roles and social organization*, Oxford: Blackwell.

Allan, G. (1986) 'Friendships and care for elderly people', *Ageing and Society*, 6: 1–12.

Allan, G. (1989) *Friendship: Developing a sociological perspective*, Hemel Hempstead: Harvester Wheatsheaf.

Allan, G. (1990) 'British studies in the sociology of friendship: A view of the past decade', paper given at the Fifth International Conference on Personal Relationships, July, Oxford, England.

Allan, G. and R.G. Adams (1989) 'Aging and the structure of friendship', in Adams and Blieszner (eds), *Older Adult Friendship*, Newbury Park, CA, and London: Sage.

Allen, K.R. (1989) *Single Women/Family Ties*, Newbury Park, CA, and London: Sage.

Altman, I. and D. Taylor (1973) *Social Penetration*, New York: Holt, Rinehart and Winston.

Andrews, B. and G.W. Brown (1988) 'Marital violence in the community: A biographical approach', *British Journal of Psychology*, 153: 305–12.

Antonucci, T.C. (1985) 'Personal characteristics, social networks and social behaviour', in R.H. Binstock and E. Shanas (eds) *Handbook of Aging and the Social Sciences*, 2nd edn, New York: Van Nostrand Reinhold.

Argyle, M. (1987) *The Psychology of Happiness*, London and New York: Methuen.

Argyle, M. (1990) 'An exploration of the effects of different relationships on mental health and happiness', unpublished paper presented at the Fifth International Conference on Personal Relationships, July, Oxford, England.

Argyle, M. and A. Furnham (1982) 'The ecology of relationships: Choice of situation as a function of relationship', *British Journal of Personality and Social Psychology*, 21: 259–62.

Argyle, M. and M. Henderson (1984) 'The rules of friendship', *Journal of Social and Personal Relationships*, 1: 211–37.

Argyle, M. and M. Henderson (1985a) 'The rules of relationship', in S. Duck and D. Perlman (eds), *Understanding Personal Relationships: An interdisciplinary approach*, London: Sage.

Argyle, M. and M. Henderson (1985b) *The Anatomy of Relationships*, London: Heinemann.

Aries, E.J. and F.L. Johnson, (1983) 'Close friendship in adulthood: conversational content between same-sex friends', *Sex Roles*, 9: 1183–96.

Arling, G. (1976) 'The elderly widow and her family, neighbours and friends', *Journal of Marriage and the Family*, 38: 757–68.

Aughingen, E.A. (1990) 'Friendship and sibling dyads in everyday life: A study with the double diary method', paper presented at the Fifth International Conference on Personal Relationships, July, Oxford, England.

Aukett, R., J. Ritchie and K. Mill (1988) 'Gender differences in friendship patterns', *Sex Roles*, 19, 1/2: 57–66.

Ayres, J. (1983) 'Strategies to maintain relationships: Their identification and perceived usage', *Communication Quarterly*, 31: 62–7.

Babchuk, N. and A.P. Bates (1963) 'The primary relations of middle-class couples: A study in male dominance', *American Sociological Review*, 21: 13–18.

Baker Miller, J. (1986) *Towards a New Psychology of Women*, 2nd edn, London: Penguin.

Baker, W. and R. Hertz (1981) 'Communal diffusion of friendship: the structure of intimate relations in an Israeli kibbutz', in H.Z. Lopata and D. Maines (eds) *Research in the Interweave of Social Roles: Friendship*, vol. 2, Greenwich, CT: JAI Press.

Bankoff, E.A. (1981) 'Effects of friendship support on the psychological well-being of widows', in H.Z. Lopata and D. Maines (eds), *Research in the Interweave of Social Roles: Friendship*, vol. 2, Greenwich, CT: JAI Press.

Barnhart, E. (1975) 'Friends and lovers in a lesbian counterculture', in N. Glazer-Malbin (ed.) *Old Family/New Family*, New York and London: Van Nostrand.

Bates, A.P. and W. Babchuk (1961) 'The primary group: A re-appraisal', *Sociological Quarterly*, 11: 181–91.

Baxter, L.A. (1985) 'Accomplishing relationship disengagement', in S. Duck and D. Perlman (eds), *Understanding Personal Relationships: An Interdisciplinary Approach*, London: Sage.

Baxter, L.A. (1987) 'Symbols of relationship identity in relationship cultures', *Journal of Social and Personal Relationships*, 4: 261–80.

Baxter, L.A. (1988) 'A dialectical perspective on communication strategies in relationship development', in S.W. Duck (ed.), *A Handbook of Personal Relationships*, Chicester: Wiley.

Baxter, L.A. (1990) 'Dialectical contradictions in relationship development', *Journal of Social and Personal Relationships*, 7: 69–89.

Baxter, L.A. and K. Dindia (1990) 'Marital partners' perceptions of marital maintenance strategies', *Journal of Social and Personal Relationships*, 7, 2: 187–208.

Baxter, L.A. and W.W. Wilmot (1985) 'Taboo topics in close relationships', *Journal of Social and Personal Relationships*, 2: 253–69.

Beauvoir, S. de (1972) *The Second Sex*, trans. and ed. by H.M. Parshley, Harmondsworth: Penguin (1st publ. 1949).

Beechey, V. (1986) 'Women and employment in contemporary Britain', in V. Beechey and E. Whitelegg (eds), *Women in Britain Today*, Milton Keynes: Open University Press.

Bell, C. (1968) 'Mobility and the middle class extended family', *Sociology*, 2: 173–84.

Bell, R.R. (1981a) 'Friendships of women and of men', *Psychology of Women Quarterly*, 5: 402–34.

Bell, R.R. (1981b) *Worlds of Friendship*, London: Sage.

Bennett, D. (1979) 'The cultural variable in friendship and group formation', *Economic and Social Review*, 10, 2: 123–45.

Berardo, D.H. (1982) 'Divorce and remarriage at middle age and beyond', *Annals AAPSS*, 464, November: 132–9.

Berg, J.H. and M.S. Clark (1986) 'Differences in social exchange between intimate and other relationships: gradually evolving or quickly apparent', in V.J. Derlega and B.A. Winstead (eds), *Friendship and Social Interaction*, New York: Springer.

Berger, P. and H. Kellner (1964) 'Marriage and the construction of reality', *Diogenes*, 46: 1–24.

Berhide, C.W. (1984) 'Women's work in the home: Seems like old times', *Marriage and Family Living*, 46: 37–55.

Bernard, J. (1976) 'Homosociality and female depression', *Journal of Social Issues*, 32, 4: 213–35.

Bernard, J. (1981) *The Female World*, New York: Free Press.

Bernard, J. (1982) *The Future of Marriage*, 2nd edn, New Haven, CT: Yale University Press.

Bernard, J. (1987) *The Female World from a Global Perspective*, Bloomington and Indianapolis: Indiana University Press.

Bettelheim, B. (1971) *Children of the Dream*, St Albans: Paladin.

Billings, A.G., R.G. Cronkite and R.H. Moos (1983) 'Social-environmental factors in unipolar depression: Comparisons of depressed patients and non-depressed controls', *Journal of Abnormal Psychology*, 92, 119–33.

Binns, D. and G. Mars (1984) 'Family, community and unemployment: A study in change', *Sociological Review*, 32: 662–95.

Bland, L., C. Brunsden, D. Hobson and J. Winship (1978) 'Women inside and outside the relations of production', in Women's Studies Group, CCCS (eds), *Women Take Issue*, London: Hutchinson.

Blau, P.M. (1964) *Exchange and Power in Social Life*, New York: Wiley.

Blau, Z.S. (1973) *Old Age in a Changing Society*, New York: New Viewpoints.

Blieszner, R. (1988) 'Individual development and intimate relationships in middle and late adulthood', in R.M. Milardo (ed.), *Families and Social Networks*, Beverley Hills, CA: Sage.

Blieszner, R. (1989) 'Developmental processes of friendship', in R.G. Adams and R. Blieszner (eds), *Older Adult Friendship*, Newbury Park, CA, and London: Sage.

Blieszner, R. (1990) 'Friendship processes in adulthood: A decade review', unpublished paper presented at the Fifth International Conference on Personal Relationships, July, Oxford. England.

Blumstein, P. (1990) 'The production of selves in personal relationships', in J.A. Howard and P. Callero (eds.), *The Self–Society Interface: Cognition, emotion and action*, Cambridge: Cambridge University Press.

Blumstein, P. and P. Kollock (1988) 'A social constructionist approach to personal relationships', paper read at the Fourth International Conference on Personal Relationships, Vancouver, Canada.

Boissevain, J.K. (1969) 'Patrons as Brokers', *Sociologische Gids*, Nov./Dec.: 379–86.

Boissevain, J. (1974) *Friends of Friends: Networks, manipulators and coalitions*, Oxford: Blackwell.

Bonney, N. (1988) 'Gender, household and class', *British Journal of Sociology*, 34: 28–46.

Booth, A. (1972) 'Sex and social participation', *American Sociological Review*, 37: 183–92.

Bott, E, (1957, 1971) *Family and Social Network*, orginal and revised edn, London: Tavistock.

Boulton, M.G. (1983) *On Being a Mother*, London: Tavistock.

Bowlby, J. (1971) *Attachment*, Harmondsworth: Pelican.

Bowlby, J. (1975) *Separation*, Harmondsworth: Pelican.

Bowlby, J. (1979) *The Making and Breaking of Affectional Bonds*, London: Tavistock.

Bowlby, J. (1980) *Loss, Sadness and Depression*, London: Hogarth Press.

Bradburn, N. (1969) *The Structure of Psychological Well-Being*, Chicago, IL: Aldine Press.

Bradford Brown, B. (1981) 'A life span approach to friendship: Age related dimensions of an ageless relationship', in H.Z. Lopata and D. Maines (eds) *Research in the Interweave of Social Roles: Friendship*, vol. 2, Greenwich, CT: JAI Press.

Brain, R. (1977) *Friends and Lovers*, St Albans: Paladin.

Brand, S. and B.J. Hirsch (1990) 'The contribution of social networks, work shift schedules, and the family life cycle to women's well being', in S. Duck with R.C. Silver (eds), *Personal Relationships and Social Support*, London: Sage.

Brannen, J. and J. Collard (1982) *Marriages in Trouble: The process of seeking help*, London: Tavistock.

Brannen, J. and P. Moss, (1988) *New Mothers at Work*, London: Unwin Hyman.

Brim, J.A. (1974) 'Social network correlates of avowed happiness', *The Journal of Nervous and Mental Disease*, 158: 432–8.

Brittan, A. (1977) *The Privatized World*, London: Routledge and Kegan Paul.

Britten, N. and A. Heath (1983) 'Women, men and social class', in E. Gamarnikow, D.H.J. Morgan, J. Purvis and D.E. Taylorson (eds), *Gender, Class and Work*, London: Heinemann.

Broderick, C.B. (1988) 'Healing members and relationships in the intimate network', in R. Milardo (ed.), *Families and Social Networks*, Beverley Hills, CA: Sage.

Brown, G.W. (1987) 'Social factors and the development and course of depressive disorders in women', *British Journal of Social Work*, 17: 615–34.

Brown, G.W., B. Andrews, T. Harris, Z. Adler and L. Bridge, (1986) 'Social support, self esteem and depression', *Psychological Medicine*, 16: 813–31.

Brown, G.W., S. Davidson, T. Harris, U. Maclean, S. Pollock and R. Prudo (1977) 'Psychiatric disorder in London and North Uist', *Social Science and Medicine*, 11: 366–77.

Brown, G.W. and T. Harris (1978a) *Social Origins of Depression*, London: Tavistock.

Brown, G.W. and T. Harris (1978b) 'Social origins of depression: a reply', *Psychological Medicine*, 8: 577–88.

Bujra, J.M. (1978) 'Female solidarity and the sexual division of labour', in P. Caplan and J.M. Burja (eds), *Women United, Women Divided*, London: Tavistock.

Bulmer, M. (1985) 'The rejuvenation of community studies? Neighbours, networks and policy', *The Sociological Review*, 33: 430–48.

Bulmer, M. (1987) *The Social Basis of Community Care*, London: Allen and Unwin.

Bunch, C. (1981) 'Not for lesbians only', in C. Bunch, J. Flax, A. Freeman, N. Hortstock and M.H. Manther (eds), *Building Feminist Theory*, New York: Longman.

Burnett, R., P. McChee and D. Clarke (eds) (1987) *Accounting for Relationships*, London: Methuen.

Buunk, B.P. and B. Van Driel (1989) *Variant Lifestyles and Relationships*, Newbury Park, CA, and London: Sage.

Caldwell, M.A. and L.A. Peplau (1982) 'Sex differences in same-sex friendship', *Sex Roles*, 8: 721–32.

Camerer, C. (1988) 'Gifts as economic signals and social symbols', *American Journal of Sociology*, 94, Supplement: 180–214.

Campbell, J.D. and A. Tesser (1985) 'Self-evaluation maintenance processes in relationships' in S. Duck and D. Perlman (eds), *Understanding Personal Relationships: An Interdisciplinary Approach*, London: Sage.

Cancian, F.M. (1986) 'The feminization of love', *Signs: Journal of Women in Culture and Society*, 4: 692–709.

Candy, S.G., L.E. Troll and S.G. Levy (1981) 'A developmental exploration of friendship functions in women', *Psychology of Women Quarterly*, 5, 3: 456–71.

Cantor, M. (1979) 'Neighbours and friends: An overlooked resource in the informal support system', *Research on Aging*, 1, 4: 434–63.

Caplan, P. and J.M. Bujra (eds) (1978) *Women United, Women Divided*, London: Tavistock.

Caplow, T. (1982) 'Christmas gifts and kin networks', *American Sociological Review*, 47: 383–92.

Case, C. (1988) 'Paddock rites: Integrative ritual in the racing community', *Sociological Inquiry*, 58, 3: 279–90.

Cauce, A.M. (1986) 'Social networks and social competence: Exploring the effects of early adolescent friendships', *American Journal of Community Psychology*, 14, 6: 607–28.

Cavendish, R. (1982) *Women on the Line*, London: Routledge and Kegan Paul.

Cheal, D.J. (1986) 'The social dimensions of gift behaviour', *Journal of Social and Personal Relationships*, 3: 423–39.

Cheal, D.J. (1987) 'Showing them you love them: Gift giving and the dialectic of intimacy', *The Sociological Review*, 35, 1: 150–70.

Chodorow, N. (1978) *The Reproduction of Mothering*, Berkeley: University of California Press.

Clancy, P. (1991) 'Irish nuptiality and fertility patterns in transition', in G. Kiely and V. Richardson (eds), *Family Policy: European perspectives*, Dublin: Family Studies Centre, University College, Dublin.

Cline Welch, R.J. (1989) 'The politics of intimacy: Costs and benefits determining disclosure intimacy in male–female dyads', *Journal of Social and Personal Relationships*, 6: 5–20.

Cobb, S. and J. Jones-Cobb (1984) 'Social support, support groups and marital relationships', in S. Duck (ed.), *Personal Relationships*, vol 5, London: Academic Press.

Cohen, C.I. and H. Rajkowski (1982) 'What's in a friend? Substantive and theoretical issues', *The Gerontologist*, 22, 3: 261–6.

Cohen, G. (1978) 'Women's solidarity and the preservation of privilege', in P. Caplan and J. Bujra (eds), *Women United, Women Divided*, London: Tavistock.

Colletta, N.D. (1979) 'Support systems after divorce: Incidence and impact', *Journal of Marriage and the Family*, 41: 837–46.

Contarello, A. and C. Volpato (1991) 'Images of friendship: Literary depictions through the ages', *Journal of Social and Personal Relationships*, 8: 49–75.

Cooper, A. (1989) 'Theorising gender', in I. Reid and E. Stratta (eds), *Sex Differences in Britain*, 2nd edn, Aldershot and Vermont: Gower.

Copperstock, R. (1978) 'Sex differences in psychotropic drug use', *Social Science and Medicine*, 12, 3b: 179–86.

Cornwell, J. (1984) *Hard Earned Lives: Accounts of Health and Illness from East London*, London: Tavistock.

Costanza, R. S., V.J. Derlega and B.A. Winstead (1988) 'Positive and negative forms of social support: Effects of conversational topics on coping with stress among same-sex friends', *Journal of Experimental Social Psychology*, 24: 182–93.

Coverman, S. (1989) 'Women's work is never done: The division of domestic labour', in J. Freeman (ed.), *Women: A feminist perspective*, 4th edn Mountain View, CA: Mayfield.

Coverman, S. and J.F. Shelley (1986) 'Changes in men's housework and child care time, 1965–1975', *Journal of Marriage and the Family*, 48: 413–22.

Coyle, A. (1984) *Redundant Women*, London: The Woman's Press.

Cozby, J.C. (1973) 'Self disclosure: a literature review', *Psychological Bulletin*, 79: 73–91.

Craven, P. and B. Wellman (1973) 'The network city', *Sociological Inquiry*, 43: 57–88.

Crawford, M. (1977) 'What is a friend?', *New Society*, 20 October: 116–17.

Crohan, S.E. and T. Antonucci (1989) 'Friends as a source of support in old age', in R.G. Adams and R. Blieszner (eds), *Older Adult Friendship*, Newbury Park, CA, and London: Sage.

Crompton, R. and M. Mann (eds) (1986) *Gender Stratification*, Cambridge: Polity Press, in association with B. Blackwell.

Cumming, E. and W. Henry (1961) *Growing Old*, New York: Basic Books.

Cutrona, C.E. (1984) 'Social support in transition to parenthood', *Journal of Abnormal Psychology*, 93: 378–90.

Daly, M. (1978) *Gyn/Ecology*, Boston, MA: Beacon Press.

Davidson, S. and T. Packard (1981) 'The therapeutic value of friendship between women', *Psychology of Women Quarterly*, 5, 3: 495–509.

Davis, K.E. and M. Todd (1985) 'Assessing friendship: Prototypes, paradigm cases and relationship description', in S.W. Duck and D. Perlman (eds), *Understanding Personal Relationships: An interdisciplinary approach*, London: Sage.

Deem, R. (1982) 'Women, leisure and inequality', *Leisure Studies*, 1: 29–46.

Deem, R. (1986) *All Work and No Play? The sociology of women and leisure*, Milton Keynes: Open University Press.

Delamont, S. (1980) *The Sociology of Women: An introduction*, London: Allen and Unwin.

Delphy, C. (1984) *Close to Home: a materialist analysis of Women's Oppression*, Trans. and ed. by D. Leonard, London: Hutchinson.

Derlega, V.J. and B.A. Winstead (eds.) (1986) *Friendship and Social Interaction*, New York: Springer.

Derlega, V.J., B.A. Winstead, P.T.P. Wang and S. Hunter (1985) 'Gender effects in an initial encounter: A case where men exceed women in disclosure', *Journal of Social and Personal Relationships*, 2: 25–44.

Dhavernas, M.J. (1987) 'Hating masculinity not men', in C. Ducken (ed.), *French Connections*, London: Hutchinson.

Dickens, W.J. and D. Perlman (1981) 'Friendship over the life cycle', in S. Duck and R. Gilmour (eds), *Personal Relationships*, vol. 2, London: Academic Press.

Dillard, J.P. and K.I. Miller (1988) 'Intimate-Relationships in a task environment', in S.W. Duck (ed.), *Handbook of Personal Relationships*, Chicester: Wiley.

Dindia, K. and L. Baxter (1987) 'Strategies for maintaining and repairing marital relationships', *Journal of Social and Personal Relationships*, 4: 143–58.

Dixey, R. and M. Talbot (1982) *Women, Leisure and Bingo*, Leeds: Trinity and All Saints College.

Dobash, R.E. and R. Dobash (1980) *Violence Against Wives: A case against the patriarchy*, London: Open Books.

Dono, J.E., C.M. Falbe, B.L. Kail, E. Litwak, R.H. Sherman and D. Siegel (1979) 'Primary groups in old age: Structure and function', *Research on Aging*, 1, 2: 403–33.

Douglas, W. (1987) 'Affinity testing in initial interaction', *Journal of Social and Personal Relationships*, 4: 3–16.

Douvan, E. and J. Adelson (1966) *The Adolescent Experience*, London: Wiley.

Duck, S. (ed.) (1977) *Theory and Practice in Interpersonal Attraction*, London: Academic.

Duck, S. (1981) 'Towards a research map for the study of relationship breakdown', in S. Duck and R. Gilmour (eds) *Personal Relationships*, vol. 3, New York: Academic Press.

Duck, S. (1982) 'A topography of relationship disengagement and dissolution', in S.W. Duck (ed.), *Personal Relationships*, vol. 4: *Dissolving Personal Relationships*, London: Academic Press.

Duck, S. (1983) *Friends for Life*, Hemel Hempstead: Harvester Wheatsheaf.

Duck, S. (1984) 'A perspective on the repair of personal relationships: Repairs of what, when?', in S. Duck (ed.), *Personal Relationships*, vol. 5: *Repairing Personal Relationships*, London: Academic Press.

Duck, S. (1986) *Human Relationships*, London: Sage.

Duck, S. (1988) *Relating to Others*, Milton Keynes: Open University Press.

Duck, S. (1990a) 'Diaries and logs', in B.M. Montgomery and S.W. Duck (eds), *Studying Social Interaction*, New York: Guildford.

Duck, S. (1990b) 'Relationships as unfinished business: Out of the frying pan and into the 1990s', *Journal of Social and Personal Relationships*, 7: 5–29.

Duck, S., D.F. Hay, S.E. Hobfoll, W. Ickes and B.M. Montgomery (eds) (1988) *A Handbook of Personal Relationships*, Chicester: Wiley.

Duck, S. and D. Miell (1986) 'Charting the development of personal relationships', in R. Gilmour and S. Duck (eds), *The Emerging Field of Personal Relationships*, Hillsdale, NJ, and London: Laurence Erlbaum.

Duck, S. and D. Perlman (1985) 'The thousand islands of personal relationships: A prescriptive analysis for future explorations', in S. Duck and D. Perlman (eds.), *Understanding Personal Relationships*, London: Sage.

Duck, S. and D. Perlman (eds) (1985) *Understanding Personal Relationships*, London: Sage.

Duck, S. and K. Pond (1989) 'Friends, Romans, countrymen, lend me your retrospections', in C. Hendrick (ed.), *Close Relationships*, London and CA: Sage.

Duck, S., D.J. Rutt, M. Hoy Hurst and H. Strejc (1991) 'Some evident truths about conversation in everyday relationships: all communications are not created equal', *Human Communication Research*, 18: 228–67.

Duck, S. and H.K.A. Sants (1983) 'On the origin of the specious: Are personal relationships really interpersonal states?', *Journal of Social and Clinical Psychology*, 1: 27–41.

Duck, S. with R.C. Silver (eds) (1990) *Personal Relationships and Social Support*, London: Sage.

Ducken, C. (ed. and trans.) (1987) *French Connections: Voices from the Women's Movement in France*, London: Hutchinson.

Dworkin, A. (1983) *Right-Wing Women: The politics of domesticated females*, London: The Women's Press.

Dykstra, P.A. (1990) 'Contributions of friends and family to older adult well-being', unpublished paper, presented at the Fifth International Conference in Personal Relationships, July, Oxford, England.

Eckenrode, J. (1983) 'The mobilization of social supports: Some individual constraints', *American Journal of Community Psychology*, 5: 509–28.

Eckenrode, J. and E. Wethington (1990) 'The process and outcome of mobilizing social support', in S. Duck with D.C. Silver (eds), *Personal Relationships and Social Support*, London: Sage.

Edgell, S. (1980) *Middle Class Couples*, London: George, Allen and Unwin.

Eichenbaum, L. and S. Orbach (1984) *What do Women Want?*, London: Fontana.

Eichenbaum, L. and S. Orbach (1985) *Understanding Women*, London: Pelican.

Eisenstein, H. (1984) *Contemporary Feminist Thought*, London and Sydney: Unwin.

Erikson, E. (1950) *Childhood and Society*, New York: Norton.

Erikson, R. and J.H. Goldthorpe (1988) 'Debate: "Women at class crossroads"': A critical note', *Sociology*, 22, 4: 545–53.

Essex, M.J. and S. Nam (1987) 'Marital status and loneliness among older women: The differential importance of close family and friends', *Journal of Marriage and the Family*, 49: 93–106.

Evetts, J. (1988) 'Managing childcare and work responsibilities: The strategies of married women primary and infant headteachers', *Sociological Review*, 36: 503–31.

Faderman, L. (1981) *Surpassing the Love of Men*, London: Junction Books.

Farrell, M.P. (1986) 'Friendship between men', *Marriage and Family Review*, 9: 163–97.

Farrell, M.P. and S.D. Rosenberg (1981) 'Friendship groups and male development', in M.P. Farrell and S.D. Rosenberg (eds), *Men at Midlife*, Boston, MA: Auburn Horse.

Feld, S.L. (1982) 'Social structural determinants of similarity among associates', *American Sociological Review*, 47: 797–801.

Ferguson, A. and N. Folbre (1981) 'The unhappy marriage of patriarchy and capitalism', in L. Sargent (ed.), *Women and Revolution: The unhappy marriage of Marxism and feminism*, London: Pluto Press.

Ferraro, K.F., E. Mutran and C.M. Barresi (1984) 'Widowhood, health and friendship support in later life', *Journal of Health and Social Behaviour*, 25, 3: 246–59.

Finch, J. (1983) *Married to the Job: Wives' incoporation in men's work*, London: George, Allen and Unwin.

Finch, J. (1989) *Family Obligations and Social Change*, Oxford: Polity and Blackwell.

Finch, J. and D. Groves (eds) (1983) *A Labour of Love*, London: Routledge and Kegan Paul.

Finch, J. and J. Mason (1990) 'Filial obligations and kin support for elderly people', *Ageing and Society*, 10: 151–75.

Fine, G.A. (1986) 'Friendships in the work place', in V.J. Derlega and B.A. Winstead (eds), *Friendship and Social Interaction*, New York: Springer.

Firestone, S. (1979) *The Dialectics of Sex: The case for the feminist revolution*, London: The Women's Press.

Firth, R., J. Hubert and A. Forge (1969) *Families and their Relatives*, London: Routledge and Kegan Paul.

Fischer, C. (1982a) 'What do we mean by "friend": an inductive study', *Social Networks*, 3: 287–306.

Fischer, C. (1982b) *To Dwell among Friends*, Berkeley: University of California Press.

Fischer, C., R.M. Jackson, C.A. Stueve, K. Gerson, L. McCallister Jones with M. Baldassare (1977) *Networks and Places*, New York: Free Press.

Fischer, C.S. and S.J. Oliker (1983) 'A research note on friendship, gender and the life cycle', *Social Forces*, 62: 124–33.

Fischer, J.L. and D.L. Sollie (1986) 'Women's communication with intimates and acquaintances', *Journal of Social and Personal Relationships*, 3: 19–30.

Fleming, R. and A. Baum (1986) 'Social support and stress: The buffering effects of friendship', in V.J. Derlega and B.A. Winstead (eds), *Friendship and Social Interaction*, New York: Springer.

Foa, U. and U. Foa (1974) *Societal Structures of the Mind*, Springfield, IL: Charles Thomas.

Ford, J. and R. Sinclair (1987) *Sixty Years On*, London: Women's Press.

Fortes, M. (1970) *Kinship and the Social Order*, London: Routledge and Kegan Paul.

Foucault, M. (1981) *The History of Sexuality*, vol. 1, Harmondsworth: Allan Lane.

Fox, M., M. Gibbs and D. Auerbach (1985) 'Age and gender dimensions of friendship', *Psychology of Women Quarterly*, 9: 489–502.

Freudenburg, N.R. (1986) 'The density of acquaintanceship: An overlooked variable in community research', *American Journal of Sociology*, 92, 1: 27–63.

Friday, N. (1979) *My Mother/Myself*, Fontana.

Friedan, B. (1963) *The Feminine Mystique*, London: Gollancz.

Friedkin, N. (1980) 'A test of structural features of Granovetter's strength of weak ties theory', *Social Networks*, 2: 411–22.

Gabe, J. and P. Williams (eds) (1986) *Tranquillisers: Social, psychological and clinical perspectives*, London: Tavistock.

Gamarnikow, E., D.H.J. Morgan, J. Purvis and D.E. Taylorson (eds) (1983) *Gender, Class and Work*, London: Heinemann.

Gavron, H. (1966) *The Captive Wife*, Harmondsworth: Penguin.

Gelles, R.J. (1974) *The Violent Home: A study of physical aggression between husbands and wives*, Beverley Hills, CA: Sage.

General Household Survey 1983 (1985) London: HMSO.

Gershuny, J.I. and G.S. Thomas (1980) *Changing Patterns of Time Use* (Occasional Paper Series no. 13), Science Policy Research Unit, University of Sussex.

Gerstein, L.H. and A. Tesser (1987) 'Antecedents and responses associated with loneliness', *Journal of Social and Personal Relationships*, 4: 329–63.

Gerstel, N. (1988) 'Divorce and kin ties: The importance of gender', *Journal of Marriage and the Family*, 50: 209–19.

Gerstel, N., C. Kohler Reissman and S. Rosenfield (1985) 'Explaining the symptomatology of separated and divorced women and men: The role of material conditions and social networks', *Social Forces*, 64, 1: 85–100.

Gilbert, S.M. and S. Gubar (1986) 'The queen's looking glass', in J. Zipes (ed.) *Don't Bet on the Prince*, Aldershot: Gower.

Giles Williams, G. (1985) 'Gender, masculinity–femininity and emotional intimacy in same-sex friendship', *Sex Roles*, 12, 5/6: 587–600.

Ginsburg, G.P. (1988) 'Rules, scripts and prototypes in personal relationships', in S.W. Duck *et al.* (eds), *Handbook of Personal Relationships*, Chichester: Wiley.

Glidewell, J.C., S. Tucker, M. Todt and S. Cox (1982) 'Professional support system: The teaching profession', in A. Nadler, J.D. Fischer and B.M. de Paulo (eds) *New Directions in Helping*, vol. 3: *Applied Research in Help-seeking and Reactions to Aid*, New York: Academic Press.

Gluckman, M. (1963) 'Gossip and scandal', *Current Anthropology*, 4: 307–16.

Goetting, A. (1986) 'The developmental tasks of siblingship over the life cycle', *Journal of Marriage and the Family*, 48: 708–14.

Goldthorpe, J.H. (1983) 'Women and class analysis: in defence of the conventional view', *Sociology*, 17: 465–88.

Goldthorpe, J.H. and K. Hope (1974) *The Social Grading of Occupations*, Oxford: Clarendon Press.

Goldthorpe, J., D. Lockwood, F. Bechofer and J. Platt (1969) *The Affluent Worker in the Class Structure*, Cambridge: Cambridge University Press.

Goodenow, C. and E.L. Gaier (1990) 'Best friends: The close reciprocal friendships of married and unmarried women', unpublished paper.

Gottlieb, B.J. (1985) 'Social support and the study of personal relationships', *Journal of Social and Personal Relationships*, 2: 351–75.

Gouldner, M. and M. Symons Strong (1987) *Speaking of Friendship: Middle-class women and their friends*, New York and London: Greenwood Press.

Gove, W.R. (1972) 'The relationship between sex roles, marital status and mental illness', *Social Forces*, 51: 34–44.

Gove, W.R. (1974) 'Sex, marital status, and mortality', *American Journal of Sociology*, 79, 1: 45–66.

Gove, W.R. (1978) 'Sex differences in mental illness among adult men and women: An evaluation of four questions raised regarding the evidence on the higher rates of women', *Social Science and Medicine*, 12b: 187–98.

Granovetter, M. (1973) 'The strength of weak ties', *American Journal of Sociology*, 78, 6: 1360–80.

Green, E., S. Hebron and D. Woodward (1990) *Women's Leisure, What Leisure?* London: Macmillan.

Griffin, C. (1985) *Typical Girls? Young women from school to the job market*, London: Routledge and Kegan Paul.

Griffin, E. and G.G. Sparks (1990) 'Friends forever: A longitudinal exploration of intimacy in same-sex friends and platonic pairs', *Journal of Social and Personal Relationships*, 7: 29–46.

Griffiths, V. (1988) 'From "playing out" to "dossing out" ' in E. Wimbush and M. Talbot (eds), *Relative Freedoms: Women and leisure*, Milton Keynes: Open University Press.

Gubrium, J. (1975) 'Being single in old age', *Aging and Human Development*, 6: 29–41.

Gubrium, J. (1976) 'Being single in old age', in J.F. Gubrium (ed.), *Time, Roles and Self in Old Age*, New York: Human Sciences Press.

Guillaumin, C. (1987) 'The question of difference', in C. Ducken (ed.), *French Connections*, London: Hutchinson.

Gullestad, M. (1984) *Kitchen Table Society*, Oslo: Universitets Forlaget.

Hacker, H.M. (1981) 'Blabbermouths and clams: Sex differences in self disclosure in same-sex and cross-sex friendship dyads', *Psychology of Women Quarterly*, 5: 385–401.

Hannan, D. (1972) 'Kinship, neighbourhood and social change in Irish rural communities', *ESR*, 3, 2: 163–87.

Hansell, S. (1985) 'Adolescent friendship networks and distress in school', *Social Forces*, 63, 3: 698–715.

Hart, N. (1976) *When Marriage Ends: A study in status passage*, London: Tavistock.

Hartmann, H.I. (1976) 'Capitalism, patriarchy and job segregation by sex', in M. Blaxall and B. Reagan (eds), *Women and the Workplace*, Chicago, IL: University of Chicago Press.

Harvey, J.H., G. Agostinelli and A.L. Weber (1989) 'Account-making and the formation of expectations about close relationships', in C. Hendrick (ed.), *Close Relationships*, Newbury Park, CA, and London: Sage.

Harvey, J.H., A.L. Weber, K.S. Galvin, H.C. Huszti and N.N. Garnick (1986) 'Attribution and the termination of close relationships: A special focus on the account', in R. Gilmour and S. Duck (eds), *The Emerging Field of Personal Relationships*, Hillsdale, NJ: Lawrence Erlbaum.

Harvey, J.H., A.L. Weber and T. Orbuch (1990) *Interpersonal Accounts*, Cambridge, MA, and Oxford: Blackwell.

Hays, R.B. (1984) 'The development and maintenance of friendship', *Journal of Social and Personal Relationships*, 6: 21–37.

Hays, R.B. (1985) 'A longitudinal study of friendship development', *Journal of Personality and Social Psychology*, 48, 4: 909–24.

Hays, R.B. (1988) 'Friendship', in S.W. Duck *et al.* (eds), *A Handbook of Personal Relationships*, Chichester: Wiley.

Hays, R.B. (1989) 'The day-to-day functioning of close versus casual friendships', *Journal of Social and Personal Relationships*, 6: 21–37.

Hays, R.B. and D. Oxley (1986) 'Social network development and functioning during a life transition', *Journal of Personality and Social Psychology*, 50: 305–13.

Heidensohn, F. (1985) *Women and Crime*, London: Macmillan.

Helgeson, V.S., P. Shaver and M. Dyer (1987) 'Prototypes of intimacy and distance in same sex and opposite sex relationships', *Journal of Social and Personal Relationships*, 4: 195–233.

Henderson, S., D.G. Byrne and P. Duncan-Jones (1981) *Neurosis and the Social Environment*, London: Academic Press.

Hendrick, C. (1988) 'Roles and gender in relationships', in S.W. Duck *et al.* (eds), *A Handbook of Personal Relationships*, Chichester: Wiley.

Hendrick, C. (ed.) (1989) *Close Relationships*, Newbury Park, CA, and London: Sage.

Hendrick, C. and S. Hendrick (1986) 'A theory and method of love', *Journal of Personality and Social Psychology*, 50, 2: 392–402.

Hetherington, E.M., M. Cox and R. Cox (1977) 'The aftermath of divorce', in J.H. Stevens and M. Mathews (eds), *Mother–child, Father–child Relations*, Washington DC: National Association for the Education of Young Children.

Hess, B.B. (1972) 'Friendship', in M.W. Riley, M. Johnson and A. Foner (eds), *Aging and Society*, vol. 3, New York: Russell.

Hess, B.B. (1979) 'Sex roles, friendship and the life course', *Research on Aging*, 1, 4: 494–515.

Hess, B.B. (1981) 'Friendship and gender roles over the life course', in P.J. Stein (ed.), *Single Life: Unmarried adults in social context*, New York: St Martin's Press.

Hey, V. (1986) *Patriarchy and Pub Culture*, London: Tavistock.

Hill, R. (1986) 'Life cycle stages for types of single parent families: Of family development theory', *Family Relations*, 35: 19–29.

Hinde, R.A. (1979) *Towards Understanding Relationships*, London: Academic Press.

Hinde, R.A. (1981) 'The bases of a science of interpersonal relationships', in S.W. Duck and R. Gilmour (eds), *Personal Relationships*, vol 1: *Studying Personal Relationships*, London: Academic Press.

Hirsch, B.J. (1979) 'Psychological dimensions of social networks: A multimethod analysis', *American Journal of Community Psychology*, 8: 159–72.

Hirsch, B.J. (1981) 'Social networks and the coping process', in B. Gottlieb (ed.), *Social Networks and Social Support*, Beverley Hills, CA: Sage.

Hite, S. (1987) *Women and Love*, London: Penguin.

Hobfall, S.E. and J. Stokes (1988) 'The process and mechanics of social support' in S.W. Duck *et al.* (eds), *A Handbook of Personal Relationships*, Chichester: Wiley.

Hobson, D. (1981) 'Now that I'm married . . .', in A. McRobbie and T. McCabe (eds), *Feminism for Girls*, London: Routledge and Kegan Paul.

Hochschild, A. (1973) *The Unexpected Community*, Englewood Cliffs, NJ: Prentice Hall.

Holmes, D.J. (1972) *Psychotherapy*, Boston, MA: Little Brown.

Homans, G. (1961) *Social Behaviour: Its elementary forms*, New York: Harcourt, Brace and World.

Homel, R., A. Burns and J. Goodenow (1987) 'Parental social networks and child development', *Journal of Social and Personal Relationships*, 4: 159–77.

Hoyt, D.R. and N. Babchuk (1983) 'Adult kin networks: The selective formation of intimate ties with kin', *Social Forces*, 62: 84–101.

Huckfeldt, R.R. (1983) 'Social contexts, social networks and urban neighbourhoods: Environmental constraints on friendship choice', *American Journal of Sociology*, 89, 3: 651–69.

Hudson, B. (1984) 'Femininity and adolescence', in A. McRobbie and M. Nava (eds), *Gender and Generation*, London: Macmillan.

Hughes, M. and W.R. Gove (1981) 'Living alone, social integration, and mental health', *American Journal of Sociology*, 87, 1: 48–73.

Hunt, G. and S. Satterlee (1986) 'The pub, the village and the people', *Human Organization*, 45, 1: 63–74.

Hunt, G. and S. Satterlee (1987) 'Darts, drink and the pub: The culture of female drinking', *The Sociological Review*, 35: 575–601.

Imray, L. and A. Middleton (1983) 'Public and private: Marking the boundaries', in E. Gamarnikow, D. Morgan, J. Purvis and D. Taylorson (eds), *The Public and the Private*, London: Heinemann.

Jaggar, A.M. (1983) *Feminist Politics and Human Nature*, Totawa, N.J. Rowman and Allanheld, and Brighton: Harvester.

Jerrome, D. (1981) 'The significance of friendship for women in later life', *Ageing and Society*, 1, 2: 175–97.

Jerrome, D. (ed.) (1983) *Ageing in a Modern Society: Contemporary approaches*, Kent and Australia: Croom Helm.

Jerrome, D. (1984) 'Good company: The sociological implications of friendship', *Sociological Review*, 32, 4: 606–715.

Jerrome, D. (1989) 'Age relations in an English Church', *Sociological Review*, 37, 4: 761–83.

Jerrome, D. (1990) 'Fraility and friendship', *Journal of Cross-Cultural Gerontology*, 5: 51–64.

Johnson, C.L. and D.J. Catalano (1983) 'A longitudinal study of family supports to impaired elderly', *The Gerontologist*, 23, 6: 612–18.

Johnson, F.L. and E.J. Aries (1983) 'The talk of women friends', *Women's Studies International Forum*, 6, 4: 353–61.

Johnson, J. (1974) *Lesbian Nation: The feminist solutions*, New York: Simon and Schuster.

Johnson, M.P. and R.M. Milardo (1984) 'Network interference in pair relationships: A social psychological recasting of Slater's theory of social regression', *Journal of Marriage and the Family*, 46: 893–9.

Jones, W.H., C.W. Covert, R.L. Snider and T. Bruce (1985) 'Relational stress: An analysis of situations and events associated with loneliness', in S. Duck and D. Perlman (eds), *Understanding Personal Relationships*, London: Sage.

Jong-Gierveld, J. de (1980) 'Singlehood: A creative or lonely experience?', *Alternative Lifestyles*, 3: 350–68.

Jorgensen, P.S. (1991) 'The family with dependent children in Denmark', in G.

Kiely and V. Richardson (eds), *Family Policy: European perspectives*, Dublin: Family Studies Centre, University College, Dublin.

Jourard, S.M. (1971) *Self Disclosure*, New York: Wiley–Interscience.

Kaplan, R.E. (1984) 'A prescription for ailing work relationships: "The Talking Cure" ', in S. Duck (ed.), *Personal Relationships Vol 5: Repairing Personal Relationships*, London: Academic Press.

Kelley, H.H., E. Bercheid, A. Christensen, J.H. Harvey, T.L. Huston, G. Levinger, E. McClintock, L.A. Peplau and D.R. Peterson (1983) *Close Relationships*, San Francisco, CA: Freeman.

Komarovsky, M. (1967) *Blue Collar Marriage*, New York: Vintage Books.

Krieger, S. (1982) 'Lesbian identity and community: Recent social science literature', *Signs: Journal of Women in Society and Culture*, 8, 1: 91–108.

Kurdek, L.A. (1989) 'Relationship quality in gay and lesbian cohabiting couples: A one-year follow-up study', *Journal of Social and Personal Relationships*, 6: 39–59.

Kurth, S. (1970) 'Friendship and friendly relations', in G.J. McCall (ed.), *Social Relationships*, Chicago, IL: Aldine.

La Follette, H. and G. Graham (1986) 'Honesty and intimacy', *Journal of Social and Personal Relationships*, 3: 3–18.

La Gaipa, J.J. (1977) 'Testing a multi-dimensional approach to friendship', in S. Duck (ed.), *Theory and Practice in Interpersonal Attraction*, London: Academic.

La Gaipa, J.J. (1981) 'A systems approach to personal relationships', in S. Duck and R. Gilmour (eds), *Personal Relationship*, vol. 1: *Studying Personal Relationships*, London and New York: Academic Press.

La Gaipa, J.J. (1982) 'Rules and rituals in disengaging from relationships', in S.W. Duck (ed.), *Personal Relationships*, vol. 4: *Dissolving Personal Relationships*, London and New York: Academic Press.

La Gaipa, J.J. (1990) 'The negative effects of informal support systems', in S. Duck and R.C. Silver (eds), *Personal Relationships and Social Support*, London: Sage.

Larson, R.W. and N. Bradney (1988) 'Precious moments with family members and friends', in R.M. Milardo (ed.), *Families and Social Networks*, Beverley Hills, CA: Sage.

Lasch, C. (1977) *Haven in a Heartless World*, New York: Basic Books.

Laumann, E.O. (1973) *Bonds of Pluralism the Form and Substance of Social Networks*, London: Wiley.

Lawton, M.P. (1977) 'Environmental and health influences on aging and behaviour', in J.E. Birren and K.W. Schaie (eds), *Handbook of Psychology of Aging*, New York: Van Nostrand Reinhold.

Lazarsfeld, P. and R.K. Merton (1954) 'Friendship as a social process: A substantive and methodological analysis', in M.Berger, T. Abel and C.H. Page (eds), *Freedom and Control in Modern Society*, New York: Van Nostrand.

Lea, M. and S.W. Duck (1982) 'A model for the role of similarity of values in friendship development', *British Journal of Social Psychology*, 21: 301–10.

Leatham, G. and S. Duck (1990) 'Conversations with friends and the dynamics of social support', in S. Duck with R.C. Silver (eds), *Personal Relationships in Social Support*, London: Sage.

Lee, S.A. (1973) *The Colours of Love*, Englewood Cliffs, NJ: Prentice Hall.

Leffler, A., S. Krannich and D.L. Gillespie (1986) 'Contact, support, and friction', *Sociological Perspectives*, 29, 3: 337–55.

Leis, N.B. (1974) 'Women in groups: Ijaw women's associations', in M. Z. Rosaldo and L. Lamphere (eds), *Women, Culture and Society*, Stanford CA: Stanford University Press.

Leiulfsrud, H. and A.E. Woodward (1988) 'Women at class cross-roads: A critical reply to Erikson's and Goldthorpe's note', *Sociology*, 22: 555–62.

Leonard, D. and M.A. Speakman (1986) 'Women in the family: Companions or caretakers', in V. Beechey and E. Whitelegg (eds), *Women in Britain Today*, Milton Keynes: Open University Press.

Leslie, L.A. (1989) 'Stress in the dual-income couple: Do social relationships help or hinder?', *Journal of Social and Personal Relationships*, 6: 451–61.

Leslie, L.A. and K. Grady (1985) 'Changes in mothers' social networks and social support following divorce', *Journal of Marriage and the Family*, August, 663–73.

Levinger, G. (1980) 'Toward the analysis of close relationships', *Journal of Experimental Social Psychology*, 16: 510–44.

Levinger, G. and J.D. Snoek (1972) *Attraction in Relationships: A new look at interpersonal attraction*, Morristown, NJ: General Learning Press.

Levy, J. A. (1981) 'Friendship dilemmas and the intersection of social worlds; re-entry women on the College campus', in H.Z. Lopata and D. Maines (eds), *Research in the Interweave of Social Roles: Friendship*, vol. 2, Greenwich, CT: JAI Press.

Levy, M.B. and K.E. Davis (1988) 'Lovestyles and attachment styles compared: Their relations to each other and to various relationship characteristics', *Journal of Social and Personal Relationships*, 5: 439–71.

Leyton, E. (1975a) *The One Blood: Kinship and class in an Irish Village*, Toronto: University of Toronto Press.

Leyton, E. (ed.) (1975b) *The Compact: Selected dimensions of friendship*, St. John's Institute of Social and Economic Research, Memorial University of Newfoundland.

Litwak, E. (1985) *Helping the Elderly: The complementary roles of informal networks and formal systems*, New York: Guilford Press.

Litwak, E. and I. Szelenyi (1969) 'Primary group structures and their functions: Kin, neighbours and friends', *American Sociological Review*, 34: 465–81.

Lock, A.J. (1986) 'The role of relationships in development: An introduction to a series of occasional articles', *Journal of Social and Personal Relationships*, 3: 89–99.

Lopata, H.Z. (1971) *Occupation Housewife*, London: Oxford University Press.

Lopata, H.Z. (1973) 'The effect of schooling on social contacts of urban women', *American Journal of Sociology*, 78: 604–19.

Lopata, H.Z. (1979) *Women as Widows*, New York: Elsevier.

Lopata, H.Z. and D. Maines (eds) (1981) *Research in the Interweave of Social Roles: Friendship*, vol. 2, Greenwich, CT: JAI Press.

Lorber, J. (1989) 'Trust, loyalty and the place of women in the informal organization of work', in J. Freeman (ed.), *Women: A feminist perspective*, 4th edn. Mountain View, CA: Mayfield.

Lowenthal, M.F. and C. Haven (1968) 'Interaction and adaptation: Intimacy as a crucial variable', *American Sociological Review*, 35: 20–30.

Lynch, K. (1989) 'Solidary labour: Its nature and marginalisation', *Sociological Review*, 37, 1: 1–14.

Maher, V. (1976) 'Kin, clients and accomplices: Relationships among women in Morocco', in D. Leonard Barker and S. Allen (eds), *Sexual Divisions and Society: Process and change*, London: Tavistock.

Mangam, I.L., (1981) 'Relationships at work: A matter of tension and tolerance', in S. Duck and R. Gilmour (eds), *Personal Relationships*, vol. 1: *Studying Personal Relationships*, London: Academic Press.

Marris, P. (1982) 'Attachment and society', in C.M. Parkes and J.S. Hinde (eds), *The place of attachment in human behaviour*, London and New York: Tavistock.

Marsden, D. (1978) 'Sociological perspectives on family violence', in J.P. Martin (ed.), *Violence and the Family*, Chichester: Wiley.

Marsden, P.V. and K.E. Campbell (1984) 'Measuring tie strength', *Social Forces*, 63, 2: 482–501.

Marsden, P.V. and N. Lin (eds) (1982) *Social Structure and Network Analysis*, Beverley Hills, CA and London: Sage.

Marshall, G., D. Rose, H. Newby and C. Vogler (1989) *Social Class in Modern Britain*, London and Boston, MA: Unwin Hyman.

Maslow, A.H. (1968) *Towards a Psychology of Being*, New York: Van Nostrand.

Matthews, S.H. (1979) *The Social World of Old Women*, Beverley Hills, CA and London: Sage.

Matthews, S.H. (1983) 'Definitions of friendship and their consequences in old age', *Ageing and Society*, 3: 141–55.

Matthews, S.H. (1986) *Friendships through the Life Course*, London and Beverley Hills, CA: Sage.

McAdams, D.P. (1985) 'Motivation and friendship' in S. Duck and D. Perlman (eds), *Understanding Personal Relationships*, London: Sage.

McAdams, D.P. (1988) 'Personal needs and personal relationships', in S. Duck *et al.* (eds), *Handbook of Personal Relationships*, Chichester: Wiley.

McCabe, T. (1981) 'Girls and Leisure', in A. Tomlinson (ed.), *Leisure and Social Control*, Brighton Polytechnic: Chelsea School of Human Movement.

McCall, G. (1982) 'Becoming unrelated: The management of bond dissolution', in S.W. Duck (ed.), *Personal Relationships*, vol. 4: *Dissolving Personal Relationships*, London: Academic Press.

McCall, G.J. (1988) 'The organizational Life Cycle of Relationships', in S.W. Duck *et al.* (eds), *A Handbook of Personal Relationships*, Chichester: Wiley.

McCarthy, B. (1986) 'Dyads, cliques and conspiracies: Friendship behaviours and perceptions within long-established social groups', in R. Gilmour and S. Duck (eds), *The Emerging Field of Personal Relationships*, Hillsdale, NJ: Lawrence Erlbaum.

McFarlane, A.H., G.R. Norman, D.L. Streiner, R. Roy and D. Scott (1980) 'A longitudinal study of the influence of the psychosocial environment on health status: A preliminary report', *Journal of Health and Social Behaviour*, 21, June: 124–33.

McKee, L. and C. Bell (1986) 'His unemployment, her problem: The domestic and marital consequences of male unemployment', in S. Allen, A. Watson, K. Purcell and S. Wood (eds), *The Experience of Unemployment*, Basingstoke: Macmillan.

McLanahan, S.S., A. Sørensen and D. Watson (1989) 'Sex differences in poverty', *Signs: Journal of Women in Culture and Society*, 15, 1: 102–22

McNally, F. (1979) *Women for Hire: A study of the female office worker*, London: Macmillan.

McRae, S. (1986) *Cross-Class Families*, Oxford: Clarendon Press.

McRobbie, A. and T. McCabe (1981) (eds) *Feminism for Girls*, London: Routledge and Kegan Paul.

Miell, D. and D. Duck (1986) 'Strategies in developing friendships', in V.J. Derlega and B.A. Winstead (eds), *Friendship and Social Interaction*, New York: Springer.

Milardo, R.M. (1983) 'Social networks and pair measurement: A review of substantive and measurement issues', *Sociology and Social Research*, 68, Oct.: 1–18.

Milardo, R.M. (1986) 'Personal choice and social constraint in close relationships: Applications of a network analysis', in V.J. Derlega and B.A. Winstead (eds), *Friendship and Social Interaction*, New York: Springer.

Milardo, R.M. (1987) 'Changes in social networks of women and men following divorce: A review', *Journal of Family Issues*, 8, 1: 78–96.

Milardo, R.M. (ed.) (1988) *Families and Social Networks*, Beverley Hills, CA: Sage.

Miles, A. (1988) *Women and Mental Illness: The social context of female neurosis*, Hemel Hempstead: Harvester Wheatsheaf.

Miller, R.S. and H.M. Lefcourt (1983) 'Social intimacy: An important moderator of stressful life events', *American Journal of Community Psychology*, 11: 127–39.

Millett, K. (1977) *Sexual Politics*, London: Virago (1st pub. 1969).

Mitchell, J.C. (1969) *Social Networks in Urban Situations*, Manchester: Manchester University Press.

Mogey, J.M. (1956) *Family and Neighbourhood*, London: Oxford University Press.

Montgomery, B.M. (1988) 'Quality communication in personal relationships', in S. Duck *et al.* (eds), *A Handbook of Personal Relationships*, Chichester: Wiley.

Morgan, D.H.J. and D.E. Taylorson (1983) 'Introduction: Class and work: Bringing women back in', in E. Gamarnikow *et al.* (eds), *Gender, Class and Work*, London: Heineman.

Morgan, D.L. (1986) 'Personal relationships as an interface between social networks and social cognitions', *Journal of Social and Personal Relationships*, 3: 403–22.

Morgan, D.L. (1990) 'Combining the strengths of social networks, social support and personal relationships', in S. Duck with R.C. Silver (eds), *Personal Relationships and Social Support*, London: Sage.

Morris, L. (1984) 'Patterns of social activity and post-redundancy labour market experience', *Sociology*, 18: 339–52.

Morris, L. (1985) 'Local social networks and domestic organizations: A study of redundant steel workers and their wives', *Sociological Review*, 33: 327–41.

Munroe, S.M. (1983) 'Social support and disorder: Toward an untangling of cause and effect', *American Journal of Community Psychology*, 11, 1: 81–97.

Murgatroyd, L. (1982) 'Gender and occupational stratification', *Sociological Review*, 30: 574–601.

Murgatroyd, L. (1984) 'Women, men and the social grading of occupations', *British Journal of Sociology*, 35: 473–97.

Mutran, E. and D.C. Reitzes (1984) 'Intergenerational support activities and well-being among the elderly: A convergence of exchange and symbolic interaction perspectives', *American Sociological Review*, 49, February: 117–30.

Nelson, N. (1978) 'Women must help each other', in P. Caplan and J.M. Bujra (eds), *Women United, Women Divided*, London: Tavistock.

Newcomb, T.M. (1961) *The Acquaintance Process*, New York: Holt, Rinehart and Winston.

Noddings, N. (1984) *Caring: A feminine approach to ethics and moral education*, Berkeley: University of California Press.

Oakley, A. (1972) *Sex, Gender and Society*, London: Temple Smith.

Oakley, A. (1974) *Housewife*, London: Allen Lane.

Oakley, A. (1980) *Women Confined*, Oxford: Martin Robertson.

Oakley, A. (1989) 'Women's studies in British sociology', *British Journal of Sociology*, 40, 3: 442–70.

O'Connor, P. (1987) 'Very close relationships', unpublished Ph.D. thesis, University of London. •

O'Connor, P. (1989) 'Images and motifs in children's fairy tales', *Educational Studies*, 15, 2: 129–44.

O'Connor, P. (1990) 'The adult mother–daughter relationship: A uniquely and universally close relationship?', *Sociological Review*, 38, 2: 293–323.

O'Connor, P. (1991a) 'Women's confidants outside marriage: Shared or competing sources of intimacy?', *Sociology*, 25, 2: 241–54.

O'Connor, P. (1991b) 'The significance of friendships amongst the elderly', unpublished manuscript.

O'Connor, P. (1991c) 'Women's experience of power within marriage: An inexplicable phenomenon?', *Sociological Review*, November: 823–42.

O'Connor, P. and G.W. Brown (1984) 'Supportive relationships: Fact or fancy?', *Journal of Social and Personal Relationships*, 1: 159–76.

Oliker, S.J. (1989) *Best Friends and Marriage: Exchange among women*, CA: University of California Press.

Orbach, S. and L. Eichenbaum (1987) *Bittersweet*, London: Century Hutchinson.

Pagel, M.D., W.W. Erdly and J. Becker (1987) 'Social networks: We get by with (and in spite of) a little help from our friends', *Journal of Personality and Social Psychology*, 53, 4: 793–804.

Pahl, J.M. (ed.) (1985) *Private Violence and Public Policy*, London: Routledge and Kegan Paul.

Pahl, J.M. and R.E. Pahl (1971) *Managers and their Wives*, Harmondsworth: Pelican.

Pahl, R.E. (1984) *Divisions of Labour*, Oxford: Blackwell.

Palisi, B.J. and H.E. Ransford (1987) 'Friendship as a voluntary relationship: Evidence from national surveys', *Journal of Social and Personal Relationships*, 4: 243–59.

Papanek, H. (1979) 'Family status production: The "work" and "non-work" of women', *Signs: Journal of Women in Culture and Society*, 4: 775–81.

Parker, R. (1981) 'Tending and social policy', in E.M. Goldberg and S. Hatch (eds), *A New Look at the Personal Social Services*, (Discussion Paper No. 4), London: Policy Studies Institute.

Parkes, M. (1972) 'Components of the reaction to loss of a limb, spouse or home', *Journal of Psychosomatic Research*, 16: 343–9.

Parsons, T. (1964) *Essays in Sociological Theory*, rev. edn, New York: Free Press.

Perlman, D. and S. Duck (eds) (1987) *Intimate Relationships: Development, dynamics and deterioration*, Newbury Park, CA: Sage.

Perlman, D. and S. Fehr (1986) 'Theories of friendship: The analysis of interpersonal attraction', in V.J. Derlega and B.A. Winstead (eds), *Friendship and Social Interaction*, New York: Springer.

Pierce, G.R., B.R. Sarason and I.G. Sarason (1990) 'Integrating social support perspectives: Working models, personal relationships and situational factors', in S. Duck and R.C. Silver (eds), *Personal Relationships and Social Support*, London: Sage.

Pilkington, C.J. and D.R. Richardson (1988) 'Perceptions of risk in intimacy', *Journal of Social and Personal Relationships*, 5: 503–8.

Pleck, J.H. (1983) 'Husbands' and wives' paid work and family roles: current research issues', in H.Z. Lopata and D. Maines (eds), *Research in the Interweave of Social Roles: Friendship*, vol. 2, Greenwich, CT: JAI Press.

Pollert, A. (1981) *Girls, Wives, Factory Lives*, London: Macmillan.

Porter, M. (1983) *Home, Work and Class Consciousness*, Manchester: Manchester University Press.

Powers, E.A. and G.L. Bultena (1976) 'Sex differences in the intimate friendships of old age', *Journal of Marriage and the Family*, 38: 739–47.

Price, F.V. (1981) 'Only connect? Issues in charting social networks', *Sociological Review*, 29, 2: 283–312.

Prudo, R., T. Harris and G.W. Brown (1984) 'Psychiatric disorder in a rural and urban population, 3: Social integration and the morphology of affective disorder', *Psychological Medicine*, 14: 327–45.

Przybyla, D.P.J. and D. Byrne (1981) 'Sexual relationships', in S. Duck and R. Gilmour (eds), *Personal Relationships*, vol. 1: *Studying Personal Relationships*, London: Academic Press.

Rands, M. (1988) 'Changes in social networks following marital separation and divorce', in R. Milardo (ed.), *Families and Social Networks*, Beverley Hills, CA: Sage.

Rands, M. and G. Levinger (1979) 'Implicit theories of relationship: An intergenerational study', *Journal of Personality and Social Psychology*, 37: 645–61.

Rapp, R. (1982) 'Family and class in contemporary America: Notes towards an understanding of ideology', in B. Thorne and M. Yalom (eds), *Rethinking the Family: Some feminist questions*, New York: Longman.

Ratcliff, K.S. and J. Bogdan (1988) 'Unemployed women: When social support is not supportive', *Social Problems*, 35: 54–63.

Raymond, J. (1986) *A Passion for Friends*, London: The Women's Press.

Raymond, J. (1990) 'Not a sentimental journey: Women's friendships', in D. Leidholdt and J.G. Raymond (eds), *The Sexual Liberals and the attack on Feminism*, New York and Oxford: Pergamon Press.

Reid, I. and E. Stratta (1989) *Sex Differences in Britain*, 2nd edn, Aldershot and Vermont: Gower.

Reis, H.T. (1984) 'Social interaction and well-being', in S. Duck (ed.), *Personal Relationships* vol. 5: *Repairing Personal Relationships*, London: Academic Press.

Reis, H.T., M. Senchak and B. Solomon (1985) 'Sex differences in the intimacy of social interaction: Further examination of potential explanations', *Journal of Personality and Social Psychology*, 48: 1204–17.

Reis, H.T. and P. Shaver (1988) 'Intimacy as an interpersonal process', in S.W. Duck *et al.* (eds), *A Handbook of Personal Relationships*, Chichester: Wiley.

Reisman, J.M. (1981) 'Adult friendships', in S. Duck and R. Gilmour (eds), *Personal Relationships* vol. 2: *Developing Personal Relationships*, London and New York: Academic Press.

Reiter, R. (1975) *Towards an Anthropology of Women*, London and New York: Monthly Review Press.

Retsinas, J. and P. Garrity (1985) 'Nursing Home Friendships', *The Gerontologist*, 25: 376–81.

Rich, A. (1976) *Of Woman Born: Motherhood as experience and institution*, New York: Norton.

Rich, A. (1980) 'Compulsory heterosexuality and lesbian existence', *Signs: Women in Culture and Society*, 5, 4: 631–60.

Ringelheim, J. (1985) 'Women and the holocaust: A reconsideration of research', *Signs: Journal of Women in Culture and Society*, 10, 4: 741–59.

Roberto, K.A. (1989) 'Exchange and equity in friendships', in R.G. Adams and R. Blieszner (eds), *Older Adult Friendship*, Newbury Park, CA: Sage.

Roberto, K.A. and J. Pearson (1986) 'Equity considerations in the friendships of older adults', *Journal of Gerontology*, 41, 2: 241–7.

Rohrle, B. and I. Hellman (1989) 'Characteristics of social networks and social support among long-term and short-term unemployed teachers', *Journal of Social and Personal Relationships*, 6: 463–73.

Rook, K.S. (1984) 'The negative side of social interaction: Impact on psychological well-being', *Journal of Personality and Social Psychology*, 46, 5: 1097–1108.

Rook, K.S. (1989) 'Strains in older adults' friendships', in R.G. Adams and R. Blieszner (eds), *Older Adult Friendship*, Newbury Park, CA: Sage.

Rosaldo, M.Z. (1980) 'The use and abuse of anthropology: Reflections on feminism and cross-cultural understanding', *Signs: Women in Culture and Society*, 5, 3: 389–417.

Rosaldo, M.Z. and L. Lamphere (eds) (1974) *Women, Culture and Society*, Stanford, CA: Stanford University Press.

Rose, S.M. (1984) 'How friendships end: Patterns among young adults', *Journal of Social and Personal Relationships*, 1: 267–77.

Rose, S.M. (1985) 'Same- and cross-sex friendships and the psychology of homosociality', *Sex Roles*, 12, 1/2: 63–74.

Rose, S. and L. Roades (1987) 'Feminism and women's friendships', *Psychology of Women Quarterly*, 11: 243–54.

Rose, S. and F.C. Serafica (1986) 'Keeping and ending casual, close and best friendships', *Journal of Social and Personal Relationships*, 3: 275–88.

Rosencrance, J. (1986) 'Racetrack buddy relations: Compartmentalized and satisfying', *Journal of Social and Personal Relationships*, 3: 441–56.

Rosser, C. and C. Harris (1965) *The Family and Social Change*, London: Routledge and Kegan Paul.

Rossi, A. (1980) 'Life-span theories and women's lives', *Signs: Women in Culture and Society*, 6, 1: 4–32.

Rostow, I. (1967) *Social Integration of the Aged*, New York: Free Press.

Rubin, G. (1974) 'The traffic in women: Notes on the political economy of sex', in R.L. Reiter (ed.), *Towards an Anthropology of Women*, London and New York: Monthly Review Press.

Rubin, L.B. (1983) *Intimate Strangers*, New York and London: Harper and Row.

Rubin, L.B. (1985) *Just friends: The role of friendship in our lives*, New York: Harper and Row.

Rubin, Z. and S. Shenker (1978) 'Friendship, proximity and self-disclosure', *Journal of Personality*, 46: 1–22.

Rubinstein, R.L. (1987) 'Never-married elderly as a social type: Re-evaluating some images', *The Gerontologist*, 27, 1: 108–13.

Ruehl, S. (1983) *Sexuality, Unit 4: The changing experience of women*, Milton Keynes: Open University Press.

Rusbult, C.L. (1987) 'Responses to dissatisfaction in close relationships: The exit-voice-loyalty-neglect model', in D. Perlman and S. Duck (eds), *Intimate Relationships: Development, Dynamics and Deterioration*, Newbury Park, CA: Sage.

Russell, D.W., E. Altmaier and D.V. Velzen (1987) 'Job-related stress, social support, and burnout among classroom teachers', *Journal of Applied Psychology*, 72, 2: 269–74.

Rutter, M. (1981) *Maternal Deprivation Reassessed*, 2nd edn, Harmondsworth: Penguin.

Ryan, M.P. (1979) 'The power of women's networks: A case study of female moral reform in antebellum America', *Feminist Studies*, 5, 1: 66–85.

Sargent, L. (ed.) (1981) *Women and Revolution: The unhappy marriage of marxism and feminism*, London: Pluto.

Sayers, J. (1983) 'Is the personal political? Psychoanalysis and feminism revisited', *International Journal of Women's Studies*, 6, 1: 71–85.

Scott, J. (1982) *The Upper Classes: Property and privilege in Britain*, London and Basingstoke: Macmillan.

Seiden, A.M. and B. Bart (1975) 'Women to women: Is sisterhood powerful?', in N. Glazer-Malbin (ed.), *Old Family/New Family*, New York and London: Van Nostrand.

Sharpe, S. (1976) *'Just like a Girl': How girls learn to be women*, Harmondsworth: Penguin.

Sharpe, S. (1984) *Double Identity: The lives of working mothers*, Harmondsworth: Penguin.

Sharpe, S. (1987) *Falling for Love*, London: Virago.

Shaver, P., W. Furman and D. Buhrmester (1985) 'Transition to college:

Network changes, social skills and loneliness', in S. Duck and D. Perlman (eds), *Understanding Social Relationships*, London: Sage.

Shaver, P.R. and C. Hazan (1988) 'A biased overview of the study of love', *Journal of Social and Personal Relationships*, 5: 473–501.

Shea, L., L. Thompson and R. Blieszner (1988) 'Resources in older adults' old and new friendships', *Journal of Social and Personal Relationships*, 5: 83–96.

Sherrod, D. (1989) 'The influence of gender on same-sex friendships', in C. Hendrick (ed.), *Close Relationships*, Newbury Park, CA: Sage.

Shlapentokh, V. (1974) *Love, Marriage and Friendship in the Soviet Union: Ideals and practices*, New York: Praeger.

Shostak, A.B. (1987) 'Singlehood', in M.B. Sussman and S.K. Steinmetz (eds), *Handbook of Marriage and the Family*, New York: Plenum Press.

Shulman, N. (1975) 'Life cycle variations in patterns of close relationships', *Journal of Marriage and the Family*, 37: 813–21.

Siltanen, J. (1986) 'Domestic responsibilities and the structuring of employment', in R. Crompton and M. Mann (eds), *Gender and Stratification*, Cambridge: Polity Press.

Simmel, G. (1950) *The Sociology of George Simmel*, trans. and ed. by K.H. Wolff, New York: Free Press.

Simmel, G. (1955) *Conflict and the Web of Group Affiliations*, trans. and ed. by K.H. Wolff and R. Bendix, New York: Free Press.

Simmel, G. (1971) *On Individuality and Social Forms*, edited and with an introduction by D.N. Levine, Chicago: University of Chicago Press.

Simmel, G. (1984) *George Simmel: On women, sexuality and love*, trans. and introduced by G. Oakes, New Haven, CT, and London: Yale University Press.

Sinclair, I., D. Crosbie, P. O'Connor, L. Stanford and A. Vicery, A. (1988) *Bridging Two Worlds: Social work and the elderly living alone*, Aldershot: Gower.

Slavin, L.A. and B.E. Compas (1989) 'The problem of confounding social support and depressive symptoms: A brief report on a college sample', *American Journal of Community Psychology*, 17, 1: 57–66.

Smith-Rosenberg, C. (1975) 'The female world of love and ritual: Relations between women in nineteenth-century America', *Signs: Journal of Women in Culture and Society*, 1, 1: 1–29.

Solano, C.H. (1986) 'People without friends', in V.J. Derlega and B.A. Winstead (eds), *Friendship and Social Interaction*, New York: Springer.

Stacey, M. (1981) 'The division of labour revisited or overcoming the two Adams', in P. Adrams, R. Deem, J. Finch and P. Rock (eds), *Practice and Progress: British sociology 1950–1980*, London: Allen and Unwin.

Stack, C. (1974) *All our Kin*, New York and London: Harper and Row.

Stanworth, M. (1984) 'Women and class analysis: A reply to John Goldthorpe', *Sociology*, 18, 2: 159–69.

Stein, P.J. (ed.) (1981) *Single Life: Unmarried adults in social context*, New York: St Martin's Press.

Stein, P.J. (1983) 'Singlehood', in E. Macklin and R.H. Rubin (eds), *Contemporary Families and Alternative Lifestyles*, Beverley Hills, CA: Sage.

Stewart, A., K. Prandy and R.M. Blackburn (1980) *Social Stratification and Occupations*, London: Macmillan.

Stokes, J.P. (1983) 'Predicting satisfaction with social support from social network structure', *American Journal of Community Psychology*, 11, 2: 141–51.

Strain, L.A. and N.L. Chappell (1982) 'Confidants: Do they make a difference in quality of life?', *Research on Aging*, 4: 479–502.

Straus, M., R. Gelles and S. Steinmetz (1980) *Behind Closed Doors: Violence in the American family*, New York: Anchor.

Strube, M.J. and L.S. Barbour (1984) 'Factors related to the decision to leave an abusive relationship', *Journal of Marriage and the Family*, November: 837–44.

Suitor, J.J. (1987) 'Friendship networks in transitions: Married mothers return to school', *Journal of Social and Personal Relationships*, 4: 445–61.

Surra, C. (1988) 'The influence of the interactive network on developing relationships', in R.M. Milardo (ed.), *Families and Social Networks*, Beverley Hills, CA: Sage.

Suttles, G.D. (1970) 'Friendship as a social institution', in G. McCall (ed.), *Social Relationships*, Chicago, IL: Aldine Press.

Tesch, S.A. (1983) 'Review of friendship development across the life span', *Human Development*, 26: 266–76.

Thoits, P.A. (1982) 'Conceptual, methodological and theoretical problems in studying social support as a buffer against life stress', *Journal of Health and Social Behaviour*, 23: 145–59.

Thoits, P.A. (1983) 'Main and interactive effects of social support: Response to La Rocco', *Journal of Health and Social Behaviour*, 24, 1: 92–5.

Thoits, P.A. (1984) 'Explaining distributions of psychological vulnerability: Lack of social support in the face of stress', *Social Forces*, 63: 453–81.

Thoits, P.A. (1986) 'Social support and coping assistance', *Journal of Consulting and Clinical Psychology*, 54: 416–23.

Thomas, G.S. and C.Z. Shannon (1982) 'Technology and household labour: Are times a-changing?', paper presented at The British Sociological Association Conference, Manchester, England.

Tiger, L. (1969) *Men in Groups*, New York: Random House.

Tolsdorf, C. (1976) 'Social networks, support and coping: An exploratory study', *Family Process*, 15: 407–16.

Townsend, P. (1957) *The Family life of Old People*, London: Routledge and Kegan Paul.

Townsend Gilkes, C. (1985) 'Together and in harness: Women's traditions in the sanctified church', *Signs: Journal of Women in Culture and Society*, 10, 4: 678–99.

Troll, L.E., S. Miller and R. Atchley (1979) *Families of Late Life*, Belmont, CA: Wadsworth.

Tschann, J.M. (1988) 'Self disclosure in adult friendship: Gender and marital status differences', *Journal of Social and Personal Relationships*, 5: 65–81.

Turner, C. (1967) 'Conjugal roles and social networks: A re-examination of an hypothesis', *Human Relations*, 20: 121–30.

Veblen, T. (1970) *The Theory of the Leisure Class*, London: Unwin.

Verbrugge, L.M. (1977) 'The structure of adult friendship choices', *Social Forces*, 56: 576–97.

Walby, S. (1986) 'Gender, class and stratification', in R. Crompton and M. Mann (eds), *Gender and Stratification*, Cambridge: Polity Press.

Walker, A.J. and L. Thompson (1983) 'Intimacy and intergenerational contact among mothers and daughters', *Journal of Marriage and the Family*, November: 841–49.

Walker, K., A. MacBride and M. Vachon (1977) 'Social support networks and the crisis of bereavement', *Social Science and Medicine*, 11: 35–41.

Wallace, C. (1987) *For Richer, For Poorer: Growing up in and out of work*, London and New York: Tavistock.

Ward, R.A. (1979) 'The never-married in later life', *Journal of Gerontology*, 34, 6: 861–69.

Webb, M. (1989) 'Sex and gender in the labour market', in I. Reid and E. Stratta (eds). *Sex Differences in Britain*, 2nd edn, Aldershot: Gower.

Weber, A.L., J.H. Harvey and M.A. Stanley (1987) 'The nature and motivations of accounts for field relationships', in R. Burnett, P. McGhee and D. Clarke (eds), *Accounting for Relationships*, London: Methuen.

Weiss, L. and M.F. Lowenthal (1975) 'Life courses perspectives on friendship', in M.F. Lowenthal, M. Thurnher, D. Chiriboga and associates (eds), *Four Stages of Life*, San Francisco, CA and London: Jossey–Bass.

Weiss, R.S. (1969) 'The fund of sociability', *Transaction/Society*, 6: 36–43.

Weiss, R.S. (1974) 'The provisions of social relationships', in Z. Rubin (ed.), *Support Systems and Mutual Help*, London: Grune and Stratton.

Weissman, M.M. and G.L. Klerman (1977) 'Sex differences and the epidemiology of depression', *Archives of General Psychiatry*, 34, January: 98–111.

Wellman, B. (1979) 'The community question: The intimate networks of East Yorkers', *American Journal of Sociology*, 84: 1201–27.

Wellman, B. (1981) 'Applying network analysis to the study of support', in B. Gottlieb (ed.), *Social Networks and Social Support*, London: Sage.

Wellman, B. (1982) 'Studying personal networks', in P.V. Marsden and N. Lin (eds), *Social Structure and Network Analysis*, London: Sage.

Wellman, B. (1985) 'Domestic work, paid work and net work', in S. Duck and D. Perlman (eds), *Understanding Personal Relationships*, London: Sage.

Wellman, B. (1988) 'The community question re-evaluated', in M.P. Smith (ed.), *Power, Community and the City: Comparative urban research* vol. 1, New Brunswick, NJ: Transaction.

Wellman, B. (1990) 'The place of kinfold in personal community networks', *Marriage and Family Review*, 15: 195–221.

Wellman, B., P. Carrington and A. Hall (1988) 'Networks as personal communities', in B. Wellman and S.D. Berkowitz (eds), *Social Strutures: A network approach*, Cambridge: Cambridge University Press.

Wellman, B. and S. Wortley (1989) 'Brother's keepers: Situating kinship relationships in broader networks of social support', *Sociological Perspectives*, 32, 3: 273–306.

Wellman, B. and S. Wortley (1991) 'Different strokes from different folks: Community ties and social support?, *American Journal of Sociology*: 96, 558–88.

Wenger, C. (1984) *The Supportive Network: Coping with old age*, London: Allen and Unwin.

Westwood, S. (1984) *All Day Every Day: Factory and family in the making of women's lives*, London: Pluto.

Wethington, E., J.D. McLeod and R.C. Kessler (1987) 'The importance of life events for explaining sex differences in psychological distress', in R.C. Barnett, L. Biener and G.K. Baruch (eds), *Gender and Stress*, New York: Free Press.

Wheeler, L., H.T. Reis and J. Nezlek (1983) 'Loneliness, social interaction, and sex roles', *Journal of Personality and Social Psychology*, 45: 943–53.

Whelan, C.T., D.F. Hannan and S. Creighton (1991) *Unemployment, Poverty and Psychological Distress*, General Research Series, no. 150, Dublin: ESRI.

Whitehead, A. (1976) 'Sexual antagonism in Hertfordshire', in D. Leonard Barker and S. Allen (eds), *Dependence and Exploitation in Work and Marriage*, New York: Longman.

Wilcox, B.L. (1981) 'Social support in adjusting to marital disruption: a network analysis', in B.H. Gottlieb (ed.), *Social Networks and Social Support*, Beverley Hills, CA, and London: Sage.

Williams, D.G. (1985) 'Gender, masculinity and emotional intimacy in same-sex friendships', *Sex Roles*, 12: 587–600.

Willmott, P. (1987) *Friendship Networks and Social Support*, London: Policy Studies Institute.

Willmott, P. and M. Young (1967) *Family and Class in a London Suburb*, London: Nel Mentor (1st pub. 1960).

Wimbush, E. (1986) *Women, Leisure and Well-being: Final Report*, Edinburgh: Centre for Leisure Research, Dunfermline College of Physical Education.

Winstead, B.A. (1986) 'Sex differences in same-sex friendships', in V.J. Derlega and B.A. Winstead (eds), *Friendship and Social Interaction*, New York: Springer.

Winstead, B.A. and V.J. Derlega (1985) 'Brief report: Benefits of same-sex friendships in a stressful situation', *Journal of Social and Clinical Psychology*, 3, 3: 378–84.

Wiseman, J. (1986) 'Friendship: Bonds and binds in a voluntary relationship', *Journal of Social and Personal Relationships*, 3: 191–211.

Wiseman, J. (1990) 'The mechanics of making up: Friendships as contrasted with marriage', unpublished paper presented at the Fifth International Conference on Personal Relationships, July, Oxford, England.

Woolf, V. (1977) *A Room of One's Own*, St Albans: Triad/Panther.

Wright, P.H. (1978) 'Toward a theory of friendship based on a conception of self', *Human Communication Research*, 4: 196–207.

Wright, P.H. (1982) 'Men's friendships women's friendships and the alleged inferiority of the latter', *Sex Roles*, 8, 1: 1–20.

Wright, P.H. (1984) 'Self-referent motivation and the intrinsic quality of friendship', *Journal of Social and Personal Relationships*, 1: 115–30.

Wright, P.H. (1985) 'The acquaintance description form', in S. Duck and D. Perlman (eds), *Understanding Personal Relationships: An interdisciplinary approach*, London: Sage.

Wright, P.H. (1988) 'Interpreting research on gender differences in friendship: A case for moderation and a plea for caution', *Journal of Social and Personal Relationships*, 5: 367–73.

Young, I. (1981) 'Beyond the unhappy marriage: a critique of the dual systems theory', in L. Sargent (ed.), *Women and Revolution*, London: Pluto Press.

Young, M. and P. Willmott (1962) *Family and Kinship in East London*, rev. edn, Harmondsworth: Pelican.

Young, M. and P. Willmott (1973) *The Symmetrical Family*, London: Routledge and Kegan Paul.

Index

Abu-Lughod, L., 14, 177
Acker, J., 34, 41, 89
Adams, R., 94, 119, 120, 121, 123, 126,
  127, 128, 130, 131, 140, 141, 155
adolescence, 2, 32, 91, 96–8, 100, 101–2,
  110, 113
age, 2, 19, 28, 29, 36, 38, 39, 42, 43, 91,
  100, 115, 118–19, 120, 121, 123–
  5, 126, 128–32, 140–1, 142–3,
  144, 154, 157, 158, 174, 175, 186
Allan, G., 19, 20, 23, 24, 28, 37, 44, 45,
  46, 47, 48, 59, 60, 64, 74, 77, 78,
  80, 85, 87, 88, 97, 103, 104, 105,
  119, 121, 124, 125, 127, 128,
  131, 140, 141, 145, 153, 154,
  156, 157, 159, 160, 161, 162,
  163, 173, 182, 184, 187
Allen K.R., 93, 94
Altman, I., 49
Argyle, M., 8, 19, 23, 29, 37, 51, 58, 84,
  110, 148, 158, 160, 180, 182
attachment, 3–9, 11, 24, 26, 27, 32, 47,
  50, 59, 60–2, 66, 71, 72, 92, 100,
  178, 193
attraction, 193

Babchuk, N., 28, 78
Baker Miller, J., 43
Bankoff, E.A., 129, 140
Barnhart, E., 170
Bates, A., 78
Baum, A., 2, 17, 31
Baxter, L.A., 50, 51, 52, 111, 116, 147
Beauvoir de, S., 35

Beechey, V., 44, 94
Bell, R., 22, 23, 28, 32, 38, 40, 48, 60,
  62
Berger, P., 189
Bernard, J., 35, 36, 72, 81, 95
Bingo, 182
Blau, Z., 49, 118, 129
Blieszner, R., 119
Blumstein, P., 42, 101, 116, 189, 191
Bogdan, J., 18, 30
Booth, A., 29, 123, 129
Bott, E., 28, 44, 78, 80
Brain, R., 2, 8, 9, 148
Brannen, J., 73, 103, 157
Brown, G.W., 2, 17, 47, 49, 50, 60, 83,
  105, 125, 127
Bujra, J.M., 2
Bulmer, M., 54, 72
Buunk, B.P., 90, 92, 93, 94, 95

Cancian, F.M., 30, 33, 70, 102, 180
Caplan, P., 2
care, 35, 48, 74, 82, 101, 106, 153–4,
  155, 159, 173, 182, 183–4, 186
Cheal, D.J., 47, 50, 85, 193
Chodorow, N., 32, 156
class, 2, 3, 19–21, 22, 28, 29, 38, 40–6,
  47–8, 55, 59, 70, 73, 76–80, 82,
  85–6, 87, 97–8, 99, 100, 101,
  105, 119, 126, 127–9, 131, 134,
  137–9, 142–4, 145, 157–9, 160,
  161, 165, 174, 178, 184, 186–7
Cline Welch, R.J., 102, 180
Cohen, G., 21, 85–6, 164

companionship, 23
conflict, 4, 32, 35, 49, 52, 56, 63, 78, 141–2, 144
confidant, 17, 48, 59, 62, 66, 69, 73, 77, 80, 83, 100, 108, 109, 111, 122, 123, 130, 140, 179, 185
constraints on friendship, 25, 58, 63, 82
context specific friendships, 160–2, 166, 171
courtship, 150
Coyle, A., 162
Crompton, R., 41

Daly, M., 169
dating, *see* courtship
Davis, K.E., 4, 23, 25, 26, 60, 150, 177
Deem, R., 44, 47
Delphy, C., 41
development of friendships, 8, 12, 38, 39, 48, 58, 82, 88, 94, 104, 143
Dhavernas, M.J., 43, 169
disengagement, 118
divorce, 17, 41, 52, 90–1, 92–3, 95, 102, 104–6, 107, 108–10, 116, 126, 130, 140, 150, 187
Dixey, R., 45, 127
Dobash, R., 105
Duck, S., 2, 17, 18, 24, 29, 38, 39, 49, 50, 51, 52, 53, 111, 113, 114, 116, 176, 189, 191

Edgell, S., 74, 78
effects of friendship, 3, 83–6, 106, 110
Eisenstein, H., 169, 173
emotional support, 5, 15, 18, 29, 35, 73, 87, 103, 110, 112, 158
employment, 20, 41–2, 48, 52, 66, 74, 79, 81–2, 96, 154, 163
ending of friendships, 12 *see also* termination of friendships
esteem, 16, 17, 141
Evetts, J., 21, 163, 189
exchange, 29, 37, 38, 49, 53, 64, 112, 148–9, 156

Faderman, L., 7, 10, 12, 13, 34, 148, 171
Finch, J., 11, 151, 152, 153, 156, 187
Firth, R., 151, 156, 157
Fischer, C., 22, 59, 77, 108, 122, 126, 145, 162
Fleming, R., 2, 17, 31
Fortes, M., 24, 151, 152

gender differences in friendship, 11, 13, 31, 55, 125, 186
geographical mobility, 48, 77, 80, 82, 88, 184
Gerstel, N., 108
Goldthorpe, J., 41, 78, 85
Goodenow, C., 15, 16, 59, 84, 95, 100, 163
Gouldner, H., 15, 16, 39–40, 44, 53, 54, 149, 150, 158, 165, 176, 179, 181
Gove, W.R., 95, 180
Granovetter, M., 166
Griffin, C., 97, 98, 101, 102, 115, 147
Gubrium, J., 175
Gullestad, M., 16, 21, 50, 65, 75, 76, 86, 114, 147, 186

happiness, 85
Harvey, J., 53
Hazan, C., 4, 11
health, 16–17, 21, 31, 81, 83–4, 88, 94, 95, 107–9, 124, 125, 126, 130, 132, 134, 140, 141, 142, 144, 176
help, 24, 29, 46, 53, 56, 64, 66, 75, 104, 106, 134, 135, 137, 141, 154, 156
Henderson, S., 6, 8, 23, 29, 51, 58, 148, 158
Hendrick, C., 11
Hess, B.B., 35–6, 54, 78, 79, 100, 148
heterosexuality, 1, 13, 22, 26, 36, 38, 56, 91, 96, 97, 119, 146, 147, 167, 168, 169, 172, 179, 192
Hite, S., 15, 20, 65, 72, 73, 169
Hochschild, A., 138, 158, 178, 183
Hunt, G., 45

intimacy, 4, 17, 19, 23, 24, 28–33, 38, 39, 49, 51, 56, 59, 63, 66, 69–70, 72, 74–5, 84, 87, 89, 94, 96, 98–100, 120, 121, 129, 133, 138, 140, 141, 148, 152–3, 156, 157, 158, 165, 170, 179, 182

Jerrome, D., 21, 23, 25, 36, 50, 119, 121, 122, 124, 125, 126, 130, 132, 137, 138, 143, 147, 155, 176, 177, 181, 184
joy, 13, 19, 84, 111, 174

kin, 5, 7, 13, 41, 55, 104, 108, 124, 125, 128, 141, 143, 145, 146, 147, 151–4, 155–6, 157, 162, 179

Komarovsky, M., 29, 62, 78, 155
Kurth, S., 22

La Gaipa, J., 18, 22, 51, 78, 141, 145, 148
Larson, R.W., 19, 77, 84, 110
Leatham, G., 24, 111, 189
leisure, 45, 47, 57, 113
Leonard, D., 93, 95
lesbian, 3, 13, 28, 33, 34, 90, 146, 167–71
life cycle, 21, 25, 80, 158
Litwak, E., 119, 145
loneliness, 5, 16, 96, 107, 109, 133
Lopata, H.Z., 5, 13, 120, 122, 123, 126, 127–8, 131, 165
Lowenthal, M.F., 29, 59, 77, 120, 123, 125, 140

maintenance of friendships, 12, 82, 88–9, 100, 143, 177, 181
Mangam, I., 160
marital status, 125, 126, 128, 130, 140, 142, 143, 174, 186, 191
marriage, 5, 15, 19, 21, 33, 51, 52, 56, 57, 62, 65, 72, 73–5, 76, 79, 84–6, 87, 88, 91, 92, 95, 98, 104–5, 107, 114, 115, 116, 139, 140, 173, 181, 182, 184, 187, 190, 191
Maslow, A., 4
Mason, J., 151–3
Matthews, S.H., 119, 121, 125, 141, 154
McAdams, D., 3, 4, 175
McCabe, T., 94, 113–4
McCall, G.J., 8, 145, 146–7, 150, 189, 191
Miell, D., 39, 51, 113
Milardo, R., 44, 46, 97, 103, 104, 108, 109, 116
mobility, 48, 124, 127, 131, 134, 136
moral discourses, 21, 86, 178, 186, 189
Morgan, D.L., 2, 50, 55, 108, 137, 190
Morris, L., 20, 81
mother/daughter, 150, 155–7, 158

neighbours, 47, 66, 109, 135, 138, 145, 149, 163–4
network, 20, 22, 28, 35, 46, 53, 77, 78, 95, 97, 101, 103, 104, 105, 107, 108–10, 114, 115, 117, 126, 190
number of friendships, 17, 58

O'Connor, P., 10, 11, 17, 22, 24, 25, 28, 30, 47, 50, 59–66, 69–71, 73–4, 83, 87, 120, 122, 124, 127, 132, 134, 135, 142, 150, 153, 156, 158–9, 164, 176, 181, 191
Oakley, A., 11, 32, 73, 164
Oliker, S.J., 15, 16, 21, 47, 50, 57, 62, 65, 73–6, 86, 114, 164, 165, 188–9
Orbach, S., 37, 156

Pahl, R.E., 49, 60, 74, 80, 106
Parker, R., 173
Perlman, D., 2, 24, 38, 49, 119, 128, 139
personal space, 21, 44
Pond, K., 50, 116
Porter, M., 177, 178
private arena, 23, 34, 189
psychological well-being, 3, 26, 83, 84, 86, 88, 139–42
public arena, 23, 45, 48, 57, 81, 182, 189

Rands, M., 29, 104
Ratcliff, K.S., 18, 30
Raymond, J., 12, 14, 31, 43, 70, 166, 169, 180
real friends, 57, 64, 69, 77, 102, 104, 116, 120, 124, 125, 130
reciprocity, 25, 37, 110, 148, 152, 154, 157
Reis, H.T., 30, 51, 96, 111
resources, 8, 19, 23, 31, 33, 40, 42, 44, 47–8, 55, 56–7, 71, 75, 81–3, 85, 87, 88, 89, 104, 126, 127, 132, 143, 186, 188
Rich, A., 43, 146, 167
Ringelheim, J., 12, 43, 188
Roberto, K.A., 49
Rook, K.S., 122, 139, 141
Rose, S.M., 22, 33, 52, 97, 98, 99, 101, 112, 114
Rubin, L.B., 32, 60, 65, 95, 102
rules (within relationships) 147, 148

Satterlee, S., 45
Seiden, A.M., 10
Sharpe, S., 97, 163
Simmel, G., 1, 8, 11, 19, 63, 177, 180, 182
Sinclair, I., 122, 132, 154
single women, 2, 3, 15, 42, 90–2, 94, 95,

99, 100, 102, 107, 111, 114, 115, 130

sister/sister, 3, 150, 153, 157–8, 160, 171

sociability, 11, 16, 19, 39, 63, 72, 79, 87, 107, 121, 126, 141, 158, 160

social networks, 18, 28, 44, 97, 157, 178

Stacey, M., 11

Stack, C., 41, 48, 148, 155

Stanworth, M., 41

status, 138

Stein, P.J., 93, 100

Suitor, J., 41

termination of friendships, 9, 44, 49, 52, 111, 116, 142, 148, 149, 171, 177, 190

Todd, M., 23, 25, 26, 60, 150, 177

Tremendous Ten, 138, 147

validation, 14, 21, 23, 49, 65, 70, 88, 89, 96, 124, 140, 142, 181

Veblen, T., 85, 187

Weiss, R.S., 4, 5, 6, 24, 29, 59, 65, 72, 77, 107, 120

Wellman, B., 22, 23, 28, 44, 59, 81, 85, 154, 158, 161, 162

Wenger, C., 120, 122, 123, 125, 130

Whitehead, A., 45, 74, 86, 188

widowhood, 52, 92, 119, 120, 122, 126, 127, 129, 180

widows, 91, 93, 118, 125, 126, 127, 128, 129, 130, 131, 132, 136, 138, 140

Willmott, P., 24, 38, 60, 62, 64, 65, 77, 78, 80, 81, 155, 156, 164

work friends, 9, *see also* context specific friendships

Winstead, B.A., 23, 29, 38

Wiseman, J., 46, 52, 95, 114, 116, 149

Wright, P.H., 22, 23, 29, 65, 69, 70, 100, 114, 124, 184